Elusions of Control

Society of Biblical Literature

Semeia Studies

Number 41

ELUSIONS OF CONTROL
Biblical Law on the Words of Women

Jione Havea

Volume Editor
Danna Nolan Fewell

Elusions of Control

BIBLICAL LAW ON THE
WORDS OF WOMEN

Jione Havea

Society of Biblical Literature
Atlanta

ELUSIONS OF CONTROL
Biblical Law on the Words of Women

Copyright © 2003 by the Society of Biblical Literature.

All rights reserved.

Library of Congress Cataloging-in-Publication Data

Havea, Jione, 1965–
Elusions of control : biblical law on the words of women / by Jione Havea.
      p.   cm. — (Society of Biblical Literature Semeia studies ; no. 41)
    Includes bibliographical references and index.
    ISBN 1-58983-033-4 (paper)
    1. Women—Religious aspects—Judaism. 2. Women in Judaism. 3. Bible. O.T.
Numbers XXX—Criticism, interpretation, etc. I. Title. II. Series: Semeia studies.
BM729.W6H38 2003
222'.1406—dc21   2003005079

03 04 05 06 07 08 09 10   5 4 3 2 1

The book is printed in the United States of America
on acid-free paper.

'I he manatu hounga mo e 'ofa tu'a
kia
'Etina Fe'aomoetoa mo Sione 'Amanaki

Contents

Acknowledgments

This book has been, and still is, all over the place—from the South Pacific Islands to the continental United States to Down Under, and in between also—but it has not gone over all the places. Much in biblical law and narrative, in transoceanic experience and island space, and in Num 30, remains to be expressed, and played.

Through the delays and redirections of this study, with the pains of arrival and the pleasures of departure, several people, alive and dead, and in between, such as the drifters and prisoners who feed me things to think, edged me along.

Because I will no doubt fail to acknowledge everyone who allowed this book to happen, to event, I write, here, now, in Tongan, *mälö e kätaki* (thanks for enduring, for enduring thanks) to all of you.

Nonetheless, there are three people whom I should not fail to acknowledge. They read earlier (d)rafts of this book and though they are not responsible for the errors and indeterminacies, illusions and elusions, that remain herein, they are responsible for their patience and encouragements.

Danna Nolan Fewell, at once editor and adviser, critic and ally, introduced me to narrative and deconstructive theories, and practices, which I extend in this study to the unfamiliar territories, for both of us, of the Hebrew Bible law and Oceania. I was obliged when she gave me room to be different, to *be stranger*.

David M. Gunn reminded me of the unstable footings of higher criticism and the significance of delays, both of which flow in this book, and David Jobling encouraged me to cross boundaries, at once in theory and in space.

Elusions of Control was also influenced, as well as coerced, by my extended family, and their families and friends, including S. 'Ungatea Fonua, Lile and Vaiola Finau, Soane 'Etu, Sione Ui Kilisimasi, Finau Lokotui, Siosaia Kongaika, and Sione Mila, all of whom died since I started my transtextual journey, hence they elude my acknowledgment, my words, my *mälö e kätaki!*

And thanks to John C. Turnbull, the way I write (and ride on words) has become less problematic. As for the rest of you, you know who you are, and the limit of words, and the elusions of acknowledgments. I continue to face your gifts.

Finally, *Elusions of Control* is dedicated to the memory of, as an alibi for, my parents, 'Etina Fe'aomoetoa and Sione 'Amanaki:

KIOKIO MEI HE LILO

Though possibilities be repressed
And responsibilities yielded,
So that subjects are abjects
Their rights denied;
Though opportunities be rejected
And obligations resigned,
So that the poor are placeless
Their voices undermined;
Still I stutter under fractures
And the marks of erasure.

To Wind and its strength
Current and its stealth,
To Earth and its breath
Darkness and its depth,
Though limits rupture
And the center conquers
I cannot help but utter
Obligations for the Other

When departure defers
Limits are maintained;
When arrival delays
Hope is sustained,
That waves may rise
And return to their places,
But the lines in the sand
Shall resist their displacing hands

Courage, tame my heart
Patience, lead my hands
Thou, look at my face
My hope, do realise!

For hope is my name
The lines on my face!

Land of the Darug people
among the Barramatugal clan, close to the river
August 28, 2003

Abbreviations

AB	Anchor Bible
ABD	*The Anchor Bible Dictionary.* Edited by David Noel Freedman. 6 vols. New York, 1992
Ant	*Jewish Antiquities* (Josephus)
BA	*Biblical Archaeologist*
BHS	*Biblia Hebraica Stuttgartensia.* Edited by K. Elliger and W. Rudolph. Stuttgart, 1983
Bib Ant	*Biblical Antiquities* (Pseudo-Philo)
BWA(N)T	Beiträge zur Wissenschaft vom Alten (und Neuen) Testament
BZAW	Beihefte zur Zeitschrift für die Alttestamentliche Wissenschaft
CBQ	*Catholic Biblical Quarterly*
Ebr	*De Ebrietate* (Philo)
ET	*Expository Times*
FCB	Feminist Companion to the Bible
HSM	Harvard Semitic Monographs
HTR	*Harvard Theological Review*
HUCA	*Hebrew Union College Annual*
ICC	The International Critical Commentary
IDB	*The Interpreter's Dictionary of the Bible.* Edited by George A. Buttrick. 4 vols. Nashville: Abingdon, 1962
Int	*Interpretation*
ITC	International Theological Commentary
JAAR	*Journal of the American Academy of Religion*
JBL	*The Journal of Biblical Literature*
JSNTS	Journal for the Study of the New Testament Supplement Series
JSOT	*Journal for the Study of the Old Testament*
JSOTS	Journal for the Study of the Old Testament Supplement Series
LCBI	Literary Currents in Biblical Interpretation

LSM	Legal Semiotics Monographs
MT	Masoretic Text (from *BHS*)
Mut	*De mutatione nominum* (Philo)
NCBC	New Century Bible Commentary
NovT	*Novum Testamentum*
OBS	Oxford Bible Series
OBT	Overtures to Biblical Theology
OTL	Old Testament Library
PG	Patrologia graeca [= Patrologiae cursus completus: Series graeca]. Edited by J.-P. Migne. 162 vols. Paris, 1857–1886
PMB	*The Postmodern Bible.* New Haven, 1995
Praem	*De Praemiis et Poenis* (Philo)
SC	Sources chrétiennes. Paris: Cerf, 1943–
Som 1	*De Somiis I* (Philo)
ThWAT	*Theologisches Wörterbuch zum Alten Testament.* Edited by G. J. Botterweck and H. Ringgren. Stuttgart, 1970–
USQR	*Union Seminary Quarterly Review*
VT	*Vetus Testamentum*
ZAW	*Zeitschrift für die Alttestamentliche Wissenschaft*

Introduction

In order to change the perspective, the established priorities are reversed. What is seen to be central will be marginalized, and what has been treated as marginal will become central. (Bal 1988a, 2)

Reading against the grain is a call to responsibility. It is a call to see how texts and their interpretations oppress people—and sometimes even creation itself—physically, emotionally, economically, theologically. It is a call to expose domination in order to bring about change. (Gunn and Fewell 1993, 204)

0.1 Mapping the Turf

Circling around and *tear*ing at Num 30, this book explores the nature of vows involving women in the Hebrew Bible–Old Testament[1] and demonstrates an alternative way of reading biblical law. Drawing upon the transoceanic leanings of South Pacific islanders, in order to explore, also, how those leanings might aid the reading of biblical texts, I propose to read law and narrative around each other, in other words, to *circumread* law and narrative.[2]

Numbers 30 "regulates" vows as if words were at once unbreakable and breakable, and as if Num 30 at once stipulates and eludes control. Its regulations may be revamped as a multivalent demand: *keep your vow!*[3] The following pages will weave different senses, and remainders, of this demand (cf. Foucault 1999, 61, 69). In part 1, I address the dominant, ig-

---

[1] The place-fullness of this political text (cf. Foucault 1999, 107), at once "Hebrew Bible" and "Old Testament" (cf. Alter 2000, 21–61), suspends readers at several places.

[2] *Circumreading* echoes Derrida's *circumfession* (circum-confession), "confession around." Using the prefix *circum-* to denote "around" and "circumcision," *circumfession* is Derrida's way of "fessing up" to his Jewishness and "talking around" it (cf. Dodaro 1999, 80–83).

[3] I begin with a double sense: "Keep your vow" may be read as a demand to uphold (fulfill, hold up) and withhold (hold back, hold up) one's vow.

1

nored, and repressed subjects in and of Num 30;[4] then, in part 2, I circum-read its regulations over vows by women with narratives involving subjects of the same status (daughter, wife, widow, and divorcée). Part 2 directs readers of biblical law to the strengths and limits of deconstructive modes of reading (cf. *PMB*, 124–25),[5] with each of the chapters, together, at once, materializing the *elusions of control.*

Circumreading law with narrative follows, and crosses, redirects, the lead of readers who cross boundaries both in the academy and in the synagogue-church (see chs. 4 and 5).[6] In part 1, I review dominant theories and practices of reading a specific segment of the Hebrew Bible law, expose the limits that critics place on texts (cf. Penchansky 1992), driven by the illusion that they control meanings, and offer alternatives in each case; in other words, I cross several boundaries. I cross more boundaries in part 2, with Num 30 as a subject, at once guide and victim, *around* narratives dealing with women's vows. Moving from *illusion of control* to *elusion of control,* this book is an event in deconstruction.

Since circumreading law with narrative focuses on particular subjects and texts, it is a call *to particularize* (cf. Jameson 1981, 9; Boer 1997, 7). And since it also exposes gaps and fractures in both law and narrative, circum-reading also, at once, calls *for disclosure* (cf. Gutiérrez 1983, 4; Ricoeur 1984, 17).[7] In other words, circumreading urges readers toward the embrace of

---

[4] I deal with different "subjects" in part 1, according to the theories I explore in each chapter. In chapter 1, I focus on the "subjects of the law" whose vows are regulated in Num 30. In chapter 2, I turn to the "subjects of the text [book of Numbers]" that positivist readers tend to ignore. And in chapter 3, I co-opt the "subjects of the unconscious" repressed by interpreters of Num 30. I differentiate and interrelate these "subjects" as I proceed in part 1; then, in part 2, I *cross* them.

[5] According to Caputo and Scanlon, "Deconstruction is a dream and a desire of something *tout autre*, of something that utterly shatters the present horizons of possibility, that confounds our expectations, that leaves us gasping for air, trying to catch our breath, the first words out of our mouth being, 'How did that happen? How was that possible?' That is what Derrida calls *l'invention de l'autre*, the incoming of the other, the coming of something we did not see coming, that takes us by surprise and tears up our horizon of expectation. Faced with the (unforseeable) prospect of this 'incoming,' deconstruction does not timidly shout 'heads up' and then head for cover; rather, it boldly and brazenly calls 'come' (*viens*), 'yes, yes' (*oui, oui*), and offers it its hospitality. The incoming of the 'same,' on the other hand, would simply further confirm the present, already familiar horizon, would be more of the dreary, pedestrian, humdrum sameness of the possible . . . and what Lyotard would call merely a new move in an old and familiar game" (1999, 3).

[6] Contexts, real and/or imaginary, are *partial* (biased and limited) *texts* that affect interpretation (cf. *PMB*, 129–35). Like readers, contexts are not neutral, nor original.

[7] "Disclosure" refers to the act of exposing, of posing out, of releasing, the gaps and fractures in the text, which, consequently, opens up, dis-closes, the text for interpretation.

the Other (Levinas 1981, 1987), always particular and already *dis*closed. It resists inflexible linear representations in order to account for the complexity of the around-and-across relations of texts. Circumreading is, in that regard, transgressive.

Circumreading law with narrative, metacritically speaking, resists autonomy (in this case, the consensus positioning of law *versus* narrative), the myth of modernity,[8] but embraces particularity, at the underside of postmodernity (cf. Žižek 1996), as if it's transmodern.[9] This alternative third position, at once *alter* and *native*, disguises, but does not hide, the current that surges at the underside of my study: liberation praxis.

0.2 Watering the Turf

Insofar as I am not the only islander who reflects on the interpretive task,[10] I write not in order to colonize *the* islanders' transoceanic perspectives but to enact our *boundary-crossing* tendencies in events of *transtextuality*.[11]

---

[8] I presume the "death of the [modern] subject" (ch. 1), which may be explained in two ways. First, that the "bourgeois individual subject" of modernity *no longer exists* in the postmodern age of corporate capitalism. And second, that the bourgeois individual subject is a myth, a subject that *never existed* (Jameson 1998, 5–7; cf. Caputo and Scanlon 1999, 5–6). In both explanations, the postmodern resistance is against the image of a bourgeois subject who parades as an autonomous subject.

Thanks to the postmodern insistence on the "death of the modern subject," we may begin to account for "other subjects" on whose shoulders the modern bourgeois subject rides and writes as if they are right. The call to particularize does not demand another autonomous subject, but it turns toward the "once-colonized" (Sugirtharajah) subject. To particularize is to face other faces at the underside of the postmodern critique of the modern subject.

[9] The transmodern turn seconds Sugirtharajah's critique of postmodernism: "Postmodernism is still seen as Eurocentric in its conceptual and aesthetic thrust. It is found wanting from a third world perspective on several fronts: its lack of a theory of resistance; its failure to cultivate a transformative agenda due to its detached attitudes; its revalidation of the local and its celebration of differences, which are liable to lead to further alienation of subalterns thus assigned to their own space and concerns; its repudiation of and skepticism toward grand-narratives, which fail to take into account liberation as an emancipatory metastory and as a potent symbol for those whose rights have been negated, circumvented, or put in abeyance" (1998, 15; so Müllner 1999, 131–32).

[10] Identity is complex (cf. Lee 1995, 29–53). In my case, I am at once in-between and at many places, at once placeless and place-full. I am Tongan, but Tonga is more than me, and the South Pacific Islands are more than Tonga. In writing as a native I may insult other natives, of Tonga and beyond, for I write as a native and *not* as a native—as an *alter-native*. I read from/at the point where the elusive Other meets, *is*, crosses, the eluding reader. I am both, and not both, Other and reader.

[11] "Transtextuality" represents the meeting, the crossing, of inter*textuality* with *trans*oceanic perspectives. It encourages the *crossings* of texts toward transformative (Danna N. Fewell) and transdisciplinary (Joerg Rieger) reading.

Transtextuality is concerned with both crossing between texts and the crossing of texts. The former imagines texts apart while the latter sees them intersecting, crossing, *a part* of, each other: Transtextuality reads texts a_part of each other; in other words, transtextuality is an event of double-crossing.[12]

Because land-space is limited, South Pacific islanders are oriented toward the ocean, our island boundary, albeit a fluid boundary, and an extension of our land. Into the ocean we search for food, under and above the surfs, from one island to the next. We are oceanic and transoceanic. We are *lured* to our island boundary,[13] a watery mass that can sometimes be hostile and unyielding, and beyond. We sing and dance as we cross our boundary (such as the Tongan *Tau-'a'alo*, a paddling chant) and when we harvest its produce (such as the Tongan *No'o-'anga*, a shark-binding [with leis and shells] chant), so celebration and merriment are parts of our lives. There is pleasure even if the fishing or travel parties are unsuccessful, because most South Pacific islanders face (look at, and give face to) challenges with calmness (*pacifically*).

I draw two connected moods of transtextuality from our transoceanic experiences: first is an orientation toward the boundary (ocean, margin, limit), and second, a tendency to celebrate, to play, to be happy, carefree, no worries, *hakuna matata!*[14] Transtextuality emphasizes the boundary (ocean) that links texts (islands), the fluid expanse in between texts, in/through which readers are encouraged to cross playfully but calmly.[15]

Transtextuality reflects Sugirtharajah's characterization of "delocalized transnationals" as "part of the diasporic culture which *moves across borders and feels at home everywhere and nowhere*" (1998, 108; my italics). Similar to postcolonial reading, transtextuality "is an active interrogation of the hegemonic systems of thought, textual codes, and symbolic practices which the West constructed in its domination of colonial subjects. . . . [Transtextual] interpretation will reject the myth of objective or neutral truth and will replace it with a perception of truth as mapped, constructed, and negotiated" (Sugirtharajah 1998, 17, 18).

[12] This reflects Foucault's *system of the transgressive:* "There is certainly, in any culture, a coherent series of gestures of separation; among these, prohibition of incest, the marking out of madness and perhaps certain religious exclusions are only particular cases. The function of these gestures is, in the strict sense of the term, ambiguous: just when they mark the limit, they open out a space whose transgression is always possible" (1999, 50; cf. Beal 1994, 172).

[13] The island boundary is a large hole, an inverted barrier, filled with salty water that flows from various parts of the globe, rather than a structure raised above the ground (as is commonly assumed when one thinks of "boundary"). Figuratively speaking, the island boundary is an inverted and inverting boundary.

[14] Transtextuality crosses Cornell's description of deconstruction as the "philosophy of the limits" with Derrida's notion of *jouissance*.

[15] The attitude of celebration should not desensitize readers to the danger and violence in crossing and harvesting practices (cf. *PMB*, 135). Transtextuality, as are

Insofar as texts share qualities and interests, and differences at once set them a_part, transtextuality focuses both on sameness and differences and resists the temptation to globalize. Globalization is problematic not because it imagines that *no text is an island* but because it tends to ignore the boundary that sets texts a_part. The transtextual reader, accordingly, dives into the boundary to expose the shoulders on which globalization rides (writes, rights). She up-anchors the underside of globalization to set adrift what readers repress and ignore, their *ignor-ances,* but over which they establish themselves and their readings (see chs. 2 and 3).

In addition to reading texts intertextually (cf. Fewell, ed., 1992; Aichele and Phillips 1995b), transtextuality adds a "third text," that which separates and links texts, the boundary, the margin, which is in between texts, to prevent the reader from (con)fusing texts.[16] On the flip side, the boundary is also a stepping stone, a medium, a conduit, real (textual) and/or imaginary (ideological), that enables the reader to leap from one text to another. I demonstrate this aspect of transtextuality by exploring the regulations (law) in Num 30 *around* and *across* biblical narratives that appear not to have anything to do with Num 30 (part 2). I will not even try to forge historical and literary relations between these texts, though I will address some of these relations, but to *cross* the limits that set them a_part. Part 2 is an *event* in, a demonstration of, and (in some places) against, trans-textuality!

Transtextuality places the weight of the reading practice on the *shoulders* of the reader's imagination (see also Fuchs 1985, 118), at once reader-responsive and text-constructing. Like an islander who is responsive to the currents while she maneuvers her raft according to her course/cause, a transtextual reader at once responds to and constructs the text. Transtextuality is *gendered* (we are conditioned readers) and *engendering* (our readings may affect the text and may affect us), demanding responsible reading (cf. West 1999, 15–16). This call involves accounting for gaps in texts and for the faces at the underside of texts.[17]

---

all reading practices, is political (Jameson), and it involves resistance (Gutiérrez, Sugirtharajah).

The transtextual reader faces the danger of being cast out of/beyond the boundary, of being out-lawed, and she poses the same threat to the text. She imposes a reading on the text, but the text may resist her reading, with the aid of other readers, whose alternative readings also impose on the text (cf. Sugirtharajah 1998, 24, 106–8, 129–32).

[16] Without margins, two or more texts overrun to become one text; in other words, they become (con)fused.

[17] Echoing the "underside of history" in liberation theologies (Gutiérrez 1983, 169–234; Rieger 1998a; 1998b, 2–5, 221–22), I imagine an "underside of the text."

0.3 Dipping into the Surfs

When an islander dips into the ocean, away from the shores of certainty, she rides up the wake (Tongan: *ma'ahi*) and down the gap (Tongan: *matua*), while looking out for breaking waves, to face the wake behind the gap. She cannot jump from one *ma'ahi* to the next without descending the *matua*, and she can not stay on a *ma'ahi* without being pushed backward.

To determine the waves to ride over and the breaking waves to ride through, she counts the number of regular waves between breaking waves. The intervals between regular and breaking wakes are not constant, however, and the islander expects some regular waves to break (Tongan: *ngalu fakaofo*). The reality of gaps and the unpredictability of wakes keep the islander on alert and enchant her task. I draw two related insights from this transoceanic view to explain transtextuality further: the *gift of gaps*[18] and the *unpredictability of wakes*.

As an islander rises on wakes and dips into gaps, so transtextuality accounts for dominant subjects (main points, wakes) and ignored and repressed subjects (the marginalized, gaps) in biblical texts.[19] Transtextuality is *more than* the uncovering of a text's main points. It also faces gaps and explores the contours under the surface that cause some of the main points (regular waves) to break into the gaps and onto the preceding, or the receding, text/wake. Transtextuality *recovers gaps* in biblical texts, a process that threatens to *re-cover* (in the sense of covering again) gaps. To use the language of Derrida, the *gift of gaps* is a consolation (medicine) that may drown (poison).

By dipping into gaps, transtextuality enjoys the complexities and ambiguities of texts.[20] In this book, I take *textual complexity* as the elements that lure (Miscall) the reader (to cross the limits) toward other texts and that encourage the crossing of texts, and *textual ambiguity* as the qualities that resist the texts' fusion.[21] These two *terms* urge readers from one text to another, and they remind readers that texts are beyond their control.

---

[18] I describe "gap" in spatial terms but I imagine it also as a temporal phenomenon, a *delay*. A *matua* (gap) allows two wakes to be separate (or individual) waves; so does a *delay* allow two happenings to be separate events. In this regard, (spatial) *gaps* and (temporal) *delays* imitate Derrida's notion of *différance*, which stands for "differ" and "defer" both.

[19] For a transoceanic reader, *sea level* and *ground zero* are never constant. There is always fluctuation, owing to the waves and the tides, and the sandy shorelines.

[20] A text is complex when it has many meanings and the reader cannot reduce it to only one meaning, making it "undecidable" (Miscall), and ambiguous when some of its meanings are not fully worked out, which makes it "indeterminate" (Clines). In most texts, undecidability is due to indeterminacy, both of which are not free of the reader's imagination.

[21] To emphasize one or the other is totalizing. Sugirtharajah writes, "[T]heories, however neat or sophisticated, have the potential themselves to become colonialist" (1998, 24).

Together, they materialize the illusions and elusions of control. In other words, transtextuality is concerned with the act of *crossing* and not just the events of *departure* and *arrival* between texts (cf. Foucault 1999, 87), as if it is an apocalyptic exercise.[22]

In spite of the *gift of gaps*, the transoceanic islander must respect the *unpredictability of wakes*.[23] Crossing over to the act of reading, the transtextual reader may playfully explore gaps, but she cannot control "main points," which may unexpectedly break upon her reading to wash it away. And texts may break away from her reading to throw her onto the next text and reading. I demonstrate in the following chapters how the *unpredictability of texts* is a joy to a transoceanic reader, breaking onto her readings and throwing her from one text to another. In the end, the transoceanic reader realizes that she can neither control nor duplicate the text. Nor can its boundaries (ocean)! Nonetheless, the reader disturbs the text (by crossing and harvesting it) and then she must let the text be. In that regard, the *alter*native that transtextuality offers is about *letting go* of the text, and one's reading of the text. Transtextuality, therefore, also participates in the *illusion* and *elusion of control*.

Accounting for the unpredictability of biblical texts sets the reader adrift in the currents of place-fullness. It transforms the risks of placelessness into the joy of place-fullness, being situated at more than one place, on the turf and in the surf, on the wakes and in the gaps. I demonstrate this place-full quality by reading Num 30 in several placements: in itself (ch. 1), in the book of Numbers (ch. 2), in its treatments by earlier interpreters (ch. 3), and in relation to vow-narratives involving a young woman (ch. 4), a wife (ch. 5), and a widow and divorcée (ch. 6). The following readings will not control Num 30 but materialize its placefullness;[24] the aim is not to capture or tame Num 30 but to discharge the *illusions of control*.

0.4 Overturning the Surfs

When regular waves break unexpectedly (*ngalu fakaofo*) the islander realizes that changes have taken place somewhere. The disturbances she faces on the surf were triggered at the underside of (that is, beneath and

---

[22] Transtextuality is apocalyptic insofar as it is future-oriented, focused on the transcendent (cf. Collins 1977, 76–77), and crisis-informed and -directed (cf. Paul Hanson 1987, 27–28). It directs the reader to what lies beyond the boundaries (at the underside of the text), without uprooting (up-routing) the reader from the gap (boundary, crisis) that she is in. In that regard, transtextuality embraces the "placefullness" of texts, of contexts, and of readers.

[23] The shorelines of Näfanua ('Eua) and Pulotu (Ha'afeva) exemplify this unpredictability. On some calm days they "lock up" and no vessel can land or depart. But once it turns rough beyond the reefs, Näfanua and Pulotu calm down.

[24] Texts are both sites (to cross) and objects (to harvest). In crossing and harvesting texts, the transtextual reader "alters" them.

beyond) the waves. She cannot determine what caused *ngalu fakaofo* but she can feel them in the *ma'ahi* (wake) and *matua* (gap). The forces at the underside are real, but they resist representation; they cannot be captured, but they touch and disturb the islander. From this view I draw two undercurrents of transtextuality: the affects (agency) and elusiveness of the Other.

Transtextuality presents the reader with opportunities to (be) embrace(d by) disturbances at the underside of the text. Like an islander who is sucked into the ocean by disturbances at the underside of *ngalu fakaofo*, a transtextual reader feels for the undercurrents of the text and, to reiterate Levinas's call (see ch. 6), overturns the text to (receive the) embrace (of) the Other.[25] I explore this aspect first, in part 1, by imagining different ways in which the underside of Num 30 *breaks* onto its interpretations, and then, in part 2, by causing three vow-narratives to break onto Num 30. I focus in part 2 on the women subjects of Num 30 and *face* the faces of "the Other" in the contexts of family relations (see ch. 1), national interests (see ch. 2), and institutional constraints (see ch. 3). In these chapters, together, disturbances at the underside of the text "have a say" in the interpretive practice (cf. Tracy 1999, 171) and point to the many faces of the Other.[26]

Metacritically speaking, transtextuality is a humbling (disarming) event. It humbles readers who realize the complexity and elusiveness of (literary, ideological, contextual) "texts" (*illusion of control*) and disarms readers who accept that sublime forces (disturbances) work at the underside of all readings (*elusion of control*).

0.5 The Limits of Transtextuality

Insofar as "the Other" resists representation, why speak of "the Other" *as if* "it" exists? This question suggests that "reading for the Other" is doomed to fail because the reader cannot capture the text and/or materialize its undersides. On the other hand, insofar as the transtextual reader sets out to cross and harvest texts, the question exposes the epistemological limits of transtextuality. As transtextuality puts the weight of interpretation on the shoulders of the reader's imagination, the transtex-

---

[25] I offer myself to, by seeking, the embrace of the Other, and I expect to be soaked, salted, and tanned—in other words, altered—in the process. In this procedure, the Other is vulnerable to my embrace. Of course, the difference between "embracing the Other" and "being embraced by the Other" exists in my imagination. I decide what and when to embrace, whether to accept or resist the embrace of the Other, but the Other may refuse to give its embrace, to keep me "at arm's length."

[26] These readings will also disclose two blind spots in liberation hermeneutics: the failure to consider the "other faces of the Other," human and divine (see also Beal 1994), and the failure to consider the "price of liberation." I demonstrate both limits in part 2.

tual reader senses, faces, "the Other" not as a "global Other" but in the faces of the text that here and there break upon her readings. And since what may be present in one reader's imagination may be absent or insignificant for other readers, transtextual readers have a chance to resist other readings and, consequently, to free the text from readers' control.

On the metacritical level, transtextuality harbors Bloom's proposal: "There is no reading worthy of being communicated to another unless it deviates to break form, twists the lines to find a shelter, and so makes a meaning through the shattering of belated vessels" (1990, 22). In the following pages I review the contentions made by notable biblical critics, past and present, drawing attention to the diversity of interests and practices that set them a_part from each other.

The faces of transtextuality I (mis)represented above threaten to suspend the reader in between places, always preparing for departure, as if she will never arrive.[27] Transtextuality can trouble the already-placed with the threats of placeless-ness, but it can also encourage the placeless with the possibilities of place-fullness (for being in between and a_part is *to be placed*). In other words, transtextuality is a disarming practice that arms the reader while she anticipates the next departure (on/to the next text and reading). Both effects are demonstrated in the following readings of Num 30 around and across legal and narrative texts.[28]

If what I have described is realized, the transtextual reader must be willing to let go of her readings, to depart, in theory and in practice. Only then will the limits become extensions, arms, of her surfs. So there! Here![29]

---

[27] I have, to this point, given an orientalist (Said) view of transtextuality; in other words, I presented transoceanic perspectives from the standpoint of "the Look" (Jameson). As such I submitted transoceanic faces to "the moment of bureaucratization" (Jameson, Foucault).

At this juncture, for the sake of other natives, I acknowledge that my representation is, at best, partial (biased, limited). I will later supplement this orientalist view by reformulating "gaps and delays" in terms of islanders' laid-back personality (see §6.1) and by means of a folk narrative (see "Afterword, My Alibi, a Story"). Those two-step alter*native* turns shift transtextuality from the focalization of "the Look" to the behaviors of natives.

[28] The following readings are unashamedly synchronic: "One way to reclaim my power as a reader, to take back the text, is to follow a synchronic strategy of reading. Synchronic approaches give the reader a great deal of latitude in making connections between texts. Central to such a semiotic theory is that the connections in the text have been made in the unconscious mind" (Bach 1999, 144; see also part 2).

[29] Though I describe transtextuality in terms of transoceanic experiences, nevertheless I do not imagine that transtextuality is unique for South Pacific islanders. But I resist globalization.

Part I
Illusion of control

[T]he Bible's thrust and forte rather lie in what I call foolproof composition, whereby the discourse strives to open and bring home its essentials to all readers so as to establish a common ground, a bond instead of a barrier of understanding. . . . By foolproof composition I mean that the Bible is difficult to read, easy to underread and overread and even misread, but virtually impossible to, so to speak, counterread. (Sternberg 1985, 50)

Biblical interpretation is never simply a religious matter, for the processes of formation, canonization, and transmission of the Bible have always been imbued with the issues of authority and power. (Kwok Pui-lan 1995, 9)

[To interpret] is to admit by definition an excess of the signified over the signifier; a necessary, unformulated remainder of thought that language has left in the shade—a remainder that is the very essence of that thought, driven outside its secret—but to comment [or, to interpret] also presupposes that this unspoken element slumbers within speech (parole), and that, by the superabundance proper to the signifier, one may, in questioning it, give voice to a content that was not explicitly signified. (Foucault 1975, xvi)

In the beginning is hermeneutics. But the shared necessity of exegesis, the interpretive imperative, is interpreted differently by the rabbi and the poet. The difference between the horizon of the original text and exegetic writing makes the difference between the rabbi and the poet irreducible. Forever unable to reunite with each other, yet so close to each other, how could they ever regain the realm? The original opening of interpretation essentially signifies that there will always be rabbis and poets. And two interpretations of interpretation. (Derrida 1978, 67)

1

Dominant Subjects in and of Numbers 30

*[S]cholarship in this area [Israelite law], in spite of an extensive litera-
ture, has reached few assured results.* (Kaiser 1977, 53)

1.0 Introduction

Lacking reliable evidence that "Israel" existed in the wilderness before the
amphictyony (Noth 1960, 53ff., 85ff.; in contrast to Mayes 1974, 8–11, 16–
31; cf. Olson 1985, 59–62) and the settlement (Mendenhall 1962, 3, and
1976; cf. Gottwald 1985, 230–88), historical critics shift their rhetoric from
the histories to the traditions of Israel, and of the Pentateuch (cf. Noth
1981b, 46–145; von Rad 1962, 105–305; 1984, 1–78). This shift of rhetoric and
interest, however, has been made problematic: "The subsequent history of
Israel in the wilderness is for the most part wrapped in obscurity; the biblical sources preserve very few [historical] traditions" (Sarna 1988, 47).

And recent turns to literary matters (Philip R. Davies 1992, 11; 1997)
suggest that the histories and traditions of ancient Israel are literary cre-
ations, ideologically constructed *biblical histories* (Carroll 1998; Philip R.
Davies 1998; Lemche 1998, 22ff.; in contrast to Dever 2001). "Israel," Philip
Davies claims, "is certainly a slippery category . . . because it is a literary
category first and foremost, and a historical and political one only by in-
ference" (1994, 24; cf. 1997, 113).

I dive into this shifting juncture with transoceanic interests. I do not
seek to determine what occurred during the wilderness period, or to determine when texts about that period were written and added to the
primary story (Genesis–2 Kings), or what demanded their inclusion. I
have a simpler focus: a legal text, Num 30, and its stipulations on a neg-
lected subject, vows by women.[1]

---

[1] This book supplements studies of vows by Cartledge (1992) and Berlinerblau, both of which address the broad and illusive areas of the Hebrew Bible and
the ancient Near East.

This chapter reiterates a conclusion reached by Spinoza, Simon, Astruc, Eichhorn, and so on: the Pentateuch is a composite of *mémoires* (cf. Nahkola 2001, 6ff.). I read Num 30 as a composite within a composite Pentateuch and composite Hebrew Bible (cf. Wellhausen 1957, 295; von Rad 1972, 75), allowing its voices to aggregate, to flow together (cf. Levinas 1985, 115; Phillips and Fewell 1997, 6), to cross. I forge a transoceanic event, seeking to release, to re-lease, to lease again, Num 30.

I first sketch the limits of *positivist* (in the empirical sense; see Dworkin 1996) readings of Hebrew Bible law (§1.1),[2] then re-lease, set adrift, Num 30 (§1.2) toward legal and narrative texts from the wilderness literature, and beyond.[3] This chapter clears a path for the following chapters.

1.1 Let the Author Die

Positivist critics assume that the Hebrew Bible law's locus of meaning is identifiable in time and space, and they see their task as a *decoding* practice (cf. Douglas 1975, 83–84, 249–50; compare Phillips and Fewell 1997, 8–9), seeking to reconstruct the law's intentional, inherent, and/or affective meanings.[4] They refer to legislators and their audience in *positive* terms, with confidence, as if they are in contact.

---

[2] Other studies take more comprehensive stabs at the HB law. See, among others, van der Ploeg 1950–51, which depicts Yahwism as the source of Israelite law, and the Decalogue as the foundation of pentateuchal laws; Boecker 1980, which views HB laws as systems of justice; Dale Patrick 1985, which claims that precepts and codes, designed for persuasion and instruction, testify to God's will, and 1989, which presents the law as a coherent and comprehensive system of thought; Sprinkle 1990, which focuses on both the regulative principle and its mode of production; and Crüsemann 1996, which examines the theology and social history of HB legal codes, focusing on the institutions assumed to have generated them.

[3] I propose to circumread law and narrative even if, especially if, they are unrelated. This is based on a deconstructive premise: a relationship exists because *the subjects may not be related*. Relations and nonrelations define each other, in the same way that Sameness and Otherness interpenetrate (cf. Engnell 1960, 19). Whether one reads inner- (cf. Fishbane 1985, 6–7; Noble 2002), inter- (cf. Fewell, ed., 1992; Aichele and Phillips 1995a), and/or counter- (cf. Bal 1988a, 9–39) textually, the reader forges their (non)relations.

[4] Historical biblical critics tend to agree with their counterparts in jurisprudence on the business of decoding law to uncover its "intentions." Critics, however, disguise how their biases, ranging from a positivist attitude (cf. Dworkin 1996; Sandy and Giese Jr. 1995) to an indeterminate attitude in what the legal expert Benjamin N. Cardozo calls "method of sociology" (1921, 98–141; cf. Scheppele 1994), influence the decoding process. The "method of sociology" examines the law as a human construct, along the lines of "justice, morals and social welfare, the *mores* of the day" (Cardozo 1921, 30–31; cf. 1924, 56–57, and [on justice] 1928, 31–32). The method of sociology is indeterminate because *justice* is constructed (cf. Geertz 1973, 5; on "indeterminacy" in law see Waldron 1994; Alexander and Sherwin 1994; Kutz 1994; Meyer 1996).

The decoding process, however, differs among biblical critics, who do not always agree where to situate each code's locus of meaning, whether *behind, within,* or *in front of* the text (cf. Philip R. Davies 1994, 23; and West 1995, 131–73). Some critics associate the locus of meaning with the legislators who wrote each law, or with the redactors who collected the law codes, and/or with the sociopolitical contexts of their audience in "ancient Israel/ancient Near East." Other critics might identify the oral pre-literary stage (e.g., Uppsala school), the received "final form" of the text (e.g., canonical criticism), and/or the receiving community of decoders (e.g., reader-response criticism), as the place where meaning is produced.

The predicament for positivist critics is the lack of socio-historical anchors in law codes. Whether one reads for the intentions and settings of the actual legislators, the growth of Hebrew Bible law codes, and/or for the ideologies of decoding communities (cf. McKnight 1988), one is limited to/by the text. Positivist critics are imaginative in this regard. They seek to identify the legislators and/or their audience with questions such as: Whose interests does the law serve? What circumstances would give rise to and encourage such interests? They U-turn from *assumed* legislators/audience to the text, claiming to be text-oriented, but the turning point exists outside the text, in their imaginations. Even critics who use the same method situate the legislators/audience at different locations, implying many authors behind the text and in its interpretation.[5]

Multiplicity of legislators/audiences is evident in the works of positivist and postmodern critics, both of whom privilege the text, but they approach it from different directions (cf. Matthewson 2002). Positivist critics begin from the text and U-turn from assumed legislators/audiences, while postmodern critics accept the "death of the real author [legislator]" and focus on the world of the text. The "death of the real author [legislator]" encourages literary analysis, which positivist critics of different colors affirm (cf. Foucault 1977; Eco 1983, 7–8; Žižek 1996, 92–93). In this connection, postmodernism does not murder the legislator/author but shows how the *death* of the real legislator/author is crucial for positivist readings (cf. Iser 1978, 27–38; 1974). The real legislator/author must die if the positivist critic is to have a case, and in order "not to trouble the path of the text" (Eco 1983, 7; cited in Olson 1994, 172). The death of the real legislator/author allows positivist discourses to flourish.[6]

---

[5] Wellhausen and van Seters (1975), for example, locate J at different places: J is a preexilic author/source for Wellhausen but an exilic theologian for van Seters. Moreover, van Seters's (1992 and 1977) exilic theologian is later than Ellis's first theologian. These critics appeal to source-critical principles but they imagine different Js, thus undermining the foundation of source criticism that Graf laid: J was the source par excellence rather than a historiographer or theologian.

[6] The "death of the real author," therefore, is a gift to positivist critics, a gift that keeps on giving and that ceases to be a gift when it is claimed (cf. Derrida 1995, 5–10, 40–52).

To speak *positively* of legislators/authors and their audience is limiting. It personifies the loci of meaning, some of which resist representation, and reduces the loci of meaning under monotonous categories. Such a double-edged practice gives critics a sense of distance, as if they are disinterested (cf. Fuchs 2000, 34–43). The foregoing review, however, reveals the ideological cover-ups of this practice; *critics themselves become the legislators/authors.*

1.2 Releasing Numbers 30

In practice, I can only begin with the text of Num 30, which is *in between* the assumed legislators and interested/legislating readers. During the reading process, Num 30 is sucked into a process of transformation, reaching a "temporary final form" when I release it, *let it be.* In other words, I continue in between, *inter-esse,* with the texts of Num 30, and *interested.*

I sift the text in this chapter to identify *dominant subjects of the law* in and of Num 30,[7] which I will rewrite in the following chapters.

1.2.1 *The Limits of Numbers 30*

There are grammatical differences among the ancient renderings of Num 30, with the text altered to harmonize (usually in terms of number and gender) the subjects of the regulations. My starting point in the following translation is the Masoretic Text (*BHS*), the least harmonized of the ancient versions. I preserve the playfulness of the text, identifying variances in the text and in the footnotes:[8]

> 1   And Moses said to the sons of Israel,
>   according to {all that Yhwh commanded Moses.}
> 2   And Moses spoke to the heads of tribes over the sons of Israel
>   saying, {this is the word that Yh}wh {commanded.}
> 3   A man,[9] when he vows a vow to Yhwh[10]
>   or oaths an oa{th to oblige an ob}ligation upon himself,

---

[7] Taking the positivist stance here, I imagine the real subjects who are regulated in Num 30. I refer to them as "dominant subjects" in order to distinguish them from other subjects that I address in the following chapters, and to debunk their evasion, or should I say invasion, by so-called dominant readers.

[8] Texts within curly brackets are preserved in 4QNum[b], according to Jastram's reconstruction, which uses the Samaritan Pentateuch (SamPent) as the default text (1990, 52–53; 1994). Differences between the MT, 4QNum[b], and a first-person rendering of Num 30:3–16 in the Temple Scroll (11QT 53:14–54:5; see reconstruction in Qimron 1996, 77–78; Yadin 1983, 240–43) will be noted in the footnotes.

[9] *Targum Pseudo-Jonathan* (*TJ*) adds "[. . .] of thirteen years [. . .]."

[10] The Temple Scroll renders the reference to Yhwh in the first person, "[. . .] to me [. . .]" (11QT 53:14), here and in 30:4 (11QT 53:16). *Targum Neofiti* (*TN*) avoids anthropological language with "[. . .] to the name of Yhwh [. . .]," twice in 30:3 but not in 30:4.

he must not break his word;[11]
    according to all that come out of his mouth, he must do.
4 And a woman,[12] when she vows a vow to Yhwh
    and obliges an obligation
      while in the house of her father in her youth,
5 and her father hears of her vow and her obligation[13]
    which she obliges upon herself
    and her father ignores her,
      all her vows shall stand
      and all obligation[14] which she obliges on herself shall
        stand.[15]
6 {But i}f her father restrains her in the day he hears it,
    all {her} vows and obligations that {she obliges on herself} shall
      not stand,[16]
    and Yhwh will release her because her father {restrained her.
7 And} if {she comes to a man} while her vow is upon her,
    or the rash utterances on her lips which she obliges up{on
      herself,[17]
8 and her man hears} in the day he hears {and ignores her,}
    her vows shall stand
      and her obli{gations which she obliges upon herself shall
        stand.
9 But i}f in the day her man hears he restrains her
    and annuls {her vow}[18] which is upon her
    and the rash utterances on her lips which she obliges upon
      herself,[19]
    and Yhwh shall release her.
10 And the vow of a widow and a divorcée,
    all which she obliges upon herself shall stand upon her.
11 But if she vows in the house of her man
    or obliges an obligation upon herself in an oath,
12 and her man hears but ignores her and so not restrain her,
    all of her vows shall stand

---

[11] So LXX, whereas SamPent uses plural form and *TJ* adds, "However, the court can release him; but if they do not release him, he must do all that come out of his mouth."

[12] *TJ* adds "[. . .] of twelve years [. . .]."

[13] SamPent, LXX, and Syriac use plural forms: "[. . .] her vows and her obligations [. . .]."

[14] SamPent and Syriac use the plural form: "[. . .] her obligations [. . .]."

[15] Verb is missing from Syriac, but in the plural form in SamPent, LXX and Targums.

[16] Verb is in the plural form in SamPent, LXX, Syriac, and Targums.

[17] *TJ* adds, "[. . .] in her father's house and her father had not freed [her] while she was still unmarried, then when she is given in marriage to a man, they shall stand."

[18] Plural in SamPent, LXX, and Syriac, thereby harmonizes 30:9 with 30:8.

[19] LXX adds "[. . .] because her husband restrained her [. . .]."

and all her obligation[20] which she obliges upon herself shall
    stand.[21]

[13] But if her man does annul them on the day he hears it
    then all that come from her lips,
    her vows and obligations upon herself, shall not stand.
    Her man annuls them and Yhwh shall release her.

[14] Every vow and every oath of obligation to deny herself,
    her man may uphold and her man may annul.

[15] And if her man does ignore her from day to day,
    he upholds all her vows or all her obligations which are upon
       her;
    he upholds the{m} for he ignores her in the day he hears it.[22]

[16] And if he does annul them after {he hears it,}
    he shall bear her guilt.[23]

[17] These are the regulations which Yhwh commanded Moses
    concerning a m{an} and his woman
    and concerning a father and his daughter
       while in her youth in the house of her father.

Textual evidences suggest that the disharmonious MT has not been revised as much as have the smoother versions of LXX, SamPent, and Syriac,
and the theologically loaded Targumîm. 4QNum[b]'s preference for
SamPent (according to Jastram) and the first-person renderings of 11QT,
which thereby transform the stipulations into direct speech events (so *TJ*
and *TN*), suggest that they too are later than MT. The linking of Num
30:3–6 (lines 14–21) to Deut 23:22–24 (lines 11–14) in the same 11QT plate
(col. LIII), presumably because of their shared interest in vows, also testifies to the lateness of 11QT.

I prefer the MT rendering for transoceanic reasons also: disharmonies
open the text for interpretation and hold back readers' control.

1.2.2 *Numbers 30 within Its Textual Limits*

Does Num 30:1 belong with Num 30:2–17 or with Num 28–29? *BHS*, followed by JPS, Smith-Goodspeed, Lamsa, and Moffat, sets Num 30:1 as the
closing verse of Num 29 and thereby eliminates the problem of having
two introductory verses (30:1 and 30:2) for Num 30.

Other ancient versions do not help determine where to draw the limits of Num 30. LXX does not attach Num 30:1 to Num 29 (so Knox), nor to
Num 30:2–17 (Rahlfs 1935, 270; so *TO*, Sperber 1959, 275), but leaves it in
between the two chapters as if it belongs to both. On the other hand, the
verses that link chapters 29 and 30 are missing from 4QNum[b].

---

[20] Plural in SamPent, LXX, Syriac, and Targums.

[21] *TJ* adds, "[H]er father shall not have the authority, at the same time, to annul
them."

[22] *TJ* explains that the husband confirms his wife's vows by his silence.

[23] The suffix is feminine in the MT but masculine in SamPent, LXX, and Syriac.

The *place-fullness* of Num 30:1 may also be explored on the basis of its referents. It may be read as closure for the sanctions that begin at Num 28:1, in which the sons of Israel are also addressed, so 28:1 and 30:1 frame the cultic rules in between. Since Num 30:2 addresses a different subject, *heads of tribes*, and since a different concern is stipulated in Num 30:2–17, the (non)binding nature of vows, the contents of the text advocate the separation of Num 30:2–17 from Num 28:1–29:39 and the use of Num 30:1 to close off Num 28:1–29:39.

The opposite limit of Num 30 is not as problematic. The summary statement in Num 30:17 indicates that what needed to be said, at that point, has been said. Numbers 31:1 picks up a different subject matter, Israel's relation with the Midianites. The opening limit of Num 30 is not as stable as its closing limit; in other words, the "limits" of Num 30 are oceanlike!

The more stable limit of Num 30, however, is not as tightly knit as it first appears. Numbers 30:17 brings closure to two forms of relations: "between a man and his wife" and "between a father and his daughter." The reversal of the identification of woman "in the house of her father in her youth" (30:4) to woman "in her youth in the house of her father" (30:17), a detail not preserved in some English translations,[24] forms an inclusion, with 30:10 as a supplement that falls within the limits of the relation "between a man and his [former] wife." On account of the gender difference between the regulated (male) subject of Num 30:2–3 and the regulated (female) subjects of Num 30:4–16, and since Num 30:2–3 is not concerned with "relations" as is Num 30:4–16, I unpack Num 30 in two units (vv. 2–3 and vv. 4–16).

1.2.2.1 *Numbers 30:2–3*

In the opening verse, Moses announces Yhwh's word (singular in MT) to the "heads of tribes over the sons of Israel." The reference to "heads of tribes" sets this stipulation apart from other laws, most of which are addressed to "sons of Israel."[25] This limited focalization gives Num 30 a tone of particularity. Yhwh's word is not given to everyone, but to a particular part of society.

The rarity of the expression "heads of tribes" makes determining its referent difficult, and its significance is open for interpretation. Eryl Davies proposes that "heads of tribes" is synonymous with "heads of the houses of their fathers" in Num 7:2, both of which echo the "head of the

---

[24] *TN*, LXX, KJV, and NRSV preserve the order and reversal of MT, while JPS (father's house then youth), NEB, and NJB (youth then father's house) synchronize 30:4 with 30:17.

[25] Israelite tribes are often addressed as "house/sons of Jacob" (Pss 77:15; 105:6; 114:1; 1 Kgs 18:31; Isa 29:22; 46:3; 1 Chr 16:13), "house/sons of Judah" (2 Sam 2:4–5; Isa 22:21; 37: 31; Ezra 1:5; 3:9; Neh 4:16; 11:4), and so forth, but to address the "heads of tribes" makes this stipulation unique.

house of his father" in Num 1:4 (1995, 316). This also applies to 1 Kgs 8:1 (par. 2 Chr 5:2), the other place where "heads of tribes" occurs in reference to a part of the "elders of Israel." The text imagines a time when Israel was organized according to tribes, each with its leaders (see census lists in Num 1 and 26), during the wilderness period. The commandments are not addressed to the Israelite masses, nor to the tribes in general, but to "heads of tribes" in particular, and I assume that "heads of tribes" is also an ideological referent rather than just a historical designation .

The straightforward command of Num 30:3 is elusive, teasing critics with its disharmonious outlook.

> A man, when [*kî*] he vows [Qal impf. 3d masc. sing.] a vow to
>   Yhwh
> or oaths [Niph. infinitive absolute] an oath to oblige [Qal
>   infinitive construct] an obligation upon himself,
> he must not break his word;
> according to all that come out of his mouth, he must do.

The command is an interpretive puzzle, for one may render it as a conditional (if . . . then) or an unconditional (since/when . . . he must) command depending on how one translates *kî*. Because of its unconditional content I read the verse as an unconditional command, "A man, when he vows . . . he must do."[26]

Numbers 30:3a uses three "binding" terms, each occurring twice: *ndr* ("vow"), *šb'* ("oath"), and *'sr* ("oblige," "bind"). These terms are reduced in 30:3b under the general category of *dbr* ("word"), pointing to "all that come out of his mouth" (30:3b), but they signify different functions and responsibilities.

Ndr is the term commonly translated as "vow." To differentiate *ndr* from the third term (*'sr*), commentators propose that *ndr* signifies *positive* commitments.[27] But a closer look at the uses of *ndr* in the Hebrew Bible (see Cartledge 1992, 36–136) suggests that *ndr* is not confined to positive commitments only. The Nazirite vows (*ndr*) regulated in Num 6, for instance, are unconditional *negative* (self-denying) vows. The one who takes the vow does not make demands on the god(s) but pledges service or abstinence from something, such as food, sex, or haircut, over a period of time and in some prescribed manner. "The supplicant places absolutely no conditions on his or her fulfillment of the vow; the votary offers to do something for Yahweh without placing any corresponding conditions on the deity" (Berlinerblau 1996, 175).

---

[26] Translating *kî* with "when" presupposes that the utterance has *already* been made, whereas "if" leaves room for future utterances.

[27] "Positive commitments" are conditional vows in which a person making vows commits an object or service as reimbursement for the fulfillment of a request(s) made to the god(s) (cf. Eryl W. Davies 1995, 316, and philological study in Berlinerblau 1996, 175–76).

Not all critics, however, find unconditional vows in Num 6. Cartledge argues that the Nazirite vows are based on the *condition* that Yhwh should grant the supplicant's petitions (1989, 409–22; 1992, 18–26). This claim makes problematic the positive-negative dichotomy that Berlinerblau proposed (cf. 1996, 176).

Notwithstanding, it is helpful to entertain a positive-negative differentiation because a positive vow makes sense in relation to a negative vow. The positive and negative poles, however, do not have to come from different vows. They can be referents of the same vow. With respect to Num 6, a Nazirite commits to perform an action ("set apart for Yhwh"; 6:2), so it is *positive,* and not to perform an action ("abstain from wine and any intoxicant"; 6:3), so it is also *negative* (cf. Wendel 1931, 31). The positive and negative elements are codependent, two referents in the same vow. Whereas the conversation between Cartledge and Berlinerblau is limited to the conditional form of the Nazirite vow, and the petitions expected of the person making the vow, I entertain the positive-negative differentiation in order to account for the *content of the vow* (see also Eryl W. Davies 1995, 316–17).

The use of *ndr* in 30:3, however, frustrates both form and content configurations. The simplicity of the regulation makes it complex and unsettling. The verb is a Qal imperfect, third-person masculine singular; the subject to whom the vow is uttered is identified, Yhwh, but the content of the vow is not defined. The undefined content of the vow points back to the act of utterance, so that the commitment, be it positive or negative, is enveloped not in the uttered but in its utterance. What is regulated is the act of vowing—not what one vows to do, or not to do, but that one vows a vow.

A vow involves three elements: the one who makes a vow, the vow he makes, and the one to whom he vows (recipient), who may (not) be himself.[28] While the content of the vow may be ambiguous or unknown, the person making the vow and the recipient are crucial for the act to be considered an event of a vow. According to this view, "Yhwh" is essential to the command because it (the name) completes, closes off, ends, ceases, (seizes?), the event of vowing a vow. Without the "to Yhwh" closure, the event of the vow is meaningless.

Nevertheless, the text does not rule out reading the significance of *ndr* as the consequence of uttering it "to Yhwh" (as subject), with *kî* pointing the emphasis onto the name of Yhwh. The force of the restriction that follows, "[H]e must not break his word, according to all that come out of

---

[28] Cf. Greimas's *actantial model*, in which an "object" (message) is transferred through a process of communication from a "sender" to a "receiver" by means of a "subject," whose effort may be assisted (by "helpers") or resisted (by "opponent") (1983, 207; cf. Jackson 1987, 1–5). In that regard, a "subject" sets senders and receivers a_part. Of course, a vow may be made in private, with no one to witness it, in which case the person making the vow is also the "recipient."

his mouth he must do . . . ," is the consequence of uttering the vow *to* Yhwh.

The other binding terms form a construct (". . . or oaths an oath [*sb'*] to oblige an obligation ['*sr*] upon himself . . ."); thus, these terms need to be read together. The second clause is an alternative to the first, with the particle "or" marking a shift from the positive-negative referents and religious connotations of *ndr*.

The alternative clause does not define the content of *šb'* (oath) nor of '*sr* (obligation). It resists decisive reading because the focus is on the one *against whom* the commitments are placed (Kottsieper 1973). The subject is also recipient, the host. While the *ndr* was uttered *to* Yhwh, the commitments of *šb'* and '*sr* are uttered *upon/against* himself. Both the '*l*-particle and the Niphal form of *šb'* (in its reflexive value) emphasize the displacing tone of the clause. Whereas *ndr* has room for positive and negative commitments both, the *šb'* and '*sr* construct signifies commitments that are negative only.[29]

But the second clause does not replace (due to the "or" particle) the previous clause. I read the "or" particle as a gap that makes the two clauses a_part of/from, as if they foreground and background, each other. The second clause is an *alter-native, alter* and *native,* bearing the *crossing* marks of transition. It points to itself and, as if it is apocalyptic, beyond itself to the previous clause.

The unconditional demand in 30:3b breaks down any distinction one may make between *ndr*, *šb'*, and '*sr*, because no matter what a man vows or swears, whether to Yhwh or upon himself, he "must not break his word, according to all that come out of his mouth, he must do." It is not *what* or *how* one commits that is crucial in 30:3, nor to whom. Rather, the force of the regulation falls on the demand *not to profane (ḥll)* one's words. Words and deeds are linked in such a way that the words of the mouth are profaned, desecrated, whenever they are not performed. As such, Num 30:3 both maintains and transcends the stipulation given in Deut 23:22–24:

> When you [masc. sing.] vow a vow (*ndr*) to Yhwh your God, do not put off fulfilling it, for Yhwh your God will require it of you, and you will have incurred guilt; *whereas you incur no guilt if you refrain from vowing.* You must observe what has crossed your lips and perform what you have vowed to Yhwh your God, having spoken the vow with your mouth.

Deuteronomy 23:22–24 is maintained in the sense that Num 30:3 echoes, or prefigures, depending on how one reads the relation between the two texts, in time/space or in book/canon, the concern to

---

[29] Milgrom suggests that '*sr* "can be either positive or negative (i.e., either performing or abstaining from a specific act)" (1990, 251). What makes it negative only here is the Niphal infinitive absolute form of *šb'* and the reflexive qualification.

uphold what one vowed to Yhwh. At the same time, Num 30:3 transcends Deut 23:22–24 by broadening the kind of words for which a man
is bound.[30] Deuteronomy 23:22–24 limits a man's obligation to his *ndr* to
Yhwh, but Num 30:3 shifts the boundary so that he must also perform
the *šb'* and *'sr* that he commits upon/against himself. Deuteronomy
23:23 (italicized above) discourages the making of vows, as does Eccl
5:3–4:

> When you make a vow to God, do not delay to fulfill it, for there is no
> pleasure in fools; what you vow, fulfill. It is better not to vow at all than
> to vow and not fulfill.

Kohelet adds a new dimension. It is better not to vow if one cannot fulfill what one has uttered; the alternative is no alternative—not to vow
at all.

Intentions, whether the vow reflects what a person making the vow
wants to express, are not taken into account in Num 30:3. This trend is
challenged in later Jewish thought with the resolution that "no utterance
is binding unless the mouth and the heart agree" (*Terûmot* iii.8, cited in
Eryl W. Davies 1995, 317). In Num 30:3, on the other hand, a man is already obligated to all that comes out of his mouth. "Once expressed, then,
words are binding, even when the expression does not correspond with
the intention" (Milgrom 1990, 251).[31]

A man has no choice but to perform what he said, bound to the
event of the word (what is said), which is independent of the *event of
speech* (saying what is said). In declaring that words are binding, Num
30:3 carries metacritical and ethical implications, drawing the critic
into its wor(l)d, its events. Numbers 30:3 draws the critic to the event
of the word to see if the text does as it says (cf. Fewell 1987). When the
text does otherwise than it says, the critic must not be indifferent, for
her involvement in the event of the word entails that she too is obliged
by what she says. Simply determining what the text says is not
enough; the critic is to say what the text says and to bind herself
accordingly.

Whereas Num 30:2–3 does not particularize its male subject, for all
men are regulated, not all words of women are binding in Num
30:4–16.

1.2.2.2 *Numbers 30:4–16*

Numbers 30:4–16 regulates vows by four subjects: an unmarried young
woman still in her father's house (30:4–6), a woman who comes with

---

[30] Numbers 30:3 echoes Deut 23:22–24 in historical-critical terms, but prefigures it in the canon. See 11QT 53:11–21, where Num 30:3–6 *follows* Deut 23:22–24.

[31] The Dead Sea sectaries offer a way out: "Everything that a man has imposed
upon himself by oath so as to depart from the Torah let him not carry it out even
at the price of death" (CD 16:9–10, cited in Milgrom 1990, 251; cf. *Nedarîm* 2.2).

vows to her husband (30:7–9), widow and divorcée (30:10),[32] and a wife who vows in her husband's house (30:11–16).[33]

•

The *first subunit* (Num 30:4–6) diverts from the pattern in 30:3. Only two of the binding terms (*ndr* and *'sr*) from 30:2–3 are used, and the stipulation is addressed to a particular subject, a woman "in the house of her father in her youth," unlike the generalized "man" of 30:3. Situating the subject *in her father's house* gives her a realistic and local (domestic) face. "Here the woman in question has not yet been married, hence she was living at home. One must here think of one old enough to make a vow in the first place. Therefore the reference must be to young unmarried women of marriageable age" (Ashley 1993, 579). *TJ* imagines this subject to be twelve years old (cf. Levine 2000, 431), whereas the man in 30:3 is thirteen years old.

The subject is a "young woman" for whom her father is responsible. If the father "ignores [be silent with] her" when he hears of her vow and obligation, they shall stand (30:5). If the father keeps his words to himself ("be silent"), the daughter must keep (perform) her words.[34] In that case, like the man in 30:3, the daughter is obliged and she must perform all that came out of her mouth.

On the other hand, if her father "restrains her in the day he hears it, all her vows and obligations that she obliges on herself shall not stand, and Yhwh will release her because her father restrained her" (30:6). In this case, if the father speaks up (gives his objection, in words), then the daughter must also let go of her words. The daughter is to keep, withhold, her words to herself.

The father does not have to be present when his daughter makes (*event of speech*) her vows, but he is given authority over her vows (*event of words*). Whether he ignores or restrains her is up to him, and he is not re-

---

[32] Numbers 30:10 does not fit with the other sections because its subjects are not mentioned in 30:17, and it does not stipulate the annulment of vows. One may thus relocate 30:10 to the end of 30:17, as in 11QT 54:2–3 (cf. Milgrom 1990, 253), or after 30:3, which does not consider situations when vows may be annulled. The *place-fullness* of 30:10 poses a threat to the (structural) stability of 30:4–16. At home at two other places, 30:10 makes problematic both the received form of 30:4–16 and any attempt to fix it *either* before 30:4 *or* after 30:17.

[33] I take into account the place where the regulated commitments were made (see also Milgrom1990, 251–54; Ashley 1993, 575, 579–82). Other readers, accounting for marital status, find three subjects: unmarried woman, married woman, and widow and divorcée (e.g., George B. Gray 1903, 415; Noth 1968, 225; Harrison 1990, 376–79). See also Levine 2000, 427–34, concerning women's legal status.

[34] Silent to the daughter, making him deaf to her, the father embodies the rabbinic dictum that "silence gives consent" (*Yev.* 87b; cited in Milgrom 1990, 252; so *TJ*).

quired to justify his objection (cf. Noth 1968, 225). But he must act on the day he learns of her vows, for he does not have the liberty to wait until the next or later day. If the father hears of her vow early, at the beginning of the day, he has time to consider his decision. The gift of delays is available to him. But if he hears of the vow toward the end of the day, he does not have much time to decide. The gift of delays is thus limited and his responsibility over his daughter's vows and obligations, as a consequence, is restricted. At the underside of this limited responsibility is the daughter, whose control over her words is restricted.

Declaring that "Yhwh will release her" because her father "restrains her" makes both the father and Yhwh responsible for the vows and obligations that are not fulfilled. But there are no clear indications if the father is also responsible when he *ignores* her (30:5). One may argue that the father is responsible for her vows in both cases, whether he restrains or ignores her, but the text does not confirm or reject such an assumption. In a text in which words are regulated, according to this reading, I imagine that silence ("ignore") is not binding upon the subject. Silence may indicate approval, but it does not regulate responsibility. In that regard, I assume that the daughter is fully responsible for her own vows even though her father may have approved them by ignoring her. She must keep, uphold, hold up, her words.

Since the father's responsibility is restricted to the vows that he annuls, 30:4–6 also regulates a father's *authority* over his house (so Sakenfeld 1995, 160; Olson 1996, 175). Yhwh too will acknowledge the father's authority, by releasing the daughter from her vows. Here, no cultic ritual is linked to the solicitation or award of the daughter's "release."

This first subunit presents *events of speech* in which one breaks upon another, as if they are ocean surf. The father's gesture to restrain may break upon the vow of his daughter, as if her words are his, but if he ignores her, his silence makes his daughter keep her words. This regulation focuses on what comes out of the father's mouth, which can "out-speak" his daughter's mouth (as if his speech can overrule her words). In saying his restraining words, the father sucks her words into his, but in *not saying* his approval ("ignore") he throws her words upon herself. By juxtaposition, 30:3 also applies to the father (in 30:4–6]): He is bound to what comes out of his mouth.

On the other hand, like a wave that passes without breaking (*ngalu heke,* in contrast to *ngalu fakaofo*), the father does not bind himself to the consequences of ignoring his daughter because he did not *say* his approval. If he speaks (to "restrain"), he is responsible for his daughter's vows. But if he does not speak ("be silent"), he washes his hands from his responsibility to her vows and obligations. At the underside of his "non-speech" is the daughter who, according to Num 30, does not have complete control over her words. Juxtaposed to 30:2–3, in which words are unbreakable, 30:4–6 makes words breakable and silence irresponsible.

According to this reading, the regulation of the father's responsibility and authority over his daughter undermines the idea that he has control over words (as suggested by 30:3). He does not control the words that his daughter vows (*event of speech*), and in ignoring some of them he releases himself from her vows.

Numbers 30:4–6 drives to personify a daughter's *events of words*, as if her words could be tamed. The foregoing reading resists that colonizing drive out of respect for her "out-spoken mouth." She is responsible for what comes out of her mouth (her words) and for what does not come out of her father's mouth (his silence). But those do not make 30:4–6 a *just* regulation (see ch. 4).

While still in her father's house, a daughter is under his limited and limiting authority and responsibility. But when she "comes to a man" (husband), her father gives up his authority and responsibility. She moves into the care and protection of another man, the shift (in place and authority) with which Num 30:7–9 is concerned.

•

The *second subunit* (Num 30:7–9) is concerned with vows that a woman makes prior to taking a husband, vows she brings into her marriage (30:7a). Vows may shift from one house to another, from one authority to another, but there is no indication if what "stands" (valid) in one also "stands" in the next (cf. Harrison 1990, 378). This subunit does not consider the possibility that the husband may annul vows approved by the father; it does not restrain the husband on behalf of the father. It thus opens up a chance for conflicts between a husband and his father-in-law, between two men.

The "shift of authority" over a daughter/wife is the product of the "shift of the vow." The text focuses on the "shift of the vow" and on how the daughter made her vows before she was taken by her husband, differentiating 30:7–9 from 30:11–16, in which "she vows in the house of her man/husband." The text invites us to imagine that the transfer of authority over a daughter/wife is not the only concern of 30:7–9. It is also concerned with authorizing male authority over transferred women. At the underside of these shifts are two types of female mouths, an unmarried and a married one, both of whom are "out-spoken" by male authorities.

Numbers 30:7 introduces a new element that qualifies the content of "what comes out of the mouth" (30:3), defining what a woman obliges upon herself as "rash utterances on her lips [*mbṭ' śftyh*]."[35] The husband's authority is limited to rash utterances, which is emphasized by the use of κατα in LXX:

---

[35] JB and NJB read "voiced without due reflection," and NRSV reads "thoughtless utterance of her lips."

But if she indeed comes to a man with vows upon her *according to* the utterances of her lips,[36] in respect of the obligations which she has
contracted upon her soul. But if she indeed comes to a man with vows
upon her *according to* the utterances of her lips or obligations which she
has contracted upon her soul, but her husband expressly disallowed her
on the day he heard them, then the vows and obligations with which she
bound her soul shall not be binding because her husband disallowed her.
And the Lord will acquit her.

To get a sense for what *mbṭ' śftyh* signifies I look beyond Num 30. The
use of *mbṭ'* in Lev 5:4 suggests that men too make rash vows (cf. Ps 106:33;
Prov 20:25; Eccl 5; tracts *Nazir* and *Nedarîm*), but rashness is not considered with respect to the vows of a man in Num 30:2–3. A man is bound to
"all that come out of his mouth" (30:3), rash or otherwise. Numbers 30:7
thus sets a different standard for a wife/woman: with her, vows may be
rash. She is different from the man in 30:2–3 and from the daughter in
30:4–6, not just because of gender or marital status but because she may
make rash vows.

The husband's authority in Num 30:8 echoes the father's authority in
Num 30:5. If the husband "ignores" his wife on the day he hears of her
vows and obligations, they stand. Since the "rash utterances" of 30:7 is not
addressed in 30:8, I imagine that the vows and obligations of a woman
that are allowed to stand were *not* rashly uttered.

"Rash utterances" is used again in 30:9, but for a different purpose.
The rashness of an utterance is a husband's justification for restraining his
wife, and he is given authority to do more than the father was allowed.
While annulment of vows is implied in the father's restraint of his daughter in 30:6, the husband's privilege is more specific in 30:9. The husband
may *restrain* his wife *and annul* ("render invalid") her vows, which are considered rash.

Nevertheless, the text does not state if the husband also has the authority to (dis)approve utterances that are *not rash*, a silence that may be
read in a transtextual manner: that the vows of a wife are (always) rash
and/or that the husband's authority is limited only to rash vows. If a wife
makes a vow that is *not* rash, she undermines both implications of this
regulation (see ch. 5).

According to this reading, 30:9 also limits the husband's privileges.
He is given some control because he does not have complete control over
his wife. But total control is not presumed in Num 30. The husband is further limited in that, if he is to restrain his wife, he must do so on the day
that he hears of her vows and obligations (cf. 30:6).

Reading 30:9 and 30:6 transtextually also discloses restrictions on
Yhwh. Whereas a reason is given in 30:6 for the release of the daughter

---

[36] LXX does not carry the sense of rash utterances, as it does in NJB: "If, being
bound by vows *or* by a pledge voiced *without due reflection*, she then marries . . ."

(her father restrained her), 30:9 does not explain why "Yhwh shall release" the wife. This silence suggests that a husband controls both his wife *and* Yhwh's capacity to release his wife from her vows. This reading insinuates who the *real author* of this stipulation is *not*. Since 30:9 restricts the wife and Yhwh, neither would have authored it. The "husband," on the other hand, as beneficiary, is most probably its author.

Both the "husband" in 30:7–9 and the "father" in 30:4–6 fit under the umbrella of the *'îš* ("man") in 30:3. The general sense of *'îš* extends the subject of 30:7–9 to *all men*, so it may become *no subject*, because to generalize is to erase the subject (insofar as subjectivity operates in the realm of the particular). If we read *'îš* (in 30:3 and 30:7–9) as *every man*, hence as *no subject*, we entertain the possibility that the real author is *no author* in any particular sense. The real author exists in the imagination, as a product of readings.

•

The *third subunit* (Num 30:10) does not have a male subject.[37] Numbers 30:10 addresses vows by widows and divorcées, women no longer under the authority of husbands (Deut 21:10–14): "And the vow [*ndr*] of a widow and a divorcée, all which she obliges [*'sr*] upon herself shall stand upon her." This stipulation echoes the earlier regulation of vows by a man (30:3), insofar as widows and divorcées are bound to their vows and obligations. But there are differences between Num 30:3 and 30:10, in addition to the gender difference of their subjects.

Numbers 30:10 does not name *to whom* ("recipient") the regulated vows were uttered, and I assume that they do not have to be made "to Yhwh" *only*, as 30:3 specifies for a man. Numbers 30:10 obliges the widow and divorcée to vows that they make to *any* subject, all subjects, including Yhwh. The indeterminacy over the "recipient" makes problematic the event of the vow. There is no place for a witness; no trace of the vow exists other than whatever the widow and divorcée are willing to admit (unless the vow is written; cf. Levine 2000, 437–41). This indeterminacy both restricts the widow and divorcée, for they are bound to *all* vows, and unsettles the event of the vow, insofar as a vow made to an unknown recipient loses containment (as though the boundaries that would hold it in place become porous). Two currents cross at 30:10a: *restriction* (of the widow and divorcée, by upholding their vows) and *unsettlement* (of vows, which can free the widow and divorcée from their words) are products of the indeterminacy of the text.

Absent from 30:10a are temporal and spatial restrictions such as those for the subjects of 30:4–6 (daughter who vows *while* in her father's house in her youth) and 30:7–9 (wife who brings her vows into the marriage). In

---

[37] I read 30:10 where it stands, suggesting that deconstructive readings do not set out only to dismantle the text.

this respect, also, 30:10a loses containment. It does not specify if the regulation is directed at vows that the widow or divorcée made *before* and/or *after* she became a widow or divorcée, some of which her father or husband may have annulled. Numbers 30:10a does not rule out vows that have been annulled by previous masters, nor consider that a woman becomes a widow and divorcée because of "broken vows." It is thus curious why the subjects who have experienced "broken vows" are obliged not to break their vows (see ch. 6).

Numbers 30:10 realizes that the widow and divorcée have moved to another authority, their own, but it does not clear them from their husband's authority. This oversight discloses a countercurrent. Against the efforts in 30:4–6 and 30:7–9 to particularize and restrict female subjects, by referring to particular places and times, 30:10 destabilizes its subjects by *not* restricting the vows to which they are obliged. This, too, is the result of the indeterminacy concerning the "recipient" of the vow in 30:10. Working against the particularization of the subjects of 30:10 is the generalization of their regulated vows.

The stipulations over female subjects (Num 30:4–16) are not directed to "all women," hence to "no woman," but to particular women. Such a drive locates Num 30 in the rhetoric of power (cf. King 1999, 1–3), in which one regulates particular subjects because it is not possible to control *everyone*. The particularization of female subjects defines the male subjects' control over them. Numbers 30:10, on the other hand, deals with female subjects who are outside the control of a male ('îš) subject. Here also, stabilization (placement) and unsettlement (displacement) coincide in that the widow and divorcée are defined categorically, but they cannot be confined by usual male constraints. They escape the realm of male control; they expose the elusions of control.

The regulation over the widow and divorcée are also different in the way that their vows and obligations are anchored *upon themselves* (30:10b). For the other women subjects, their vows and obligations shall stand, but *upon whom* they stand is not specified (see 30:5b and 30:8b).[38] A widow or a divorcée has no husband to ignore or restrain her and, as a consequence, she is responsible for her vows and obligations. Numbers 30:10 does not consider the possibility that a widow or divorcée may return to her father's house (see ch. 6), that she is still a daughter. At the underside of 30:10 is the double displacement of the ex-wife: from the house of her husband and, by implication, from the authority of her father. She becomes her own master and, like a man (30:3), she cannot be released from her vows.

---

[38] In the case of wives and daughters (30:5, 8), responsibility for annulled vows shifts to Yhwh (who must release them). But for the widow and divorcée, responsibility falls on the woman alone. She has no husband (nor father?), and she is not privileged to receive Yhwh's release.

There is a slight difference, moreover, between the regulation over a man (30:3) and that over a widow and divorcée (30:10). The man must do all that came out of his mouth, but the widow and divorcée have their vows and obligations "stand [as if words materialize] upon/against them." The man may opt *not* to do his words, but the widow and divorcée are obliged to the words that stand upon/against them, as if they have no choice but to shoulder them.

According to this reading, in which differences between stipulations disclose the ideological makeup of the text, Num 30:10 unsettles the drive to control female subjects under the authority and care of a man. The subjects of 30:10 stand in contrast to the subjects of 30:7–9 and 30:11–16, for whom a husband (*'iš*) is responsible. In that regard, 30:11–16 supplements 30:7–9, making 30:10 both disruptive and transgressive.

As a rupture, Num 30:10 unsettles the regulation of vows by a married woman.[39] It closes the previous subunit (30:7–9), which announces that Yhwh shall release the wife who is restrained by her husband (30:9a), and unsettles it by referring to "ex-wives" who can no longer be restrained by a husband. Authority shifts from the house of the husband to the "house of words" and, consequently, frees the husband from his responsibilities to his (ex-)wife. The disruptive 30:10 brings closure to 30:7–9 and prefigures (disfigures?) the next subunit and its attempt to make the man *more* responsible. This reading is harbored by the different consequences of the annulment process: In 30:6, 9, and 13, Yhwh will release the women whose vows have been annulled. But in 30:16, "guilt" will fall on the husband. The disruptive 30:10 marks a shift from the unrestricted privilege of a father (30:4–6) and a husband (30:7–9) to "restrain" the women subjects under their authority, to making the husband bear the consequence of annulling his wife's wows (30:11–16) as if his privileges were restricted. In addition to his wife and her vows, the husband in 30:16 is also responsible for *his own actions* of restraining his wife and annulling her vows.

•

Concerning the *final subunit* (Num 30:11–16), I first note a fracture, a gap, in 30:13, marked by the announcement of the woman's release by Yhwh, which recalls the points of closure at 30:6 and 30:9. But it is not necessary to read 30:13 as the closure of a subunit that must be read separately from 30:14–16. Numbers 30:14–16 both supplements the concern of 30:11–13 with responsibility for annulled vows and shows dissatisfaction with resolutions proposed there. I read these subsections (30:11–13 and 30:14–16) as distinctive but supplementary, paying attention to similarities and differences between them and between 30:11–16 and the previous stipulations.

---

[39] In this reading, Num 30:10 is both *place-* and *play-full*.

The use of the binding terms (*ndr*, *šb'*, *'sr*) in, and the verse structure of, 30:11, in spite of their different subjects, invite crossing with 30:3:

30:3   ". . . when he vows a vow . . .
        or oaths an oath to oblige an obligation upon himself."
30:11   ". . . when she vows . . .
        or obliges an obligation upon herself in an oath."

Numbers 30:11b reverses the word order of 30:3b as if to disarm the regulating tone of Num 30. An ideological struggle lurks at the underside of the text, encouraged by the gender difference of its subjects, suggesting that the difference between these subunits is deeper than the rhetorical artistry of the text. In 30:3, the string of regulations points toward the anchoring *upon himself.* But in 30:11, the anchoring *upon herself* is moved in, shifted, as if to disclose, to open up, the regulation. In the case of the man (30:3), his "obligation" (*'sr*) is the (outward) manifestation of the "oath" (*šb'*) he made. But for the wife (30: 11), her "obligation" is the (inward) content of her "oath," which points inward (in the verse) to the anchoring *upon herself.* Numbers 30:3 points the man to himself, but 30:11 points the wife to her "oath." From a transoceanic viewpoint, shifting the anchoring clause (*upon herself*) destabilizes the oath of the wife, making her words annullable.

The close resemblance between 30:11–13 and 30:7–9 also has a disarming effect. They address the same subject, a married woman, and in both cases her husband is given authority to affirm or annul her vows and obligations as he sees fit. But the disruptive 30:10 points me to another reading. The justification of a husband's authority to restrain his wife and annul her vows in 30:7–9 ("rash utterances on her lips") is not a feature in 30:11–13, as if the vows pledged while under the authority of a husband cannot be rash. The text invites this reading by preserving a trace of 30:7–9 in 30:13a ("all that *come from her lips*"). The annul-able vows come from her lips, but they do not have to be rash before they could be annulled. A claim of authority, defined along the gender divide (cf. Levine 2000, 435–37), lurks at the underside of the attribution of authority to the husband. Rash or not, the husband may annul her vows if he wants. According to this reading, 30:11–13 both *regulates* the vows by wives and *confirms the authority* of husbands over their women.

A trace of the husband's authority (from 30:7–9) is also preserved in 30:12 (" . . . and her man hears but ignores her *and so does not restrain her* . . ."). Compared to the authority of the father in 30:6, which is defined in terms of his decision to *restrain* his daughter and *annul* her vows, 30:12 twists the question of authority so that the husband's decision *not to restrain* his wife defines his authority over her. The husband in 30:11–13 also stands in contrast to the husband in 30:7–9. Whereas the husband in 30:8 may annul his wife's vows by simply ignoring her, the husband in 30:12 must not restrain her. If he chooses not to restrain her, in addition to ignoring ("be silent") her, he also chooses not to annul her vows. Here lies a transtextual opening: In not restraining his wife he restrains her, for his nonactivity obligates her to keep, to hold up, her vows. On the other hand, if the husband restrains his wife then her vows shall not stand and Yhwh shall release her (30:13; cf. 30:6 and 30:9). The wife is released if her husband restrains her! In this reading, *restraining* and *not restraining* are two referents of the same regulation (30:11–13). To restrain is not to restrain, and vice versa. This opening, this gap, however, is closed in 30:14–16.

Numbers 30:14–16 broadens the authority of the husband by adding something that is implied in 30:7–9 and 30:11–13: "*Every* vow and *every* oath of obligation to deny herself, her man/husband may uphold and her man/husband may annul" (30:14). The husband gets a blank check![40] His authority is extended to *every* vow-oath-obligation in 30:14, and his responsibility is simplified in 30:15–16: If he *ignores* his wife he upholds her vow (30:15), but if he *annuls* her vows *after* the (implied) one-day limit, he bears her guilt (30:16). Ignoring (being silent) and annulling are contrasted, and the husband is responsible for what he annuls ("bear her guilt"; 30:16b), but 30:15 is "silent" about whether he is also responsible for what he ignores. Judging from the anchoring *upon herself/himself* clause (cf. 30:3, 5, 8, 10, 12), I assume that the burden of fulfilling the upheld vows falls on the wife.[41] She is the subject *upon whom* the vows were made and upheld. In this case, appealing to 30:16, she bears her guilt.

Referents to the husband's privilege (*not*) *to restrain* his wife are erased from 30:14–16, distinguishing this subsection from 30:4–9 and 30:11–13. In 30:14–16, the husband must uphold his wife's vows and obligations if he ignores her on the same day he hears of them (30:15), but the expected qualification, not to restrain his wife (cf. 30:12), is not included in the regulation. Moreover, 30:16 does not explain how the husband may annul his wife's vow, a process that includes restraining in 30:6 and 30:9. In this regard, 30:16 oversimplifies the regulation by excluding the expected qualifications ("they are annulled if he annuls them" and "if he restrains her on the same day he hears of them") that we find in 30:6 and 30:9. In other words, 30:14–16 undermines the drive of Num 30 (and Hebrew Bible law in general) to restrain (control) its subjects. On the other hand, 30:16 replaces the traces of "[not] restrain" (as [in]activity) with the question of "guilt" (as consequence), and there is a consequence for this shift of rhetoric. Whereas Yhwh "releases" the daughter in 30:6 and the wife in 30:9 and 30:13, 30:16 only explains what will happen if the husband annuls the vows *after* hearing them: He shall bear her guilt. The shift from "release" to "guilt" (or "penalty"; Levine 2000, 427) suggests

---

[40] I use "check" in a double sense: as a bank draft (checkbook) and as a mark (score). In the former, the husband is given unlimited power; in the latter, he is not given any.

[41] One may assume that the husband is also responsible for making sure that his wife's vows are fulfilled (so Levine). But the text "ignores" that assumption.

that Yhwh does not always release subjects whose vows are annulled for them, and that the annulment of vows *after* the one-day time limit has consequences ("guilt" on the subjects who annul vows). On the flip side, by juxtaposition, the husband (*'îš*) takes over the position of Yhwh in the annulment process. Numbers 30:16 implies that the wife is released from her vows if her husband annuls them within the time limit, leaving Yhwh out of the picture, and instructs the husband on how to avoid bringing guilt on himself. Here also, the husband gets a blank check!

The husband bears the burden of the process. But since the vows regulated in 30:14–16 are without content, I cannot determine which (whether to uphold the vow or to bear the guilt for annulling it) has more burden. The underside of 30:14–16 suggests that the husband shall *not* bear her guilt if he annuls her vows when (i.e., within the one-day limit) he hears them, but it does not give him unlimited control over his wife and her vow. According to this reading, 30:16 ends with a deterrent: it warns the husband that he may bear his woman's guilt (cf. Rakover 1992, 122), discouraging him from annulling his wife's vow because of the guilt he may bring upon himself. The authority and responsibility of the husband (con)fuse in 30:16 in such a way that this (con)fusion deters husbands from abusing either, for to abuse one is to abuse the other.[42]

The juxtaposition of Num 30:11–13 and Num 30:14–16 gives us a glimpse of the workings of "legal revisions." In 30:11, the regulated vows are those that a wife makes in the "house of her man," but in 30:14, they include "every vow." In 30:12, the husband upholds his wife's vows by ignoring *and* by not restraining her, but in 30:15, the husband upholds her vows only by ignoring her. In 30:13, the annulment of vows leads to release by Yhwh, but in 30:16, the annulment of vows beyond the one-day time limit brings guilt upon the husband. According to 30:11–16, there is nothing wrong if a husband annuls his wife's vows. It is only "wrong" if the husband transcends the time limit. In this second reading, 30:16 is both deterring and stirring. It also encourages husbands to annul the vows of their wives within the time limit, for if they wait until the next day they will bear *her* "guilt." Numbers 30:16 suggests to a husband who hears of his wife's vow toward the end of the time limit that it is better to be safe (by annulling it immediately) than to be guilty later.

Legal revisions also occur in the gender- and status-specific regulations in 30:4–16. As a woman moves from one "house" to another, 30:4–16 shifts the authority over her vows from one man to another. The shifting of authority and the process of legal revisions, however, are made problematic at two places. First, the widow and divorcée are set beyond the realm of male authority and responsibility, as if they cease to be "daugh-

---

[42] Fusion is complete when one can no longer tell the difference between the fused elements, that is, when they are *confused*. The elements are not (con)fused if they are still separate. In this regard, *(con)fusion* indicates inability to tell and set apart both their differences and sameness.

ters" when they become wives. The widow and divorcée represent *women whose vows cannot be annulled* and *subjects who resist legal revisions* (see also ch. 6). And second, splitting the regulation over a wife (30:7–9 and 30:11–16) undermines the attribution of authority and responsibility to the husband. In its received form, the regulation over the widow and divorcée (30:10) splits (dis-closes) the regulations over a "wife" (30:7–9 and 30:11–16), the status that removes a "daughter" from her father's house. In this regard, the widow and divorcée (30:10) link the wife both to her father (under whose authority she made the vows regulated in 30:7–9) and to her husband (under whose authority she made the vows regulated in 30:11–16). In other words, the wife is under several authorities (compare the different "husbands of Hannah" in ch. 5). According to this reading, the "widow and divorcée" (of the "disruptive 30:10") set the women subjects of Num 30 a_part from each other.

The authority of fathers and husbands over their women's vows is made problematic in a text that grants authority (cf. Rakover 1992). Words that grant authority to the father and husband also deauthorize authority. This viewpoint begs two transtextual questions: Why did it become necessary to legislate, to *regulate,* words? Why grant that control (i.e., the power to confirm and annul words) to fathers and husbands? Numbers 30:4–16 makes explicit what is not apparent—male authority and responsibility—which needed to be regulated; in other words, authority and responsibility are both granted and limited.

According to this transtextual reading, Num 30 is unsettled and unsettling. Controlling words and vows is an ambiguous, and elusive, task. How does one annul words already uttered? How does one take back commitments already spoken? How does one un-speak speech? How does one reverse vows and obligations already committed, in words and/or in deeds? Even if one assumes that the annulment of words and/or vows is possible, how does one know when their annulment has taken place? How does failure to perform words and vows become their annulment? What if words and vows could not be broken or annulled, as presumed in the stories of Daniel and Esther? What if the words and vows of women are like the word of God?

> So is the word that issues from My mouth:
> It does not come back to Me unfulfilled,
> But performs what I purpose,
> Achieves what I sent it to do. (Isa 55:11 JPS)

On the other hand, what if words do not return because their utterance is their annulment, as if they are compromised in the event of speech? In the foregoing reading, Num 30 affirms that words are both breakable and unbreakable. When words are unbreakable, the person making the vow must keep, up hold, hold up, his/her vow. And when words are breakable, the person making the vow must keep, withhold, her vow to herself.

I have explored the *wakes* and *gaps* in 30:4–16, paying attention to the repetition of the regulations, how one understates some and overstates others, reading them a_part of each other. In its received form, 30:11–16 points to an *'îš* (in 30:16) and the "guilt" that his woman may bring upon him. This "man" opens up the constraints set in 30:2–3, as if to inform "men" that vows may be annulled if they are willing to bear the guilt. On that note, the call to "keep your vow" has several tones. It at once involves upholding and withholding, keeping and observing (as in the Hebrew *šmr*, "to keep," "to watch"; cf. Gen 4:2 and 4:9, in which both Abel and Cain are "keepers") one's vow. This playful crossing and harvesting of the word "keep" invites a transtextual turn: the vows of women in Num 30 are up for keeps (playing upon Penchansky 1992)!

1.2.2.3 *Numbers 30:1–17*

The difference in word choice reveals differences (openings) between the enveloping frames of Num 30:2–17.

30:2b   . . . this is the word (*dbr*) which Yhwh commanded (*ṣwh*) . . .
30:17a   These are the regulations (*qymḥ*) that Yhwh commanded (*ṣwh*) Moses . . .

The closing frame fractures the opening frame at two places. First, the singular "word" of 30:2b is transformed in 30:17a into the plural "regulations." In between 30:2b and 30:17a, we find both the dissemination of "word" into many words and the crystallization of words into regulations, "incisions" ("inscriptions"; Levine 2000, 439). In between the frames of Num 30, *words to be heard* become *regulations to be observed*. These alterations legalize (i.e., authorize) and multiply the word of Yhwh to accommodate the stipulations that come in between—the words of men. And since textual frames (limits) have the capacity to control how one reads a text, they grab the reader (cf. Penchansky 1992); the foregoing reading portrays Num 30 with a different kind of control. Because of the fractured and fracturing tendencies of its frames, Num 30 presents a transtextual form of control. Imitating the authority of the husband in 30:11–13, it controls (restrains) by not controlling (silencing, ignoring). It controls by letting go, by letting loose, by re-leasing; *control is elusive, it is up for keeps, kept by elusions!*

The second point of fracture, also an authorizing move, involves the redirection of the command given to "heads of tribes" in 30:2 to Moses alone in 30:17. It authenticates the regulations as commands *of Yhwh* and justifies their preservation by relating them through Moses, Israel's authoritative law mediator (cf. George B. Gray, 1903, 414; Eryl W. Davies 1995, 316). This second fracture opens Num 30 to 30:1, where "Yhwh commanded Moses" occurs, shifting the limits of Num 30 from 30:2 to 30:1. While 30:2 anticipates closure in 30:17, 30:17 pushes our attention beyond 30:2 to 30:1. The textual limits shift; in other words, 30:17 reopens, discloses, Num 30 to itself. The textual frames cannot *contain* Num 30. In the following chapters, I explore how its fractures, its gaps, open Num 30 to texts *beyond* its limits.

Numbers 30 breaks the opening frame by saying more than "the word that Yhwh commanded" (30:2b). It uses the "word that Yhwh commanded" to promote the authority of male subjects over their women, as well as Yhwh (insofar as Yhwh releases based on what fathers and husbands do; cf. 30:6, 9, 13).

Numbers 30 also breaks the closing frame by saying more than the summary remarks of 30:17 ("man" and "widow and divorcée" are not named in 30:17). The closing frame also says less than what was said after the opening frame. The more stable limit (Num 30:17) identified above opens Num 30 to itself. In other words, the closing frame cannot close off Num 30.

Numbers 30 has the capacity to do other than what is said in between its frames, including the capacity to resist the foregoing reading,[43] pointing this transtextual reader to the ideological nature of texts and interpretations. It is necessary, therefore, once again, to let the real legislators-authors of Num 30 die in peace, for their deaths give their texts new life.

I acknowledge the overflowing nature of the text in order to illustrate how textual limits fail to contain what the text says, in other words, to expose the *place-fullness* of Num 30. No matter how hard textual limits (frames) may try to restrain what comes in between, the text (i.e., words) can break through to say more and less. The overflowing characteristic of the text invites reading Num 30 beyond itself, a task I pursue in the following chapters.

1.3 Re-leasing Numbers 30

The majority of positivist critics argue that Num 30 is the work of priestly writers, giving it a late date, for they find stylistic characteristics of P in Num 30.[44] Words like "tribe" (מטה; 30:2) and "deny oneself" (ענה נפש; 30:14) suggest priestly writers (George B. Gray 1903, 413), and *šb'* ("oath") is a referent to testimonies in court and in worship (e.g., Lev 5:4, 22, 24; Num 5:21; 32:10, 11). In court, a *šb'* supports a testimony (oath of witness), and in worship a *šb'* signifies determination to perform as one has committed (oath of clearance; cf. Magnetti 1969, 27–46).[45] This double

---

[43] Just as the text has the capacity to say more than what was said, so must I invite it to resist the "more than" that I say it says.

[44] See George B. Gray 1903, 413; Budd 1984, 323; Eryl W. Davies 1995, 316. Other critics stop short of, as if they are uneasy with, attributing Num 30 to P (Snaith 1967; Noth 1968; Plaut 1981).

[45] Obligation (*'ssar*) and vow (*neder*) are distinguishable. "The *neder* may have been concerned predominantly with religious matters, whereas the *'ssar* was perhaps applied to social or secular concerns, but this distinction is at best uncertain" (Harrison 1990, 376).

placement delineates the *place-fullness* of Num 30, in which *šb'* identifies subjects who set obligations on themselves (30:3, 11, 14). A *šb'* binds a subject to an obligation (*'sr*), *confined to his or her words,* in a manner similar to ancient Near Eastern international treaties and Israelite covenant relationships (cf. Magnetti 1969, 65–143; see also ch. 3).[46]

The stipulation over the *šb'* of a male subject (30:3), announced to "heads of tribes over the sons of Israel" (30:2), may have been earlier than the stipulations over female subjects (30:11 and 30:14). The straightforwardness of 30:2–3 and the absence of legal revisions within 30:3 suggest that 30:3 is the earliest of the *šb'* occurrences. I assume that 30:3 was constructed to assert the irreversibility of commitments, over against which stands 30:4–16.[47] Unlike the *šb'* of a male subject, the *šb'* of female subjects is reversible.[48] The uses of *šb'* fracture Num 30 into two units, 30:2–3 and 30:4–16, with the latter unsettling the former. Here, the recurrence of *šb'* does not signify authorship but transtextual maneuvering. In Num 30, *šb'* shows that words are at once binding and nonbinding, breakable and unbreakable. Numbers 30 is playful in that way.

The linguistic argument cannot be used to identify, or deny, the real author/legislator of Num 30 with certainty because priestly writers, or any circle of writers, do not control the use of words. No writer, or reader, controls language. There are phrases in Num 30 that are not usually associated with P, such as "break words" (חלל דבר; 30:3), "oblige" and "obligation" (אסר), and "rash utterances" (מבטא שפתה; 30:7) (George B. Gray 1903, 413), but priestly writers could have used them, regardless of how critics define their linguistic preferences.

The reference to "heads of tribes over the sons of Israel" (30:2), preserved in the ancient versions (LXX, SamPent, *TO,* and *TN*), implies a time when Israel was (perceived to be) organized according to tribes. The rare "heads of tribes" is the distinguishing element of 30:2, without which 30:2a simply repeats 30:1a.

> 30:1a And Moses said [*'mr*] to the sons of Israel,
> 30:2a And Moses spoke [*dbr*] to *the heads of tribes over* the sons of Israel,

---

[46] Mendenhall (1955) was one of the first critics to argue for a relationship between ancient Near Eastern vassal treaties and Israelite covenant. His theory, however, has been revised by McCarthy (1963 and 1972), who finds aspects of Hittite vassal treaties absent from the Israelite covenantal formula, and vice versa.

[47] In the received form of Num 30, however, the regulating tone changes. It shifts from the irreversibility of commitments (30:2–3 and 30:10) to conditions when commitments are reversible (30:4–9, 11–16). The focus again shifts with the summarizing 30:17, from conditions for the annulment of vows to the relationship between family members.

[48] Because Num 30:10 shares the unconditional tone of Num 30:2–3, even though *šb'* is *not* used in 30:10, the text equates a widow and divorcée with a man. Neither of these subjects, however, is mentioned in Num 30:17.

A legal system in the modern sense, with judicial principles and decisions, may not have existed in "early Israel," but "heads of tribes" would have maintained order in a similar manner. This goes to show, as Plaut argues, "that P contains many old strands and traditions (probably predating J and E) but also later additions when the document was put into final written form after the return from exile" (1981, xxii–xxiii; cf. Kaufmann 1966 [that P is early]). This challenges the popular assumption that legalism was only a late institution of Judaism (cf. Wellhausen 1957, 77–78, 294–95, 423–24, 438–39) and complements Daube's claim (see ch. 3) that some narratives reflect existing (earlier) legal codes (cf. Z. Falk 1964).

Also problematic for attributing Num 30 to P is the absence of the essential marks of the priestly strand. Eryl W. Davies voices the judgment of scholarly consensus when he insists that P

> exhibits *an intense interest in cultic and ritual institutions and in the rules and regulations governing the activities of the priests and Levites.* This interest in cultic matters is one of the features that distinguishes this source from the other sources of the Pentateuch, but P's individuality is also apparent from its stereotyped and repetitive language, its measured, prosaic style, and its distinct theological outlook. (1995, xlviii; my italics)

Numbers 30 shows no interest in cultic institutions, nor in the activities of priests and Levites. It does not demand sacrifices with the making or annulment of vows, as in the case of Nazirites in Num 6, nor as prerequisite or restitution for release from obligations by Yhwh, as in the laws of Lev 1–7.[49] Numbers 30 does not require mediators (priests) to sanction what transpires between a person making a vow and Yhwh, or between family members (cf. Num 5). Rather, it falls on individuals to carry out what comes out of their mouths. The authority figures in Num 30 are fathers and husbands, operating at the family level (van der Toorn 1996, 182), not priests and Levites. Because no cultic tenets are preserved in Num 30,[50] and since laws are not only the work of the priestly class, I cannot confirm if Num 30 is the work of P (cf. Rofé 1986, 3).

The legislators/authors of Num 30 are not as determinable as positivist critics assume. I imagine the legislators' shadows in the text, but I cannot pinpoint their faces, nor their interests. Even if it was possible to determine the *Sitze im Leben* of Num 30, significant for cultural critics in both the socio-anthropological (cf. Douglas 1984, 1993; Mendenhall 1955; Gottwald 1979) and postmodern (cf. *PMB*; Fish 1989; Iser 1978) camps (see also Matthewson 2002), an interpretive leap is required to link Num 30 to its (assumed) *Sitze*

---

[49] The demand of sacrifice is crucial in Num 29, underscoring the demand's absence from Num 30. Nonetheless, sacrifice is not the only concern of priestly writers.

[50] In contrast to Milgrom, who does not speak of a priestly writer but associates "vow to the LORD" (30:3) with conditional dedications made at the sanctuary (1990, 251), a cultic setting.

im Leben. Critics' interests encourage such a leap, and this reading is no different. Since the legislators/authors of Num 30 are difficult to determine, and because I am more interested in the text, I too re-lease them to death.

A wife faces different stipulations, one for vows made in the house of her father (30:7–9) and the other for vows made in the house of her husband (30:11–16). The stipulations over women split the male subject into "father" and "husband," with the unsettling regulation for a time when no male subject is in control (30:10). The foregoing readings also make problematic the assumption that Hebrew Bible laws are static. I offer this augury with a transtextual caveat: I did not seek to destabilize Num 30 and/or its subjects but to call attention to their instability. Numbers 30 is dynamic, place-full and playful, hence unstable![51]

Nothing in the text prevents us from reading Num 30 in the context of the wilderness narratives, as if Moses were addressing the "heads of tribes over the sons of Israel." The text lures us in that direction at three places where Moses is named: 30:1, 30:2, and 30:17, the ebbing boundaries of Num 30. This proposal allows 30:1, which I ruled out in my first reading, back into Num 30. It brings closure to Num 29 *and* opens Num 30 to itself and to other texts, which I will unpack in the coming chapters.

The foregoing reading, which is both in between and interested (*inter-esse*), gave up trying to image the real authors in order to make explicit the ideologies *in* and *of* Num 30 (cf. Boer 1997, 7).[52] I began this chapter by exploring the positivist drive to identify authors of Num 30, and I close by acknowledging that critics have a say about where to locate its loci of meaning.[53] In between, I too author Num 30, not as a foolproof composition (in contrast to Sternberg 1985, 50) but as an unsettled and unsettling textual event.[54]

---

[51] Insofar as I assume that Num 30 is inherently dynamic, the readings in the following pages are also positivist; in other words, I can neither control nor escape limits.

[52] The more specifically we try to identify the authors, the less certain we become. As in the stipulations in Num 30, to be more specific (to particularize) is to exclude. In other words, to restrict Num 30 to specific authors is to make the text say less than it is capable of saying.

[53] I reserve for the next chapter two subjects that positivist readers of Num 30 ignore, but whose absence is elusive: (1) the wilderness narratives and law events in the book of Numbers, and (2) the "literary contexts" of Num 30. Ignoring such loci of meaning contributes to the crisis in contemporary biblical criticism (cf. Wink 1973, 1–18; West 1995, 21–46; Brett 1991). Moreover, to focus only on the discontinuities between different approaches and loci of meaning can be, indeed, has been, counterproductive (cf. Stephen D. Moore 1994, 65–83).

[54] Paradox, ambiguity, and incoherence are the stuff of transtextuality, and the reason for the endurance of biblical interpretation. I am reminded of Irigaray's embrace of ambiguity: "Be what you are becoming, without clinging to what you could have been, might be. Never settle. Let's leave definitiveness to the undecided; we don't need it" (1980, 76).

2

Ignored Subjects in and of Numbers 30

One of the most distinctive characteristics of Old Testament law is that it is enclosed by narrative. . . . The law does not stand in independence from that story. It is not even presented as a single chapter within that story but is woven into the narrative throughout. (Fretheim 1991, 201)

2.0 Introduction

What is *dominant* to one reader another may *ignore*.

I turn in this chapter to "subjects of the Book" of Numbers that readers of Num 30 ignore, without deserting the "subjects of the law" addressed in chapter 1,[1] upon the assumption that ignoring is interested, even if it is unintentional (so Lacan 1977; cf. Goodman 1986, 55). Nonetheless, I admit that *ignored subjects are elusive.* They are elusive absences, ignored but not erased; they are ignored because they are elusive, elusive because they are ignored.[2]

This chapter crosses positivist readings to face subjects that readers ignore in order to privilege their dominant subjects. Both modes of reading are products of the imagination: one aims to stabilize (dominant subjects) while the other drives to foreground (ignored subjects). In other words, seeking to face ignored subjects in and of Num 30 will disclose blind spots in the reading in chapter 1; these chapters unsettle and resettle each other.

I first map the place of the book of Numbers in the wilderness narra-

---

[1] The "subjects of the law" are constructed by the text, in this case, Num 30, just as the "ignored subjects" I address in this chapter are constructed by the book of Numbers.

[2] Because each reading has its own ignored subjects, its rem(a)inders, all readings are "ignor-ant" by nature.

tive with its complex composition and narrative tensions (§2.1), then turn to two subjects ignored by dominant readers of Num 30: the story of Israel's wilderness wandering (§2.2) and legalized events in the book of Numbers (§2.3). I close by exposing some of the blind spots in my reading (§2.4).

By revis(it)ing my own reading I turn the transoceanic process on myself, in order to account for the meeting of text with interpretation. This turn manifests the shift from meta-criticism to self-criticism, which makes problematic the assumed autonomy and stability of interpretation. The role that ignored subjects play in defining the text, and in enhancing its reception, points toward chapter 3, where I examine some of the "repressed subjects" in and of Num 30.

2.1 Mapping Numbers

The book of Numbers narrates Israel's transition between two places, in the wilderness, two years after the exodus from Egypt (1:1), and prior to the crossing of the Jordan (36:13; Josh 3:1–2). The complex composition of, and tensions in, the book suggest that complexity is inherent in biblical history, inviting us to cope with inconsistencies in the text and its interpretations. Elliot Binns made a similar judgment early in the study of Numbers:

> Any conception of the Historical Value of Numbers, as of any other O.T. book, which we may adopt *will depend almost entirely upon the critical position which we occupy.* . . . On the whole our knowledge of the real history of the Exodus period is very slight, and indeed until the period of the kings we can hardly dare to assert that we have much definite historical material to work upon. (1927, xxxviii–xxxix; my italics)

For Binns, whose interpretation is determined by the critical position that he prefers, the book of Numbers has more to say about the postexilic period when it was composed than the period that it claims to portray (1927, l). This view does not suppose that Numbers is *non*historical. Rather, it challenges us to account for the text's *historical conditionings*, to "cross and harvest" the conditionings of the text by events in history, some of which resist representation. In this chapter, I shift the focus of reading the wilderness narrative from *reading history as a textual product* toward *also reading the text as a historical product.* Being conditioned, biblical texts are ideological and interested (cf. Flanagan 1976, 17).[3]

I read Num 30 as it is, a chapter in the book of Numbers, taking the conditionings of the text seriously and recognizing that the wilderness narrative is an ignored locus of meaning for Num 30. I circumread a legal

---

[3] I bypass the debate whether texts have ideologies in themselves or whether they are products of the reading process. See the challenge by Stephen Fowl, who divorces the text from its mode of production and suggests that readers insert the so-called textual ideologies. On the other hand, I relate the text in the following reading to its modes of production, viewing the text and its interpretation as overflowing moments.

text with one of Israel's stories. In that regard, this chapter explores what McCarter calls "evidence of tradition" (cf. Shanks 1997). Evidence of tradition is not historical in the strict sense (cf. Herberg 1964), but imagined to be historical over many generations; it is *historical in the ideological sense.*

The transtextual readings that follow present a double shift, from historiography to ideology and from narrative to legal texts. This double shift is radical on two fronts. First, it is radical in proposing to circumread a legal text with a story whose credibility, as dominant critics claim, is difficult to substantiate, a story that evades historical ties (cf. Noth 1981b, 58–59); thus, I may end up with ghost readings. But since I read for ideologies at the underside of Num 30, I am encouraged by elusive readings.

Second, proposing to circumread a legal text with an old story is also radical because it is like setting up strangers that have nothing in common. I should expect them to go their separate ways! But these "strangers" coexist in the biblical text, making this transtextual shift a canonical argument also. In that regard, there are grounds for reading Num 30 *around* and *across* events of the wilderness wandering. I read for points where Num 30 coincides with the wilderness story, especially when they *cross* each other.

●

The structural outline proposed below emphasizes the admixtures of law and narrative texts in the book of Numbers, and it is highly subjective. Another critic may see as "law" what I propose as "narrative." The censuses in Num 1–4 and 26 are a case in point. For Milgrom, who perceives a regular alternation of law and narrative, the censuses (1:2–3; 3:15–16; 4:2, 21; 26:2), which Yhwh ordered, fall under the category of "law" (xv–xvi). On the other hand, I read the censuses as narratives because they serve crucial functions in the plot. As Israel prepares to march to Kadesh and on to Canaan, the censuses provide opportunities to organize the people by setting the Levites apart from the rest of the people (Num 3–4), and from everyone under Moses and Aaron (and Eleazar in Num 26).[4] By categorizing the censuses as "narratives" I resist reading all commands by Yhwh as "laws," in order to account for the story world that anchors them. Laws too have and/or create story worlds. In that regard, the structural outline I propose presumes the following working definition: *"Law" refers to instructions about behaviors or functions given by a figure of authority to subjects under her/his leadership, which may be enforceable beyond, in time and space, the confines of the story world.*[5]

---

[4] The censuses organize Israel by drawing lines that identify and divide the sectors (classes) of society; organization is by means of division (cf. Havea 2000, 111–17).

[5] This working definition intends to be "practical," viewing "law" as *prescription* (for order) rather than *decision* (legislation) (Knierim 1989, 8; cf. Dale Patrick 1985, 4).

This working definition is helpful in two ways. First, it emphasizes a delay between the law's utterance (command) and its actualization.[6] By speaking of command and actualization I acknowledge that some laws may be observed more than once, in contrast to other laws that may never be actualized. With regard to the latter, I maintain that a law is not defined by its actualization but by the *possibility* that it may be actualized beyond the immediate story world. As such, the Decalogue is still law even though its terms were actualized (through obedience *and* disobedience) in the story worlds of Exod 20 and Deut 5. A later generation that actualizes a commandment testifies to the durability of the Decalogue, sustained by the delay between command and actualization (cf. Jackson 1987, 10, on the continuity of legal codes).

The delay between command and actualization is a transtextual place at which laws may be examined in relation to each other and to some narratives.[7] At this (or some other) transtextual place, a second law may arise to clarify, supplement, undermine, and even replace the existing law. This is the place of legal revision and what Brin calls "double laws" (see also Levinson 1997; Nahkola 2001). In this chapter, the place of the delay is symbolic of the drive to exclude, to outlaw, persons that defile the community in some of the law codes in Numbers (see §2.3.1).

Second, my working definition is helpful in its openness. It enhances the flow of the narrative. I heed the warning that attempts to fit texts into tight categories are doomed to fail. I leave room for mixed categories (Gunkel's *mixed types;* cf. Linton 1991; Collins 1992), as in the following outline of Numbers according to its narrative (N) and law (L) texts:

Chs. 1–10:   preparation and march from the wilderness of Sinai
   1–2:   census and camp arrangements, by Moses and Aaron (N)
   3–4:   census of Levites under Moses and Aaron (N)
   5–6:   removal of defilement, and dedication to God (L)
   7–8:   consecration of tabernacle and cleansing of Levites (N)
  9–10:   paschal sacrifice, march to the wilderness of Paran (N)

Chs. 11–19:   delay in the wilderness of Paran
 11–14:   rebellion against God; Israel fails to penetrate Canaan (N)
    15:   laws in anticipation of entering Canaan (L)
 16–17:   rebellion against Moses and Aaron, on leadership (N)
    18:   subjugation of Levites under Moses and Aaron (N/L)[8]
    19:   rites for the purification of the (rebellious) people (L)

---

[6] I speak of "actualization" instead of "observation" because I see "law" as having to do with functions and tasks. I am concerned more with the *effect* of the law than its *principles.*

[7] This "transtextual place" is a place I insert with my reading, an imagined place; thus, it is an ideological placement, a place that I imagine because of my interests.

[8] Mixed categories also reflect the transitory and disclosing natures of Numbers. Numbers 18 (N/L), for example, is crucial in advancing the narrative by subjecting the Levites under Moses and Aaron in response to the rebellion by

Chs. 20–25:　transition from Kadesh to the steppes of Moab
　　20–21:　trials and wars during march to the steppes of Moab (N)
　　22–24:　Balaam and Balak's failed opposition against Israel (N)
　　　25:　apostasy at Baal-peor, the problem of foreign women (N)[9]

Chs. 26–36:　preparation for the dispossession of Canaan
　　　26:　second census, by Moses and Eleazar (N)
　　　27:　further anticipation of entering Canaan (N/L)
　　28–29:　cultic calendar (L)
　　　30:　fulfillment/annulment of vows (L)
　　31–32:　defeat of Midian and division of spoil; claiming the
　　　　　　Transjordan (N)
　　　33:　wilderness stations, preparation to dispossess
　　　　　　Canaanites (N)
　　34–36:　land boundaries and property holders (L/N)

The book of Numbers is a narrative with law texts supplementing the plot as its points of focalization shift from the wilderness of Sinai to the wilderness of Paran and finally to the steppes of Moab.[10] Numbers picks up the story of Israel's journey and does not have a final arrival to bring closure to that story, which is common in ancient epics. When Odysseus returned to Ithaca, for instance, it was not the home he had left. He had to fight the suitors of his wife Penelope and, instead of the homecoming he desired, he faced a reception to a strange home (*Odyssey* I:3–5). He returned to Ithaca but he did not arrive home, then he prepared to leave again. Similar was Israel's arrival at the steppes of Moab at the end of the book of Numbers, where it was poised to cross the Jordan.[11]

Korah, Dathan, and Abiram in Num 16–17. And its instructions may still be used at a later time to restrain rebellion. The same may be said of Num 34–36 (L/N), which has the qualities of law but serves the plot by dividing up the land to which Israel has been traveling since (before) Num 1. Both cases indicate that labeling a text "law" or "narrative" depends on the critic and her/his goals.

[9] Judges 11–12 (see ch. 4) lures us to read Num 20–24 as a unit that deals with Israel's wars against Edom (Num 20 [P]), the Amorites (Num 21, [P]), and the Moabites (Num 22–24 [JE]), which are referent points in Jephthah's speech (Judg 11:14–33). One may also add Num 25 (JE), also situated in Moab but outside the Balaam narrative. However, I yield to the traditional ways of treating the Document of Balaam (Num 22–24) independently from Num 20–21 (cf. George B. Gray 1903, xxviii–xxix; Milgrom 1990, xv; Levine 1993, 62–63; see below).

[10] Ingalis argues for the unity of Numbers based on its rhetorical structure. He suggests a three-part division (chs. 1–10, 11–25, and 26–36) that accounts for the temporal and geographical markers in the story. Compare with Snaith (1967, 4–5) and Budd (1984, xvii–xxi), who argue for a three-part division on geographical bases, although they differ from Ingalis on the extent of each division. The number of parts remains the same but the textual limits shift, because of the method and interests of each critic. See also Olson (1985, 31–32), who found twenty-four different outlines in forty-six commentaries!

[11] There are excesses to this intertext, for, in the strict sense, Israel was not returning home, as Odysseus did.

Along that line, I read Numbers as if it shares in legal traditions that do not require actual presence in order to sustain (land) claims. In the Roman legal *traditio* dealing with transfer of ownership, for instance, it "was not even necessary for me to step on the land or touch it with my hands: I might seize it, it was held, with my eyes" (Daube 1947, 27). Withholding Canaan from Moses therefore did not signify failure: "Moses saw the land full well, that in spite of his age he was capable of controlling and validly taking it with his eyes" (Daube 1947, 39), and Moses' eyes were not dim. In that regard, it was not necessary for Israel's journey to be completed in order for the book of Numbers to be meaningful.

I also read Numbers as a narrative that is open for future actualization. The subdivisions account for points of transition in the plot of a story that does not bring itself to closure. Both the transitory and open-ended natures of the book reflect the concern for reinstatement in some of its law codes (cf. §2.3.2).[12]

In mapping Numbers, I direct attention away from P, assumed to be responsible for the laws and part of the narratives, and for the final redaction of the book. And I downplay the differences between JE and P narratives, which disrupt the narrative flow of the book. My interests assault the unity of P, by exploring its diverse (in terms of genre) contents, and break down the barrier between JE and P, insofar as (according to most source critics) "narrative" crosses the source divide (there are narratives in both JE and P) while "law" does not. I direct this double assault below upon the story of Zelophehad's daughters, a narrative that was turned into the announcement and revision of a law, and vice versa (§2.2.2; cf. Levine 1993, 68–69).

There are also inconsistencies in the narratives of Numbers which would unsettle systematic and positivist readers (cf. Jackson 1973, 8–9), such as in the story of the spies. The spies were sent from the "Wilderness of Paran" (Num 13:3) at the northern end of Sinai, but they returned to "*Kadesh* at the Wilderness of Paran" in 13:26 (MT, LXX, SamPent). The inconsistency concerns the placement of Kadesh (Barnea), assumed to be located in the Wilderness of Zin in the southern Negeb (cf. 20:1; 33:36; 34:3–4), which Israel did not reach until a later time (cf. 20:1–2 [P]). If the spies *returned* to Kadesh, then they must not have *departed* from the Wilderness of Paran.

The Israelites passed through Kadesh on their way to the steppes of Moab, but Numbers does not confirm when they arrived at Kadesh or how long they stayed there. According to one witness (P), Israel wanders around the Sinai Peninsula and arrives at Kadesh toward the end of the

---

[12] My reading echoes the rabbinic "call to imagine arrival" which Susan Slater, following Cynthia Ozick, sees as the heart of Deuteronomy's rhetoric. Slater argues that in Deuteronomy "the call to imagine arrival in all its aspects is yoked with a powerful imperative for active love of God in covenant obedience, and this is understood as the way from imagination to actualization" (Slater 1999, 107).

wilderness sojourn. But in another witness (JE), Israel arrives at Kadesh earlier on,[13] and settles there for most of their time in the desert (Levine 1993, 53–57; cf. Snaith 1967, 23–26). The book of Numbers says that Israel spent most of the wilderness time at Sinai *and* at Kadesh.[14] These traditions, read with positivist eyes, resist each other.

Levine imagines geographical fudging in 13:26, with Kadesh slipping southward into the Wilderness of Paran (1993, 54). But one may also argue for the Wilderness of Paran slipping northward to the Wilderness of Zin. The narrator shifts the boundary as if he were a later writer (P) who reworked 13:26 (JE). Assuming that "Kadesh" was original to 13:26, Israel arrived at Kadesh earlier than P proposed (Levine 1993, 54). This early arrival justifies the divine decree to delay their entry into Canaan as punishment for the spies' report (14:26–38). In that regard, we have both geographical fudging and a drive to postpone Israel's arrival at Kadesh. The boundaries shift in the narrator's account, and under the critic's pen.

When accounts conflict, systematic historiographers usually favor what they believe to be the earlier witness. Such judgments are based on three biases: (1) that an earlier witness is more reliable, (2) that an earlier account is not as interested as later ones (cf. McEvenue 1971, 91–92), and (3) that conflicting accounts cannot both be historical. These biases confuse earlier with reliable witnesses, which are taken to be historical only and not also ideological, and consequently blind critics to certain subjects in the text.

Everyday experiences teach us, on the other hand, that reality (as in what is historical) contains conflicting witnesses, so we should also expect conflicts in earlier claims. We read conditioned texts, and it is not uncommon for claimants to have different opinions about an event due to obscurity on the part of the event, uncertainty on the part of the claimant, and ambiguity on both parts. The Balaam narrative makes explicit the differing opinions, and desires, that the biblical narrator and characters have about the same event.[15]

The narrator presents God as a character who does not know everything around him when he asked Balaam, "What do these people want of you?" (Num 22:9). Told of Balak's desire to curse Israel, God objects (22:12) but then allows Balaam to go (22:20).[16] Then he changes his mind again

---

[13] See George B. Gray 1903, xxix–xxxix, for the distribution of JE and P in Numbers, which is the starting point for many source critics. Compare Levine 1993, 48–50, and Milgrom 1990, xvii–xxii.

[14] It is possible that these are locations with the same name, just as there is a Toronto and a Newcastle in New South Wales, Australia. On the other hand, "Kadesh" may just be an ideological placement that should not be defined locally.

[15] On reading for desires, see Jobling 1994. Since the Balaam narrative contains conflicting voices, it is a fitting critique of the bias that earlier texts are always reliable.

[16] Because of repetitions and conflicts (e.g., the messengers are "elders" in 22:7 but "princes" in 22:8, 15, 21), commentators have argued that Num 22–24 is not a

the next morning: "God was incensed at his going" (22:22). God has differing opinions, accented by the opposite claim that "God is not man to
be capricious, or mortal to change his mind . . ." (23:19). God did not
change his mind concerning Israel and Balak, but he changed his mind
concerning Balaam and his mission. Balaam is the central character—also
an outsider and a foreigner—who is in contact with Israel's guardian
God, as if he is both a hero and villain. These tensions are the consequences of the excessiveness and elusiveness (fluidity) of the text.

The relation between God and Balaam is complex. At first Balaam
says only the word God gave him (22:20; 23:5, 16), but then he "takes *his*
[God's?] theme (*mšl*)" and the words that follow are not identified with
God but Balaam: "Word (*n'm*) of Balaam son of Beor, word of the man
whose eye is true" (24:3, 15). Word of God, or word of Balaam? I find
Balaam resisting God's destabilizing responses by (con)fusing the word of
God with his own.

The details of the narrator's representation of God and Balaam are
not as consistent as a systematic reader would prefer. As God's opinion toward Balaam's expedition changes, so does the source of Balaam's
utterances. The narrative is elusive. On the other hand, if we read the
story from the side of Balak and the Moabites (who are "outsiders"), a consistent picture emerges. God is determined to bless Israel in spite of the
repeated sacrifices. God's inconsistency hurts Balaam and his consistency
hurts Balak and the Moabites.

This reading finds uncertainty in the voice of the narrator. But this is
a different kind of uncertainty from the one we found in the spy stories,
in which the narrative tension involves different voices (JE and P).[17] In the
Balaam story, the tension exists within the same narrative voice (or voices
[JE]). Upon these narrative inconsistencies I take a transtextual leap; I surf
from one wave to another. A similar tension exists in the priestly material
(P) due to the two types of material it contains: narrative and legal texts.
P has two faces, as narrator and as legislator. Critics who explore the relation between these two types look to see if they come from the same settings (cf. Crüsemann 1996), and if narrative and legal texts are from different situations they imagine that the narrative was earlier (cf. Carmichael
1985; 1992) or later (cf. Daube 1947; 1981). This cross-type kind of study
has not been undertaken with Num 30, a gap that this chapter fills.

---

literary unit. But it is impossible to distinguish the different voices without dis-
mantling the story. In the following reading, I read the Balaam narrative as a *single
complex account* (cf. Sturdy 1976, 157; Wenham 1981, 164–65). I read the text with
its disharmonious voices.

[17] The "narrator" transcends the "sources" in order to tell the story in its
"canonical" form (cf. Gunn and Fewell 1993, 52–63; Bal 1985, 120–26; Miscall 1998).

2.2 Circumreading Numbers 30 with the Wilderness Motif

To circumread Num 30 with the wilderness narrative, I build on Noth's reconstruction of pentateuchal traditions. Noth argues that these traditions, from different tribes, were originally independent of each other but they "manifestly have *only* an *all-Israel* significance" early in the development of the traditions (1981b, 43). He arranged his five traditions diachronically, between the *terminus a quo* at the emergence of the twelve tribes in Canaan and the *terminus ad quem* at the time of statehood: guidance out of Egypt, guidance into arable land, promise to patriarchs, guidance in the wilderness, and revelation in Sinai (which is not the foundation of Israel's faith-election).[18] Each theme has its distinct core of tradition and history of development, which later writers reworked in order to "historicize" and "Israelitize" the account (Noth 1981b, 46–145). The fourth theme sets the following reading in motion.

2.2.1 *Of Guidance*

In its received form, "guidance in the wilderness" fills the gap between, as if to hold a_part, "guidance out of Egypt" and "guidance into arable land." These two themes share the motif of *guidance*, with God as the *guide* and Israel as the *guided*. But the wilderness theme differs in the sense that it "seems to lack any cultic rootage, even though individual stories with a cultic content have clearly contributed to its narrative development" (Noth 1981b, 58, 59). Von Rad adds that the accent of the divine-guidance motif falls on God's salvation acts in history, *Heilsgeschichte*, in which *guidance* is manifested as "essentially statements of belief . . . [as] a *creed*, a summary of the principal facts of God's redemptive activity" (1966, 2, 106; see also 1958, 68–78).

Coats also finds divine guidance in murmuring stories, whose intention was to present God as Israel's provider in the wilderness (1968, 38–39). Graham Davies's study of Deuteronomistic itinerary notes, which he contrasts with P's attention to the turning points of the story (cf. 1979, 62–93), suggests that the idea of wilderness *journey* "is found not only in the historical retrospects of Deut. i–ii and Judg. xi but also in the theologoumenon of Yahweh as *hammôlîk*, the guide, in the wilderness (Deut. viii 2, 15, xxix 4)" (1983, 12).

The initial wilderness event in Exod 15:22–27 roots divine guidance in the wilderness tradition.[19] The story is framed with itinerary formulas,

---

[18] For von Rad, a "very long process of literary crystallisation" led by Deuteronomy's homiletical interest in the will of God made Sinai prominent (1966, 33; cf. Olson 1994, 172ff.). These cultic traditions legitimize Israel's claim to the land (von Rad 1966, 46–47) and explain why the Yahwist introduced them with the patriarchal promise of land (cf. 1966, 56–57); hence, the traditions form a promise-and-fulfillment Hexateuch (cf. von Rad 1962, 304).

[19] Most critics limit the wilderness tradition in Exodus to 15:22–18:27 (cf. Noth 1962, 127; Hyatt 1971, 17; Childs 1979, 170), but Coats 1972 takes it back to Exod 12.

marking Israel's departure (15:22a) and arrival (15:27), while the middle part sets up the basis for an etiology (15:23–25a [J]) and demands the observance of "a fixed rule" (15:25b–26 [D]). After Israel travels for three days without finding water (15:22b), it arrives at Marah, where water is bitter and the people "grumbled against Moses" (22:24). The murmuring motif may be read back to this pericope, but the focus falls upon Yhwh's ability to provide and restore the sweet water that Israel lacks. Israel's complaint is not out of rebellion but the repercussion of its existential plight: for three days, Israel cannot find water (cf. 17:1–7). Moreover, the text does not propose that the sweetened water was given as *punishment* for Israel's rebellion. Coats consequently concludes that

> the whole section of response to the murmuring seems to be dominated by the gift of Yahweh's gracious aid. And this . . . has no intrinsic negative connotation. The only contact in this unit with the murmuring motif, and thus with a negative view of the people's request for water, lies in the narrative introduction. (1968, 52; in contrast to McCurley 1979, 95)

Two readings are possible. A *negative* reading relates this story to other water narratives in which Israel rebels against Yhwh and Moses (e.g., Exod 17:1–7; Num 20:1–13), while a *positive* reading will have "as its content the quite positive request for something to drink and Yahweh's gracious response to that request" (Coats 1968, 52). Both readings imagine that Yhwh is in control in the wilderness. He guides Israel by providing what they lack, water, and by punishing them for their rebellions.

> Yahweh is repeatedly portrayed as providing for Israel's needs in the desert in the most dramatic ways: these include guidance by the pillar of cloud and fire (Exod 13:21–22) and by the movement of the ark (Num 10:33), as well as the provision of food and drink. Even the hardships of the journey are seen positively as divine discipline (Deut 8:3–5). (Graham I. Davies 1992, 914)

Protection of Israel from enemies in the wilderness (Exod 17:8–16) also falls within the realm of divine guidance (cf. Noth 1981b, 119–22). Between Egypt and Canaan, Israel marches under divine guidance.

But the motif of divine guidance is not limited to the wilderness tradition. It is also present in the exodus tradition, which overlaps with the wilderness tradition. The event that separates these traditions, the deliverance at the Reed Sea (Exod 13:17–15:21), cannot keep them apart, and critics do not agree how to read this transoceanic event. For Noth, the exodus climaxes with the deliverance at the Reed Sea, and he treats "guidance out of Egypt" as independent of other pentateuchal themes (1962, 105; cf. Coats 1967, 254). Childs (1970b) too ties the Reed Sea to the exodus, based on Exod 14:1–2 (P), in which Israel is ordered to turn back and camp in Egypt, thus linking the Reed Sea to Egypt. Moreover, Exod 13:20 and Num 33:5 mention Israel reaching Etham at the "edge of the wilderness," suggesting that "the wilderness" did not begin until Israel left the Reed Sea region, the point where the exodus from Egypt reaches its conclusion.

Other critics link the Reed Sea to the wilderness tradition instead (Coats 1979). Burden provides textual support for this argument: "The setting for the Reed Sea in all three sources (Exod. 13:17–18 [E], 13:20ff. [J], 14:1–2 [P]) also places Israel outside of Egypt and in the wilderness" (1994, 21). Nonetheless, Burden also claims that the exodus concludes with the Reed Sea event (23). This invites reading the event that separates the exodus from the wilderness as an event that links them; the limit that sets apart also brings together, to be a part of each other. According to this reading, the Reed Sea is both the climax (end) of the exodus and the beginning of the wilderness tradition. This reading reopens, it discloses, the Reed Sea back to Egypt and forward to Canaan.

By recognizing the double link between the exodus and wilderness traditions, I insert an ethical demand into the wilderness narrative. Yhwh should be responsible for the people he guided out of Egypt during their passage in the wilderness (cf. Num 11:10–15).[20] In this sense, divine guidance is the expression of Yhwh's redemptive acts in history and the enactment of his responsibility toward Israel. It is thus misleading to speak of the wilderness period as the *wanderings* of Israel, for Israel proceeded under the guidance of God. Graham Davies is quick to point out that "[o]nly in the latter stages is the idea of aimless wandering present, where it is regarded as a divine punishment for the Israelites' failure to make a direct assault on southern Palestine (Num 14:33–34; 32:13; Deut 2:1–3). In the wilderness itinerary in Num 33:1–49 the notion of 'wandering' is completely lacking" (1992, 912).

What, then, is the contribution of the motif of divine guidance for reading Num 30?[21] Where does this theme guide Num 30? These questions require an interpretive leap, made possible by two ideological stepping stones.

First, one may read a father's right to annul his daughter's vow as a figure of the motif of guidance. As Yhwh provided provisions and protection for Israel in the wilderness, so should a father take care that his daughter does not commit herself to something that will hurt her. This reading pacifies the sense of "restrain" in Num 30:6. The father restrains his daughter in order to guide her away from trouble. In that sense, the

---

[20] I am reminded of Wiesel's lament on behalf of Jews, who felt that God drew them into a covenant so that God could press them harder: "Either You are our partner in history, or You are not. If You are, do Your share; if You are not, we consider ourselves free of past commitments. Since You choose to break the covenant, so be it" (1979, 194).

[21] In its received form the motif of guidance surrounds, is the context for, Num 30. This circumreading allows the narrative to inform my reading of Num 30. I later allow the wilderness narrative and Num 30 to "cross" (cut) each other.

annulment of a daughter's vows is not harsh punishment for misbehavior but caring guidance through the wilderness of her youth. A guardian father who ignores his daughter and her vows (30:5) is not negligent, if he thinks that her vows and obligations are not hazardous. One may also read the husband's right to annul "rash utterances" or to uphold his wife's vows in the same manner (30:7–9, 11–16). Like the father, the husband too may "ignore" his wife if he finds no objections against her vows (30:12, 15). Numbers 30 also defines the functions of the *hammôlîk*, the guide, over daughters and/or wives. The guide must also care and provide for his subjects.

A second stepping stone leads from the ethical sense of the motif of guidance. Numbers 30 circumscribes the responsibility of a father for his daughter (30:4–6) and of a husband for the wife who comes to (30:7–9), or is already in (30:11–16), his house. As Yhwh was bound to Israel in the wilderness because he had guided them out of Egypt, so fathers and husbands are bound to the daughters and wives they bring into their houses. It is not their *privilege* to establish or annul the vows and obligations, the words, of their dependents, but their *responsibility*. This responsibility is irreversible, implied in the firm decree over the moment of decision: both the father (30:6) and husband (30:8, 9, 13, 15) must decide on the same day if the vows are to be established or annulled. Once they decide, they must abide. The motif of responsibility suggests a resisting current at the underside of Num 30, disclosing a double voice at the event of reception. A text that defines occasions when commitments (by women) may be reversed also stipulates binding responsibilities (on men).[22]

The binding nature of responsibility (response-ability) requires one to act with regard to another subject, in response to an other. The face of the other obliges one's responsibility. This conjecture extends my transtextual reading: As Yhwh's acts of deliverance in the exodus and guidance in the wilderness were *in response* to the cries of Israel, so should fathers and husbands relate to the women within their houses (Num 30). In other words, they should "ignore" and/or "restrain/annul" *in response* to their female subjects.

In Num 30, however, the matter of responsibility is compromised. Numbers 30 does not require fathers and husbands to justify their responses to the vows by the(ir) women, as if they do not have to respond to the face of the other. As such, a daughter/wife may experience her father's/husband's responsibility to ignore (30:5, 8, 12, 15) or restrain her (30:6, 9), or to annul her vows (30:13, 16), as an irresponsible act that fails to account for her face and interests. Multiple readings of Num 30 are thus allowable.

---

[22] The irreversibility of responsibilities crosses the gender divide, since the widow and divorcée have no choice but to perform as they have committed (30:10).

When fathers and husbands affirm/annul vows, they disturb intact relations. To be responsible, fathers and husbands insert a "third subject" (themselves) that prevents the meeting of daughters/wives with Yhwh (to whom vows were made). To perform their responsibilities, fathers and husbands displace Yhwh as the one to whom female subjects must respond. In that regard, Num 30 is elusive in asserting that the regulation of these disruptions was commanded by Yhwh (30:1, 2, 17). This reading finds Num 30 substantiating the placement of fathers and husbands, who overtake the place of the other, converting their function from having to respond to female subjects into having daughters and wives respond to them. Numbers 30 anticipates that daughters and wives will observe their guardians' judgments. Yhwh too is expected to comply with the male subjects, by releasing the daughter (30:6) and wife (30:9, 13) from vows that they made. Yhwh is doubly displaced.

The motif of responsibility urges us beyond the realm of phenomena to the realm of praxis. When readings fail to enter the latter, readers end up with conceptualizations that fall short of what *response-ability* embodies. But in the realm of praxis we discover that texts are more complex then we would prefer. Texts often do more than they say (Fewell). The foregoing reading suggests that fathers and husbands displace Yhwh from the place of the other, and oblige him to them. The one who releases daughters and wives from their vows and obligations is in the end *restrained!*

On the other hand, texts also have the tendency to say more than they do. Numbers 30 *says* that fathers and husbands are to be responsible for their female subjects, but it does not allow daughters and wives to be in the place of the other, where they might become subjects to whom fathers, husbands, and Yhwh respond. This reading finds the guardians responding to their interests instead of the face of the other (daughters and wives). What those interests may be are not defined, just as the contents of the vows are undefined, but I assume that the interests of the guardians will benefit the ones who overtook the place of the other. Initially, I expected fathers and husbands to be responsible for "their women," but Num 30 subordinates daughters and wives to their *hammôlîk* instead. I also expected Yhwh to respond to subjects who made vows to him, but in Num 30 Yhwh is directed to respond to the judgments of fathers and husbands. The text unravels my expectations by not doing all that it says. This text also says more than it does. It is elusive.

2.2.2 *Of Rebellion*

Complementing the motif of divine guidance is the murmuring motif, which is Israel's response to the absence of their *hammôlîkîm*. This motif portrays the wilderness as a place where Israel tested Yhwh and Moses, provoking Yhwh's anger (Exod 16:28; Num 14:11; and Moses', Exod 16:20b) and punishment (Num 20:12; compare Exod 15:22–25; 17:1–7; cf.

Num 14:11ff.; see Coats 1968, 21–28). Israel's complaints did not always provoke anger (in Exod 3:7–10, Israel's outcry led to deliverance from Egypt), but those that did are presented as rebellions against Yhwh's purpose (Num 14:3; cf. Josh 7:7; 22:16) and/or the leaderships of Moses (Exod 15:24; Num 15:36) and Aaron (Exod 16:2–3).

The murmuring motif, also, is not unique to the wilderness tradition. It has counterparts in other texts before and after the wilderness story, against humans and Yhwh both (cf. Gen 3:13; 12:18; 20:9; 26:10; 29:25; Exod 1:18; 5:15; Josh 7:7; 22:16; Judg 8:1; 12:1; 2 Sam 12:21; Neh 2:19; 13:17; and so forth). The charges vary in form and content according to each setting, but they all have to do with a party's perception that it has been mistreated. In that regard, the murmuring motif is ethically and existentially motivated. The complainant demands both explanations and accountable conducts from the opposition.[23]

The murmuring motif accentuates God's role in Israel's passage from Egypt to Canaan. Since God brought Israel out of Egypt, he is *liable* to them in the wilderness. The complaints then express Israel's sense that the god who should be liable is, for the time being, here, no longer *reliable*, even if the complaints do not reflect Israel's general perception of God.

Israel's complaints stem from existential needs: for water, food, and security (Noth 1981b, 115–22; Coats 1968, 47–127). Faced with the elements of the wilderness, Israel calls on God for explanations and for relief. Israel demands response in both words and deeds from God and Moses, who are assumed to be capable of meeting their complaints. Israel also demands transformation of societal procedures in order to prevent similar situations from reoccurring. From the sides of God and Moses, however, Israel's discontent assaults their authority and suggests failures in their leadership. So defined, one may find the murmuring motif in nonrebellion stories also, such as the story of Zelophehad's daughters, a story that exhibits discontent and dissension on the parts of female subjects as they demand transformation of societal procedures. The following reading performs a double leap: from the murmuring motif to the story of Zelophehad's daughters, then to the stipulations of Num 30.

The story of the daughters of Zelophehad begins in Num 26:29–33, where we learn that Zelophehad only had daughters: Mahlah, Noah, Hoglah, Milcah, and Tirzah.[24] They are first named in the census of the

---

[23] Begrich (following Gunkel) addresses the move from informal questioning to a formal legal process in his study of the *Gerichtsrede* form (1938, 18ff.). Informal challenges later develop into the formal process of law, with plaintiffs and defendants coming with witnesses to the public square to be judged by citizens (elders) of the community (cf. Deut 21:18–21; 22:13–21). For a fuller sketch of the legal process within the biblical traditions, see Jer 26.

[24] Their names appear in a different order in Num 36:11, and they are left out of 1 Chr 7:14–19, as if in an attempt to erase their names from biblical memory.

Israelites, including those from the age of twenty years up who are able to bear arms (26:2), as members of the "new generation" who will inherit the land God promised (Olson 1985, 174–75). As the only descendants of their father, they should inherit his portion like the other persons named in the census.[25] Accordingly, I assume that the focus at this stage of the story is not on the placement of the inheritance, whether at Transjordan or Cisjordan (in contrast to Snaith 1966, 126; 1967, 309–10; cf. Jobling 1980, 203–4), but with ancestral rights (so Eryl W. Davies 1995, 300).

In Num 27:1, the daughters of Zelophehad bring a complaint before Moses and the officials, at the entrance to the tent of meeting, as if they are seeking God's hearing. Both the location and the persons present testify to the seriousness of their complaint. They challenge the customs that deny daughters the right to inherit their father's holdings (cf. Deut 21:15–17; 25:5–10).

The daughters clear their father first: Zelophehad had died in the wilderness for his own sin, and he was not involved in Korah's faction (Num 16–17). By disassociating themselves from those rebels, the daughters align themselves to Yhwh (27:4) and Moses (cf. 16:3). One could almost hear them murmuring, "If only we had died by the hand of Yhwh in the land of Egypt, where we had a place, a home, in which we felt safe. For you have brought us out into the wilderness where our father died for his own sin, and we will not be able to inherit his holdings . . . let us keep what is already ours, for we have no brothers. Give us land to make our home, among our father's brothers" (cf. Exod 16:3; 17:2–3; Num 20:3–5; Josh 2:12–13; Judg 1:15).

Moses' hesitation to pass judgment on their complaint (compare Exod 17:1–7) does not suggest that he was afraid of breaking with tradition for fear of retribution (27:2). Moses could have said, simply, that such a thing is "not done in Israel" (cf. 2 Sam 13:12; Mathew 1984, 51). The text suggests, on the other hand, that Moses is not in a position to counter their claim so he brings "their case [mišpat] before Yhwh." Their claim is already mišpat (read: just), and Moses has to seek Yhwh's endorsement. Though the murmuring motif is present in their case, Moses and Yhwh are not threatened because the daughters have already shown that they are allies. In return, Yhwh acknowledges their claim and tells Moses to transfer their father's share to them (27:6–7). Yhwh sides with Zelophehad's daughters, and together they transgress old customs that limit the rights of women.

Yhwh's judgment is then transformed into a procedural law for the whole of Israel (27:8–11). Here we find the legal process at work. A complaint that began informally grows into "the law of procedure for the

---

[25] Other ancient Near Eastern cultures recognized that a daughter had the right to inherit her father's property when there was no male heir (Eryl W. Davies 1995, 302; Westbrook 1985, 262).

Israelites, in accordance with Yhwh's command to Moses" (27:11b). The ruling in 27:8–11 exceeds the situation against which the daughters complain, by addressing the cases of a man who dies without a son (27:8) and of a man who dies without any children (27:9–11a). In the first case, a daughter has right of inheritance before her father's brothers and kinsmen, who are privileged in the second case.

Both Zelophehad's daughters and the women of Num 30 face the threat of dispossession: Num 30 regulates the dispossession of words, while the story of Zelophehad's daughters confronts the dispossession of property.[26] By transference, as if they were widows and divorcées, the daughters of Zelophehad have lost their father and are seeking "to establish a home" for themselves. Numbers 30 gives regulations that may result in the dispossession (of the words) of daughters and wives by their fathers and husbands, while Zelophehad's daughters fight to prevent the dispossession of their father. While Num 30 brings female subjects under the control of their men, Num 27:1–11 bring the inheritance of a man under the control of his daughters.

Both texts introduce procedural laws for Israel, but the legal process in Num 27:1–11 (transformation of a complaint into a regulation) is absent from Num 30. Nonetheless, in the received form of Num 30 Yhwh endorses the regulations as proper procedures for Israel. In this reading, the story of Zelophehad's daughters discloses fractures in the regulations of Num 30, and vice versa.[27] The following reading will cross these two texts.

First, unlike the decisive rules of procedure in response to the petition by Zelophehad's daughters, Num 30 does not stipulate the total reversal of the norms in question, words of daughters and wives, but leaves the final decision to the discretion of fathers and husbands. In the case of Zelophehad's daughters the primary beneficiary is the dead father, whose name should not be "lost to his clan because he had no son" (27:4). The daughters want to preserve his name through them, but the rule aims to preserve their father through his property. The ensuing law of procedure is concerned with naming the legal inheritors of a dead man's property (27:8–11a), hence the rule exceeds the petition. By making the man who dies without a son or daughter the primary subject of the rules (27:8–9), this code reflects the kind of gender bias visible in Num 30. The male subject of 27:8–11a corresponds to the father and husband who are the "real subjects" in Num 30. This transtextual link implies that the 27:8–11a rules are rigid *because they privilege a man*, while the rules of Num 30 are conditional *in order to privilege a man*.

---

[26] The crossing of a vow-event and land claims takes place in Judg 11 also, the story of the multilayered dispute among Jephthah, his daughter, the Gileadites (a Josephite clan; cf. Num 36:1), and the Ammonites, to which I turn in chapter 4.

[27] Since the story of Zelophehad's daughters continues in Num 36, Num 30 is a delay (in terms of the received form of the narrative) in the closure of their case.

Reading further to the restrictions on Zelophehad's daughters in Num 36, we find a second fracture in Num 30. Because of a counterpetition by family leaders, the ruling is revised on behalf of the tribe of Joseph. The family heads were worried that Zelophehad's daughters may marry into another tribe and thus relinquish Zelophehad's portion to that other tribe. This would diminish the portion of the Josephite tribe. The daughters are not consulted in this second story, though it concerns *their* share. Yhwh heeds the plea of the Josephites and commands the daughters to marry anyone they wish, provided that they marry into a clan of their father's tribe (and they comply in 36:10–12). The same goes for all daughters who may inherit an ancestral share, in order that "Israelite tribes shall remain bound each to its portion" (36:5–9).

Several critics view Num 36 as a necessary amendment to the "bad law" in 27:1–11, which failed to secure Zelophehad's portion to the tribe of Joseph (Snaith 1966, 127; cf. Eryl W. Davies 1995, 368; Weingreen 1966, 519). To these critics, Num 36 delivers what the daughters wanted in the first place, so the petition of the Josephites is just in their eyes (cf. Sterring 1994, 93; Sakenfeld 1988, 46). Such a reading favors the reflection by tribal family heads, *many days after they heard the daughters' complaint,* and brings the daughters' desire under their control. On the other hand, if as I suggested above the daughters were concerned with the name of their father rather than the holdings of the tribe, then Num 36 shifts the focus of the story, and the subject of the law, from Zelophehad and his daughters to the Josephite tribe, from women of a particular family to the domain of the tribe where decision makers are male.

Reaction to Num 36 will be mixed, depending on one's point of view. What one views as an attempt to secure the common good for the most people may be seen by another as the deprivation of the privileges of certain individuals. Numbers 36 privileges the kinsmen whose right to a dead man's property was deferred in Num 27:8–11a, and makes the women whose petition initiated the legal process serve the purpose of the tribe. The women become nonentities (cf. Wegner 1990, 23–24); the *particular* is subjected to the *general.*

In principle, Num 36 is a gendered attempt to give a hearing to a silenced voice and displaced subject. That a similar revision does not exist in Num 30, which would return to daughters and wives the control over their vows, discloses gendered blind spots at the underside of the law. The corrective and redeeming functions of the legal-revision process are not afforded the silenced voices in Num 30. Daughters and wives do not have control over their will in Num 30, just as Zelophehad's daughters lose their petition and story to the interests of their tribe and family heads. I assume that it would have been different if the silenced voices in Num 30 had been male voices.

The reference to the celebration of jubilee in 36:4 identifies a third element that Num 30 lacks. Some critics find this reference inappropriate because the jubilee law (cf. Lev 25) has to do with land sold to another party, but it does not apply to inherited land (Snaith 1966, 127; Noth 1968, 257; Eryl W. Davies 1995, 369). On the other hand, Sakenfeld argues that the reference to jubilee is the appropriate climax for the counterpetition by the family heads. It is necessary for the daughters to marry within their tribe because their land was not sold to them, so it will not return to the tribe of Joseph even in the year of jubilee. If their land was under the law of jubilee, then there will be no problem because they will not concede their land to the tribe into which they marry (1988, 45–46). Sakenfeld too buys into the argument of Zelophehad's kinsmen.

I read the jubilee reference differently, as a sign that the focus has shifted *from* the desires of Zelophehad's daughters *to* the property of the tribe.[28] The daughters said that they were concerned with their father's name, and they were objecting to the possibility that his holdings would end up in the hands of the clan because he had no son (27:4). On the other hand, by lamenting the inadequacy of the jubilee law to prevent the loss of their ancestral portion (36:3–4), the family heads ensure that Zelophehad's property remains in his clan. Observing the kinsmen's demand will result in the erasure of the daughters' concern.

A jubilee reference is not demanded from the father or husband in Num 30. Rather, their own interests are the "law of jubilee," which allows them to "reverse ownership" over the vows of a daughter or wife. Whereas Zelophehad's daughters and their kinsmen had just reasons for murmuring, no corroboration is demanded for the murmuring of a father or husband in Num 30. And there is no parallel "law of jubilee" in Num 30 for a man, widow, and divorcée, even though they too may marry into another tribe (cf. 36:3–4). According to this reading, these texts (Num 27, 30, 36) are set a_part in textual space and in gendered blindness.

The counterpetition by the "sons of Joseph" implies that the daughters' petition was not as just as Yhwh judged, using the jubilee law to bring Yhwh to their side. But this is not a simple insider-versus-outsider case. Yhwh did not declare the case of the daughters unjust as a consequence of the case of the sons of Joseph. In justifying the sons' counterpetition, Yhwh restricts the privilege of the daughters. Such a dynamic interaction is not offered in Num 30 to the daughters and wives, whose vows may either be established or annulled. If annulled, Yhwh will side with the decision makers against the ones making the vow.

This reading entertains the complexity of (counter)petitions. A petition becomes "rebellion" when Yhwh and/or the leaders are threatened

---

[28] The story turns into a story about property and the implications of granting inheritance to women (cf. Weingreen 1966, 519). Sterring picks up on this economic view with respect to the use of "cleave" in Num 36:7, 9. What Gen 2:24 prescribes for a man, that he abandons his parents but "cleaves" to his wife, is given in Num 36 with respect to the relation between a man and his land (Sterring 1994, 93–94).

by it. And like the reading process, they make their judgment at the event of reception. Sometimes the judgment unravels a previous petition, as in the foregoing reading, and sometimes the judgment does not require the rejection of other judgments (as with Num 27 and 36).

Drawing upon the *mišpaṭ* of Zelophehad's daughters, I exposed gaps and delays in Num 30. The story of Zelophehad's daughters illustrates the "flexibility of the tradition and the warrant for reinterpreting the past for the sake of the new. . . . Past traditions require reinterpretations" (Olson 1985, 176).

2.3 Circumreading Numbers 30 with Law Events

The previous section accounted for the wilderness narrative as a locus of meaning for Num 30. In that locus, law events sustain the flow of the narrative. I address two such law events (read: ignored subjects) in the following sections.

2.3.1 *On Defilement*

The "doctrine of defilement" develops from the Hebrew Bible law's concern for purity and social purgation, which has been the subject of several studies. Jacob Neusner (1973) traces the development of "purity" and "impurity" in three stages: "biblical legacy" (limited to the Hebrew Bible), postbiblical literature produced before the destruction of the second temple (70 C.E.), and Talmudic literature.[29] It is his treatment of the first stage that concerns me here.

Neusner agrees with Levine that impurity in the biblical legacy is not a state of being but an active demonic force (in contrast to W. Robertson Smith, who claims that im/purity is a psychological state) that may invade a person. "That a man is impure means only that there are certain things he must not do, others he must do in order to return to a state of purity" (Neusner 1973, 11). Influenced by the priestly class, purity became an aspect of the cult in which the ideas of cult and land were linked to the people: "[A]ll three must be kept free of impurity. The purity of cult, land, and people signifies God's favor; the divine favor is joined to the specific rules concerning purity in food and sex" (1973, 21). In this regard, im/purity rules are products of priestly propaganda (so Mary Douglas).

---

[29] Neusner analyzes the first two stages in order to place the third in the context of ancient Judaism. He senses a shift of focus in the Second Temple literature because "going to the Temple no longer was important among the reasons for keeping the laws" (1973, 32). The language of im/purity provided a polemical theme for sectarian discourse, and a means for defining a sect's relationship to the Jerusalem temple (uncleanness is a metaphor for exile). "In biblical and post-biblical literature, purity serves as a metaphor for morality, impurity for sin. It is only with the rabbis that we find full articulation of the notion that impurity both results from and punishes sin" (1973, 126).

Neusner quotes Mary Douglas's *Purity and Danger* (1966) in conclusion: "Pollution is a type of danger which is not likely to occur except where *the lines of structure, cosmic or social, are clearly defined*" (1973, 28; my italics). Purity is established when the boundary, the lines of structure, cosmic or social, is honored; on the flip side, impurity threatens the community when the boundary is clearly defined. If the boundary is not clear, or if it ebbs and flows like the fluctuating island boundary (Havea 1995), im/purity becomes meaningless.

Douglas concurs that a symbolic system may be drawn from the totality of the biblical im/purity rules, but warns that a string of metaphors does not constitute a symbolic system: "A symbolic system consists not at all of verbalisations about goodness. It consists of rules of behaviours, actions and expectations which constitute society itself" (quoted in Neusner 1973, 138). Those rules create hierarchy and structure the society. Douglas's critique discloses a gap in Neusner's analysis, that is, his failure to account for the function of the law in structuring society, which may be read in two ways: first, that law brings order to society and, second, that law fractures, that it creates sects in, society.[30] The second reading accounts for those individuals repressed by a hierarchy and those ousted (outlawed) from a social structure.

Douglas suggests "that the further from membership of a sectarian group, the more the tendency to turn purity rules into metaphors of spiritual good instead of regulations for daily entrances and exits and rankings" (quoted in Neusner 1973, 141). If one views the spiritualizing process from outside the membership group, one may take the translation of cultic rules into moral principles as an attempt to discriminate. Spiritualizing the sectarian rules shifts the focus from the communal (cult) to the individual (moral) and sets the membership group apart, as if they are better than nonmembers. On the flip side, spiritualizing the rules give nonmembers an opening to join the group.

The *doctrine of defilement* is a religion's defense against images and powers (magic) that threaten the lines of structure to take a hold of (control theory) and pollute (contagion theory) its members. The exclusionary thrust of the doctrine is the basis for Israel's monotheistic faith and anti-icon principles (Douglas 1993, 25). Priests use this doctrine to enforce the boundary and social structure of the community, and in the end create a hierarchy. The function of the priestly hierarchy differs from the enclave and individualist cultures. "An enclave is usually formed by a *dissenting minority*, it becomes a social unit which maintains a strong boundary but unlike the hierarchy it tends to be egalitarian, and so to have a weakly articulated social structure" (Douglas 1993, 45; my italics). In contrast to individualist cultures, hierarchy and enclave cultures are aware of their

---

[30] A second gap in Neusner's analysis is his failure to address the role of Second Temple and Talmudic societies in the canonization of priestly propaganda.

exclusionary behaviors. But whereas, in a hierarchy, exclusion is based on a grading process, the habit of enclaves "is outcasting rather than down-grading: their exclusions all work on the outer boundary, the difference between belonging and not belonging" (Douglas 1993, 46–47). An enclave is threatened by the possibility of defection, which it averts by stressing the voluntary nature of membership and the value of each member. It resists fragmentation by widening the gap between itself and its neighbors, and it governs by consensus and equality. It uses the doctrine of defilement to reinforce its antipathy to outsiders and to discourage defection.

A priestly hierarchy's solution is reconciliation (Douglas 1993, 61), toward assimilating dissenters: "Whereas in an enclave, tension is explicitly on the relation of inside to outside, in a hierarchy it is on the up-down dimension of authority" (76).

The doctrine of defilement and hierarchical disposition of the priestly culture are discernible in Num 5–6. Persons who had an eruption or discharge, or who had been in contact with a corpse (cf. Bloch-Smith 1992, 107), had to be removed before they defiled the camp (5:1–4; cf. 19:11–12; Lev 13, 15). Those who broke faith with Yhwh by wronging another person (5:5–10), and the wife who is suspected of breaking faith with her husband by having carnal relations with another man (5:11–31), were treated as sources of defilement. These cases move from certainty to uncertainty: Defilement is visible in 5:1–4, confessed in 5:5–10, but suspected and must be tested in 5:11–31. Each case carries a different consequence: expulsion (5:3), restitution with a chance to remain in the camp (5:7b–8), and the risk of being a curse among one's people (5:27). In all three cases, we see the priestly drive to exclude defiled and defiling members from the community in order to maintain its boundary.

The matter of boundaries is also exercised in the rules for a man or woman taking a Nazirite vow, but the focus shifts from the outcast to the in-group. The function of the boundary in Num 6 is not to "keep out" the defiled but to regulate how to "keep in" one who "sets oneself apart" (6:2b) for Yhwh. When a Nazirite crosses the boundary, whether defiling him- or herself by food or drink, or by contact with dead corpses, the individual may reenter through rededication to Yhwh (6:11–12). At the completion of the term of Nazirite service, the Nazir presents offerings to Yhwh then reenters the (boundary of the) society at large, in which both shaving and consumption of wine are then allowed (6:13–20). In Num 6 the Nazirite "in-group" is graded above the rest of the community, by means of clearly defined social lines of structure that they break when they return to the community.

With gender interests, one may also detect characteristics of enclave cultures in Num 5–6. The Nazirite rules are directed to a "man or woman" (6:2), as if the rules are egalitarian, but they are constructed with a man in mind. The regulation of consecrated hair would discourage women from taking a Nazirite vow, since one must shave one's hair at the completion of the term (6:18). For a Nazirite "man," a shaved head signifies his return to "common" status, but for a woman, a shaved head is also a sign of shame. It signifies defilement (Lev 13:33; 14:8, 9; cf. bearing of a woman's head in Lev 10:6 and Num 5:18) or being desired as a wife by one's captor (Deut 21:10–13; cf. Num 31:17–18). The "woman" who is included but then ignored reveals the gender biases of the rules. The same may be said for Num 5:5–10, also addressed to "a man or woman" (cf. "male and female" in 5:3). As a subject who is addressed in a regulation constructed for a man, this "woman" represents a dissenting presence within the rulings of the priestly hierarchy (propaganda).

A dissenting tone may also be read in the rules concerning a jealous husband (5:11–31). He may bring his wife to the priest if "a fit of jealousy comes over him," but he is not required to bring evidence or a witness (5:14). His suspicion is enough to set the process in motion (5:13; compare 31:30). The rules serve the husband's jealousy, but do not give the suspected wife a chance to clear herself. She is subjected to the curse of adjuration (5:19–22) and the drink of bitter water (5:17, 23): these are supposed to determine her guilt. If she has defiled herself, then her belly shall distend and her thighs sag, otherwise she shall not be harmed and will retain his seed (5:27–28). The rules trap accused wives. Guilty or not, accused wives will be defiled (in body and in mind, by the harsh curse of adjuration). The husband's jealousy is privileged, and the other man is presumed innocent; the two are (con)fused in 5:31: "The man ['iš; husband? other man?] shall be clear of guilt; but that woman shall suffer for her guilt." It falls on the woman to clear her man or herself, and in both cases she is an outcast. She brings shame on herself if she clears her man, and guilt upon herself if she does not clear her man.

Similar privileges are given to the male subjects in Num 30. Neither a father nor a husband is required to justify his desire to annul the vows of his daughter or wife. In light of the foregoing discussion, annullable vows may be taken as figures of defilement indicating that the daughter or wife has "broken faith" with her father or husband. As the shaving of the head at the completion of the Nazirite term also implies that one has endured a period of defilement, so would the annulment of vows signify that those vows defiled the daughter or wife. In the priestly hierarchy, the privileges of annulling vows fall within the responsibility of family heads in upholding family boundaries. Nonetheless, the "outcasting" tendency of enclave cultures is present insofar as, to borrow 5:31, "the man shall be clear of guilt; but that woman shall suffer for her guilt." Numbers 30 traps the daughter or wife. When the vows of a daughter or wife are annulled, the father or husband is also cleared from having to uphold those vows. But if the vows of a daughter or wife are upheld, she is responsible for keeping her vows. In both cases, according to this reading, the daughter or wife clears her father or husband. In this regard, also, the regulation over the vows by a widow or divorcée (Num 30:10) is disruptive in Num

30. In other words, the widow or divorcée is a defiling subject (see also ch. 6).

This reading exposes dissenting tones, both *affirming* (priestly) and *dissenting* (enclavist). Whether these are independent voices, or two tones of the same voice, in the way that a piano key has different values depending on the scale in which it is played, is ambiguous. In the following section I turn to the process of purification, which marks the end of the period of defilement.

2.3.2 On (Re)purification

Douglas argues in her study of Leviticus that the symbolic systems of primitive societies are systems of order, according to which purity is defined. Whatever falls outside the standard of purity (the lines of structure, cosmic or social) threatens the society's system of order, and its elimination is "not a negative movement, but a positive effort to organise the environment" (1984, 2). When matters (dirt, impurity) get out of place, reorganization is necessary to recover the pattern of *order* (40).[31]

Impurity carries a system of meaning that gives purity meaning, and vice versa: "Holiness and unholiness after all need not always be absolute opposites. They can be relative categories. What is clean in relation to one thing may be unclean to another, and vice versa" (1984, 8–9). The system of distinction is circular, not binary, and one should not speak of a universal standard of purity.[32] "Defilement is never an isolated event. It cannot occur except in view of a systematic ordering of ideas" (1984, 41). Douglas adds that

> Any interpretations will fail which take the Do-nots of the Old Testament in piecemeal fashion. The only sound approach is to forget hygiene, aesthetics, morals and instinctive revulsion, even to forget the Canaanites and the Zoroastrian Magi, and start with the texts. Since each of the injunctions is prefaced by the command to be holy, so they must be explained by that command. *There must be contrariness between holiness and abomination which will make overall sense of all the particular restrictions.* (1984, 49; my italics)

---

[31] Douglas also challenges negative views toward "primitive cultures," as in the work of Sir James George Frazer, who "thought that confusion between uncleanness and holiness is the distinctive mark of primitive thinking. . . . If primitive, then rules of holiness and rules of uncleanness were indistinguishable; if advanced then rules of uncleanness disappeared from religion" (1984, 10–11; see also 1982, 272–89). Douglas argues, on the other hand, that the primitives lived by rules and principles; that is, they were organized (1984, 16).

[32] As one who crosses cultural boundaries I cannot imagine a universal system of order. But I do not assume the extreme "everything goes," against which Bauman (appealing to Katie Soper) suggests that "it is quite conceivable (though it still remains to be seen whether it is realistic as well) to give up on 'the grand narrative idea of a single truth, without giving up on the idea of truth as a regulative ideal'" (1995, 6).

Douglas links *holiness* (*qdš*) to *wholeness* (*kds:* "separateness"): "Holiness requires that individuals shall conform to the class to which they belong. And holiness requires that different classes of things shall not be confused" (1984, 53). The dangers to holiness come in the forms of hybrids and in confusion about what is set apart, the threats that *anomaly* and *ambiguity* pose (1984:37). An anomaly threatens the system from the outside, but an ambiguity is a liminal subject whose presence destabilizes the system (cf. Stahl 1995, 11–12).

Drawing upon van Gennep's idea that thresholds symbolize beginnings of new status, Douglas suggests that the human body is "a symbol of society, and to see the powers and dangers credited to social structure reproduced in small on the human body" (1984, 115).[33] Bodily margins and thresholds reflect the fears of the society, and the dangers associated with shifting societal margins (cf. ch. 4). Rules concerning bodily excretions and sexual behavior determine membership in the community, as if the boundary of the body defines the community: "To which particular bodily margins its [society's] beliefs attribute power depends on what situation the body is mirroring" (1984, 121). Body and society image each other.

Sometimes the system of order is at war with itself, and the boundaries are sometimes blurred. On female pollution, for instance, a tension arises when a female is seen as a person and as the currency of male transactions (Douglas 1984, 152; cf. Wegner 1988, 10–19; Pomeroy 1975). In such situations there is usually a yearning for rigidity, for hard lines and clear concepts:

> The final paradox of the search for purity is that it is an attempt to force experience into logical categories of non-contradiction. But experience is not amenable and those who make the attempt find themselves led into contradiction. . . . The moral of all this is that the facts of existence are a chaotic jumble. (Douglas 1984, 162–63)

The priestly hierarchy responds to the blurring of boundaries with rituals intended to restore order/purity, rites intended to normalize the outcast so that they may be reinstated into the society. There are incidences of the normalizing process in the book of Numbers, both for reinstatement and separation: setting the Levites apart (3:1–4:49; 8:6–12; 17:1–26; 18:1–32); reconsecration of Nazirite vows (6:10–12); return to the community after the Nazirite term (6:13–20); readmission after period of impurity (9:6–12; 12:15; 19:1–22; 31:24); Israel's entry into the land (15:1–16); restitution for wrong to a fellow (5:7–8); separate cities of refuge for the manslayer (35:9–33); and renumbering of the people after a plague (25:19–26:65). These texts echo the priestly call upon Israel to become holy

---

[33] The burial rite is a reminder of the connection between body and land— they come together at the boundary markers, that is, graves, which signify thresholds on the boundary.

as their God is holy (cf. Lev 11:44–45; 19:2; 20:7, 26; 21:8). The state of holiness is beyond, yet attainable. This demand differs from the Deuteronomic view that "Israel *is* the holy people of Yahweh, a status that carries obligations with it rather than an ideal to be striven for" (Houston 1993, 56; cf. 227). P drives to establish order, while the Deuteronomist seeks to defend (stabilize) an order assumed to be in place. But who stabilizes whom? For Houston, the holiness of God is the basis for the stabilization of Israel's holiness. To which one may add that the holiness of Israel is the basis for stabilizing God's holiness. They stabilize each other because, according to Leviticus, God cannot maintain presence among unholy conditions.

Traces of the principle of purity are evident in the stipulations of Num 30. In contrast to the "man or woman" (6:2) who are subjected to the same regulations, in Num 30 the regulation for a man (30:3) is distinct from those for a woman (30:4–16). The sexes are set a_part. Moreover, the stages of a woman's life are taken into account: young woman, married woman, divorcée, and widow. Nonetheless, the elusive status of a divorcée or widow threatens to confuse the "order" of the sexes. A divorcée or widow is elusive because she does not have a male lord over her, and she may be placed in two categories: that of a woman and a man. She is regulated together with other women, but she is regulated like a man, as if in order to *normalize* her. She is no longer on the outside, neither anomalous nor ambiguous, because she is now manlike.

Though annullable vows are treated as abominations, with no chance for reinstatement, the privileges of a father or husband to annul vows are stipulated *as if they were restoring the daughter or wife into the family circle.* In this regard, the repeated demand that a father or husband must annul on the day that he learns of the vow signifies the urgent need to restore his daughter or wife. In all of these cases, annulment of vows effects release from Yhwh. Two boundaries cross: family and *theo*logical circles of relations. Restoration into the family is accompanied by release in the *theo*logical realm.

I have spoken of the annullable obligations and vows in Numbers as *empty* commitments, suggesting that the *act* of making vows is more significant than *what* was committed. But Douglas's proposal that specters of the body are imbedded in (im)purity rules opens an interesting channel for imagining the contents of these commitments. I imagine that the annullable vows would be similar to the Nazirite vows in setting oneself apart for Yhwh, or for another person or for a function, by abstaining from some products and privileges.

The differentiation of the stages of a woman's life draws our attention to what a young or a married woman may have that a widow or a divorcée may not have, in other words, something that sets them apart. The simplicity of the temporal condition for the annulment of vows, to annul on the same day, suggests that the terms of the vow have to be critical enough not to require reflection. The terms would also have to be so impure that they are not named (cf. Goodman 1986), so severe that their annulment requires no justification, and the terms must involve a *tapu* that is critically important for men.

The above qualifications suggest that annullable vows probably had to do with sexual abstinence. No commitment would be as significant to a father or a husband, and no *tapu* is so simple yet critical, so exalted yet unspeakable, as something that involves sex. A daughter's vow of sexual abstinence makes problematic her father's chance to give her away in marriage, which has economic implications (cf. Wegner 1990, 26), and a wife's vow of sexual abstinence can torment her husband. Numbers 30 properly gives fathers and husbands privileges to annul such vows as they see fit. According to this reading, vows of sexual abstinence by a widow or divorcée are irrelevant because she is no longer an economic source for a father, or a sexual object of a husband. She must, therefore, keep all her vows and obligations, like a man.

As there are more to a woman than her private parts, one may also fill the regulated vows with things that a woman might control: food, land (as in Zelophehad's daughters) and house (see ch. 4), children and personal labor (see ch. 5), the difference between right (purity) and wrong (impurity) (see ch. 6), and so forth. Numbers 30 gives fathers and husbands control over these matters, with the widow and divorcée as fractures in their legal control.

Numbers 30 defines the bodily and social boundaries that meet at a woman's body as figures of control. In this regard, annulment of vows restores daughters and wives to "family and social order." Two worlds meet, and how one views their crossing is a matter of judgment, whether the restoration process *sanctifies the secular* or *profanes the sacred* (cf. Douglas 1975, xv). What is purification to one may be defilement to others. The insatiability of categories exposes the elusive nature of boundaries and barriers, both the bodily and textual types.

2.4 Transtextual Wander

I circumread Num 30 with two ignored "subjects of the book" in the Numbers narrative, motifs and law events from Israel's wilderness experience, and I bring this wandering reading to closure, for now, with two metacritical observations.

First, I read Num 30 *back* to the wilderness story because I also read Num 30 *from* the wilderness story. I started from many texts, and I did not seek to delimit the points where texts, themes, or traditions begin or end, because they interpenetrate. I read for the traces and erasure marks of ignored pentateuchal and wilderness motifs and events in Num 30 and, in the wandering spirit, I offered readings that complain against the regulations of Num 30. I led a guided wandering that tried to be responsible to the text while realizing that responsible and/or irresponsible readings depend on judgments made at the *event of the text's reception.*

Second, I claimed that I was analyzing wilderness traditions, but I was actually rewriting literary texts. What, then, constitutes a tradition? The problem is not with claiming to read biblical traditions, but in imagining that biblical traditions exist beyond some form of textuality. As text, traditions are open for interpretation. Nonetheless, a tradition is more than the texts that bear it, and at the event of reception we face both the tradition that the text claims to represent as well as the traditions of the text itself. It is thus more appropriate to speak of *traditions,* in and beyond literary texts, which readers cannot fully capture. This admission draws attention to the limitations of my interpretive practice and the elusive nature of texts and traditions, *the elusions of control.*

This second observation sets circumreading against the traditio-historical method, insofar as I maintain that text and tradition are inseparable. I do not advocate the "developed book-view" which traditio-historical critics resist (cf. Shanks 1988, xviii; Engnell 1960, 24; 1969, 10–11). Rather, I offer these observations in order to call attention to the dependence of tradition critics on literary texts. Even Engnell's preference for oral tradition, which he assumes reached fixed form before it was written down, presupposes a literary text (1969, 7). For Engnell too, text and tradition interpenetrate. I differ from Engnell concerning where one begins reading, for I begin from many places. I have read Num 30 around texts from its "book" context, and in the following chapters I circumread it with other historical phenomena.

•

I attended to ignored subjects out of my interest in exposing how readers' interests guide events of reception, and in order to define the contents of the annullable vows, which I was not able to do earlier. This creates an interpretive dilemma. On the one hand, in reading for ignored subjects I accounted for a lack in the positivist attempt. On the other hand, I made Num 30 say more than it says! In any case, reading for ignored subjects exposes new thresholds for the interpretive practice.

Nevertheless, reading for ignored subjects has blind spots. On the one hand, I restabilized two subjects of the book of Numbers by bringing them to bear on Num 30. They are no longer strangers to each other. On the other hand, I destabilized Num 30 by rereading it *around* and *across* subjects that brought out resisting tones and "lacks" from within. The restabilization of ignored subjects discloses "strangers" within Num 30 (cf. Kristeva 1991).

By circumreading Num 30 with some of the ignored subjects of the book of Numbers, I supplement and expand arguments proposed in chapter 1. I presented *more readings* of Num 30. Having said all of that, ig-

nored subjects still lurk at the underside of this chapter, demanding response-ability. Since we cannot read without ignoring something, this
chapter is a rem(a)inder of the blind spots in readings. We read as ignoring readers, and we read with ignorances.

3

Repressed Subjects in and of Numbers 30

For history is not only the story (histoire) *of triumphant kings and heroes, of the powerful; it is also the story of the powerless and dispossessed. The history of the vanquished dead crying out for justice demands to be told.* (Ricoeur 1984, 17)

But Sihon King of Heshbon would not let us pass through, because Yhwh your God stiffened his will and hardened his heart in order to deliver him into your hand, as at this day. And Yhwh said to me: See, I have begun to give Sihon and his land to you. Begin to possess, occupy his land. (Deut 2:30–31 [my translation]; cf. Exod 10:1; Dan 5:20)

3.0 Introduction

Critics who read with "the tendencies toward atomism and toward geneticism" (Clines 1978, 7) seek to tame, control, the Pentateuch. These tendencies, or obsessions to be more exact, unravel the Pentateuch by not treating it as a whole. David Clines offers an alternative approach that subjects the complex Pentateuch to a theme that threatens to monotonize it (cf. Whybray 1987, 221–42).

> The theme of the Pentateuch is the partial fulfilment—which implies also the partial non-fulfilment—of the promise to or blessing of the patriarchs. The promise or blessing is both the divine initiative in a world where human initiatives always lead to disaster, and a reaffirmation of the primal divine intentions for man. (Clines 1978, 29)

Both approaches, despite their different obsessions, assume that the Pentateuch is a multifaceted work in which some texts foreground and/or repress other texts, and both have unraveling effects. A third alternative is to read for the repressed, which is what I propose in this chapter.

To read for the repressed presupposes, first, that the text has multiple layers (or "lines"; cf. Alter 1981, 131–54; Gunn and Fewell 1993, 147–73) in between which the repressed are stuffed; second, that "traces" (cinders)[1] of the repressed are discernible in the text; and third, that one reads against the grains of the text (cf. Fewell 1987).[2] To read for the repressed places the critic in a dilemma: She risks *displacing* the repressed because to account for the repressed is to turn them into something that the text refuses. On the other hand, to ignore the repressed is to yield to the repressing program of the text. The critic risks romanticizing the repressed in the former (cf. Sugirtharajah 1998, 22–23), and she risks romanticizing the text in the latter.

Subjects may be repressed in the text and/or re-pressed at the events of reception, and sometimes the repressed in the first (textual) moment are ignored at the second (interpretive) moment. In that case, the text's attempt to repress prevails. I opt to read for the repressed in (§3.2) and of (§3.3) Num 30 because I opt to err on the side of ethics.[3]

3.1 The Repressed Shall Rise

Douglas's observation in anthropology also applies to pentateuchal studies:

> If there is any one idea on which the present currents of thought are agreed it is that at any given moment of time the state of received knowledge is backgrounded by a clutter of suppressed information. It is also agreed that the information is not suppressed by reason of its inherent worthlessness, nor by any passive process of forgetting: it is actively thrust out of the way because of difficulties in making it fit whatever happens to be in hand. The process of "foregrounding" or "relevating" now receives attention from many different quarters. But for obvious reasons the *process of "backgrounding"* is less accessible. (1975, 3; my italics)

---

[1] Cinder erases itself as it presents itself: "If a place is itself surrounded by fire (falls finally to ash, into a cinder tomb), it no longer is. Cinder remains, cinder there is [*Il y a là cendre*], which we can translate: the cinder is not, is not what is. It remains *from* what is not, in order to recall at the delicate, charred bottom of itself only non-being or non-presence" (Derrida 1991, 39). Moreover, cinder differs from smoke: "[T]he latter apparently gets lost, and better still, without perceptible remainder, for it rises, it takes to the air, it is spirited away, sublimated. The cinder—falls, tires, lets go, more material since it fritters away its word; it is very divisible" (Derrida 1991, 73; cf. Žižek 1996).

[2] "Exegesis has already accustomed us to the idea that a text has several meanings, that these meanings overlap, that the spiritual meaning is 'transferred' (Saint Augustine's *translata signa*) from the historical or literal meaning because of the latter's surplus of meaning" (Ricoeur 1978, 97).

[3] "Whether we speak or remain silent is always a matter of a choice. The problem is not to choose between speech and silence, but to try to make sure that speech does not become the enemy of silence and that silence does not become a betrayal of speech. We must strive for a deep inner harmony between the two" (Wiesel 1990, 7).

The process of backgrounding echoes Marx's critique of ideology and Lacan's notion of the Real, both of which deal with areas in which human consciousness is no longer the master in its own house (Lacan 1977, 49–56; cf. Žižek 1989, 161–90; 1992, 1–66).[4] For Lacan (so Freud), the unconscious affects thoughts and deeds: "What we teach the subject to recognize as his unconscious is his history—that is to say, we help him perfect the present historization of the facts that have already determined a certain number of the historical 'turning-points' in his existence" (52; cf. Rieger 1994, 127–57; Lyotard 1984, 74). "In this connection [Lacan] (re)discovers the primacy of the unconscious over the conscious: What is repressed . . . obviously has a considerable bearing on the shape of reality" (Rieger 1994, 128–29; cf. Michael Clark 1984, 67). It thus seems necessary to *always historicize* (Jameson 1981, 9; cf. the call to *always materialize* in Boer 1997, 7–8) in order to restore the repressed in literary texts:

> Interpretation proper—what we have called "strong" rewriting, in distinction from the weak rewriting of ethical codes, which all in one way or another project various notions of the unity and the coherence of consciousness—always presupposes, if not a conception of the unconscious itself, then at least some mechanism of mystification or repression in terms of which it would make sense to seek a latent meaning behind a manifest one, or to rewrite the surface categories of a text in the stronger language of a more fundamental interpretive code. (Jameson 1981, 60; cf. Lyotard 1984, 75; see also Gutiérrez 1983, 4; Ricoeur 1984, 17)

Turning to the repressed, however, is risky business. One is in danger of romanticizing and homogenizing them, both the ideological and actual, persecuted and condemned (cf. Pixley and Boff 1989, 1–13). The classification and explication of their perspectives are at the mercy of privileged critics. The wilderness narrative, for instance, is a wandering account told from different Israelite points of view, involving people from other nations, their kings and peasants, with every class and gender in between, who are repressed on account of Israel. Even lords and rulers are dispossessed, as in the case of Sihon in Deut 2:30–31 (and Balak in §2.2). Because the repressed in/of biblical literature are products of textual processes, the representation of "the repressed" in and of the text calls for strong rewriting (Jameson) and militant reading (Gutiérrez). This is not a daring assumption. It mimics Ricoeur's hermeneutical circle,[5] in which

---

[4] The *real* is Lacan's alternative to the *imaginary* and *symbolic* orders, freeing him from binary thinking (cf. Sheridan 1977, ix–x). The *imaginary* deals with the world of images (Lacan 1977, 1–7; cf. Rieger 1994, 24–32), the *symbolic* deals with the world of language (Lacan 1977, 30–113; cf. Rieger 1994, 45–53), and the *real* deals with the realm of the unconscious (Lacan 1977, 148–78; cf. Jameson 1988, 75–115; Rieger 1994, 127–37, and 1998b, 75–77).

[5] "The contribution of Ricoeur—who, for that matter, rereads Heidegger—consists in 'closing the circle' of linguistics (looking not only at what lies 'behind'

critics move from a "first [primitive] naïveté" (referring to unquestioned dwelling in the world of symbols) to a "second [modern] naïveté":

> For the second immediacy that we seek and the second naïveté that we await are no longer accessible to us anywhere else than in a hermeneutics; we can believe only by interpreting. It is the "modern" mode of belief in symbols, an expression of the distress of modernity and a remedy for that distress.
>
> Such is the circle: hermeneutics proceeds from a prior understanding of the very thing that it tries to understand by interpreting it. (Ricoeur 1967, 352; cf. Mudge 1980, 6–7; see also "hermeneutics of testimony" in Ricoeur 1980, 142–53)

This chapter drives from the stage of "second naïveté," as if to set a place for "critical naïveté"; it is, nonetheless, a stage of naïveté. As another event of reception, this chapter participates in the repression of (interpretations of) Num 30. In other words, metacritically speaking, I too risk repressing and restoring the repressed. Yet the repressed shall rise!

3.2 The Repressed in Numbers 30

The absence of cultic influences in Num 30 suggests that legislators domesticated their principles and rules of conduct as Num 30, seeking in private affairs the meaning and guidance they used to find in the cult. Notwithstanding, Num 30 is still a religious text; in other words, I read it as biblical propaganda: it challenges some of the existing (cultic) teachings (traditions) within and beyond the Bible.

This proposal is not totally radical (cf. Fishbane 1985, 5–6; Pardes 1992, 2–6). The rewriting of the Books of Samuel by the Chroniclers is (biblical) evidence of the working of biblical propaganda, an observation already made by modern critics (cf. Wellhausen's 1870 dissertation; McKenzie 1984, 1–32). Along this path, Collins presents the book of Daniel as a "political manifesto" (1977, 191–224), Power suggests that Job offers an attack on religious authority (1961, 166–95), and Heym (1973) portrays the Books of Samuel as propaganda on behalf of Solomon (cf. Rost 1982). The interplay of dissenting voices in midrashic traditions also manifests the tendency to counter existing texts and myths (cf. Fishbane 1993b) and/or to challenge existing readings (cf. Fishbane 1985, 465–66).[6] Such transtex-

---

a text, but at what lies 'in front of' it) in the construction of a fertile theory of hermeneutics" (Croatto 1987, 3; see also West 1990).

    [6] " 'Midrash' is a fundamental habit of mind, imagination, and creativity for rabbinic culture" (Fishbane 1993a, 3). Gruenwald refers to a *midrashic condition* that "entails more than a concern for lexicological or plain-sense meaning of a text or piece of information. What really matters, therefore, is not the mere act of understanding texts, but the creation of the meaning that is attached to them. . . . The act of creating meaning is a vital part of that process of appropriation" (1993, 7; on the midrashic imagination, see Idel 1993; Fishbane 1993b; on the parabolic quality of the midrashic tradition, see Stern 1993).

tual tendencies also appear in the "trickster" and "revision" models of feminist criticism (cf. Trible 1978; Niditch 1987; Camp 1988; 1993, 166–69; Ostriker 1993; 1997) and in deconstructive and poststructural criticisms (cf. Caputo 1987, 120–206; *PMB* 119–48; see also chs. 5 and 6 in this volume). To circumread Num 30, therefore, is to embark on a path well-traveled.

In the following subsections I address the opening to circumread law with other laws and narratives in theory (§3.2.1) and in practice (§3.2.2).

3.2.1 *Circumreading in Theory*

In proposing to circumread Num 30 with other legal and narrative texts I place myself in the shadows of David Daube and Calum Carmichael.

Daube was one of the first modern critics to explore the relation between Hebrew Bible narrative and law. Presuming that the Hebrew Bible is a literary product from a small community whose ideals may (not) reflect universal values, Daube argues that priests and prophets subordinated secular laws to their religious values, thus turning those laws into "religious rules, destined to guide God's chosen people" (1947, 1). He maintains that biblical (legal) historians need to study how ancient laws are preserved in sagas and annals, and how "legal ideas developed into religious ideas under the hands of priests and prophets" (3). In this developmental theory, Hebrew Bible narratives must be chronologically later than the biblical (religious) and secular laws from which they developed.

Pertinent to my study is the distinction that Daube draws between *locatio conductio rei* (letting and hiring of an *object*, at a price, for use or enjoyment) and *locatio conductio operarum* (letting and hiring of *services*, also at a price) (1947, 16–17). The *locatio conductio rei* was applicable to houses, mules, slaves, and so forth, whereas the service prescribed in *locatio conductio operarum* was limited to what a free person (usually a man of authority) could have rendered. These categories are not diametric because a free person may have ended up being given as an object under *locatio conductio rei*, as in Gen 30:15–16, in which Leah hired Jacob from Rachel for the price of Reuben's mandrakes: "Jacob was the *res*, the object of the compact: Rachel was his owner, she owned him as one might own a slave" (1947, 20). If the transaction was to involve *service* (*locatio conductio operarum*), on the other hand, Jacob had to make the transaction himself. The story resists this possibility because Jacob, who was a free person, is given as *res*. *Locatio conductio operarum* finds its way "into religion and was there applied to the relationship between man, God's labourer, and God, the employer who will pay him his reward" (25).

I digress to redirect our attention to the "vow-events" in Num 30, as "religious manifestations" of Daube's *locatio conductio* principles. A religious being vows an object (*res*) or service (*opera*) to God, or upon oneself, as payment for, or in anticipation of, a favorable response with objects and/or services. The vow is the "register" of the pact between parties.

Failure to fulfill the vow may be seen in the legal setting as an attempt to trick the other party that, in the religious setting, leads to guilt (cf. Num 30:16). The demand to fulfill vows, in that regard, parallels the legal and religious motivations of the *locatio conductio* principles. "Trickery" may be domesticated by legalizing the annulment of vows, which Num 30 grants a father or husband. Yhwh's implied approval is the religious sanction for the annulment of vows. In other words, Num 30 makes trickery legally and religiously acceptable. And the privileges to annul vows substantiate the idea that a daughter or wife is the *res* (property) of her father or husband (masters).

Daube appealed to his background in Roman legal principles, but those principles may not have been used (the same way) in the societies that produced the Hebrew Bible laws and narratives. It is one thing to argue that narratives developed from civil laws, and another to be certain which narratives developed from which laws. I follow Daube's claim for the relationship between different laws, secular and religious, and between law and narrative, but I cannot confirm the nature of their relationships. Daube argues for some *developmental* interrelations between them, and I add the possibility for counterdevelopment (i.e., narratives rewrite laws). On that note, I turn to Carmichael.

•

Since "old literary and historical" ways of studying the law generate illusory results (1985, 13–14), Carmichael proposes to read the law in its "final form" in order to show that rules are *inventions based on old rules* for quite specific reasons (1985, 15; so Daube). Nonetheless, he preserves two assumptions of the old order: that rules are both interrelated and intentional. Carmichael imagines that his theory will draw a consensus among critics, but he cannot warrant that it will lead to nonillusory readings. Two questions make his drive for consensus problematic: Which final form should we read? Whose final form?

For Carmichael, "The laws in both Deuteronomy and the decalogue arise not as a direct, practical response to the conditions of life and worship in Israel's past, as is almost universally held, but from a scrutiny of historical records about these conditions. The link is between law and literary account, not between law and actual life" (1985, 17). This position affirms the source-critical claim that the law is later than the historical records (narratives), but overlooks the possibility of earlier (than P) laws that some historical records scrutinize. Moreover, to deny direct relations between Hebrew Bible laws and Israel's "conditions of life" is to downplay the ideological dimensions of the law. The place of historical records in Carmichael's thesis defers Hebrew Bible law to a position where it "dies," removed from "conditions of life." This creates another illusion, the idea that a text (law or narrative) may be read without re-creating the "world" it offers as its anchor. Literary texts have the ability to create story and legal worlds, even if only in the imagination of critics.

There are rough spots in Carmichael's readings, testifying to difficulties in the transition from theory to method and application. One of his problematic readings concerns Deut 12:13–14, which decrees that burnt offerings must be offered at "proper places" assigned by Yhwh. He argues that this law is based on the story of Saul's burnt offering in 1 Sam 13:8–14 (1985, 41–42), and his reading is problematic at two places. First, the conflict between Samuel and Saul in 1 Sam 13 has to do with *time* rather than *place*. Samuel was upset because Saul did not wait for him, even though the seven days they agreed upon had passed (1 Sam 10:8; 13:8). Second, Saul *had to* offer the sacrifice before Samuel arrived to prevent the scattering of his army. He was in an uncompromising position. These observations suggest that 1 Sam 13 is not concerned with "proper place" as is true of the law in Deut 12:13–14.

On the other hand, assuming that these texts have something to do with each other, one may argue that 1 Sam 13 scrutinizes Deut 12:13–14 insofar as Saul's sacrifice, at the proper place, was not acceptable because it was offered without Samuel's presence. In that regard, proper place (in terms of Num 30, be it a father's or husband's house) is not as crucial as proper authorities. This alternative reading operates within the limits of Carmichael's theory, but reads in the opposite direction, making the narrative scrutinize the law.

Carmichael's theory emphasizes the relation between law and narrative, setting the stage for studies that cross, that is, *transgress*, genre boundaries. He endorses deconstructive reading by seeing in law the scrutiny of historical records, but his theory is restrictive by imagining scrutiny only in the law-over-narrative connection, and not scrutiny in law-over-law and narrative-over-law connections also. This chapter, along with coming chapters, explores scrutiny in both directions, from law to narrative and vice versa, and between different laws.

I presume on the basis of the foregoing arguments that Num 30 is an attempt to "scrutinize," in other words, *to repress*, existing stories and/or laws. In its received form, also, Num 30 provides subject matters for later ([post]biblical) rewritings. Autonomy is not a feature of circumreading!

3.2.2 *Circumreading in Practice*

I first presume a late date for Num 30 and imagine that its regulations issue from traditional stories and teachings (rules, laws). Based on word choice and common interests, two texts are relevant for this reading: Gen 28:20–22 and Deut 23:22–24. Both texts use *ndr* (vow)[7] and, insofar as

---

[7] Other places in the Pentateuch where *ndr* appears are Lev 22:18, 21; 27:2; Num 6; 15:3, 8; 21:2; 30; and Deut 12. The references in Lev 22, 27 and Deut 12 are not helpful for this reading because they are concerned with *cultic* votive offerings.

Num 30 sits in between Gen 28:20–22 and Deut 23:22–24, as if to set them a_part, I also explore how Num 30 fractures both texts.

Genesis 28:20–22 comes from the JE narrative of Jacob's flight from Esau after Jacob had deceived Isaac, with the help of Rebekah (Gen 27:1–28:9), reaching a turning point at Bethel (Gen 28:10–22). This is the story of a fugitive who utters a vow (cf. Num 21:2) and is later urged to fulfill his vow (Gen 31:13).

Deuteronomy 23:22–24, which demands that vows be fulfilled, the starting point of Num 30, is part of the Deuteronomic law code. The following reading assumes that Num 30:3 was responding to something like Gen 28:20–22 and Deut 23:22–24. Similarities and differences between these texts become evident when they are set beside each other:

Gen 28:20–22	Num 30:3	Deut 23:22–24
Jacob then makes a vow, saying, "If God remains with me, protects me on this way that I am taking, and gives me bread to eat and garments to wear, and I return in peace to my father's house—Yhwh shall be my God. And this stone, which I set up as a pillar, shall be God's house; and out of all that you give me, I will set aside a tithe for you."	A man, when he vows a vow to Yhwh or oaths an oath to oblige an obligation upon himself, he must not break his word; according to all that comes out of his mouth, he must do.	When you vow a vow to Yhwh your God do not delay to fulfill it, for Yhwh your God will indeed require it of you and guilt will be with you; but when you refrain to vow, no guilt will be on you. You must keep what crossed your lips and do what you vowed to Yhwh your God, having spoken with your mouth.

Jacob's vow occurs at a place of transition, in between Beersheba and Haran, during a delay in his journey (Gen 28:20–21). He wanders in flight, prefiguring the wilderness events (cf. Gen 4). Jacob's vow is conditional, pledging to take Yhwh as his 'elohîm if Yhwh remains with, protects, feeds, clothes, then returns him safely to the house of his father (28:20–21). Jacob obliges Yhwh to be a parent to him until he returns in peace to his father's house, at which time Jacob will reward Yhwh with a house (a stone) and a tithe out of all the things that he expects Yhwh will give him (28:22).

Jacob's vow signifies a moment of transition, a point at which a man wanders from one house into the care of another authority. The terms of the vow will end when he moves to another house or, in Jacob's case, returns to the previous one. The same is true concerning Yhwh, who is expected to move into a new house (Gen 28:22a).[8] The effect of moving from one house to another is presumed in Num 30:7–9, in which a daughter leaves her father's house and enters the house of her husband. The situations are similar but they concern subjects of different genders, which may be the reason for Yhwh's different responses in these events—he releases the daughter in Num 30:9 but safeguards the son in Gen 28. These literary traces allow these two texts to cross.

A simple reading reveals that Jacob demands more from Yhwh than from himself, and makes more demands of Yhwh than what Yhwh is willing to give: Jacob's demand for food and clothes is more than what Yhwh offers in 28:13–15.[9] Jacob also compromises Yhwh's offer to assign "the ground on which you are lying" (28:13) to him (Jacob) and his offspring by vowing to erect a pillar for Yhwh there (28:22). Yhwh will *not* be free from Jacob once the vow is fulfilled, for he (Yhwh) will be placed in Jacob's land. The weightier matter of this encounter falls upon Yhwh, who must uplift Jacob if he (Yhwh) is to be rewarded in return. Jacob is a calculating subject, a trickster, effective with words, captive of (his) desires, and manipulative of (Yhwh's) emotions.

Jacob's terms are problematic insofar as he has already acknowledged Yhwh's presence, which he did not realize at first, pronouncing that place to be "none other than the house of God" (Gen 28:16–8). This testimony comes after Yhwh volunteers, "Remember, *I am with you: I will protect you wherever you go* and will *bring you back to this land*. I will *not* leave you until I have done what I have promised you" (28:15, Tanakh; my italics). Jacob vows something he is offered, offering Yhwh's gifts back before he receives them;[10] he transforms a giver into a beneficiary, he returns his promises (in contrast to Noble 2002, 243). Jacob makes an event of gifts

---

[8] This narrative suggests that Yhwh will dwell *in person* rather than *in name* at this house, as suggested in the Deuteronomistic name theology (cf. Weinfeld 1991, 37).

[9] Commentators explain this textual tension according to two different sources—Gen 28:10, 13–16, 19 are from J and Gen 28:11–12, 17–18, 20–22 are from E (cf. Speiser 1964, 217–18; and Westermann 1995, 453). J focuses on Yhwh's commitments to Jacob, while E focuses on Jacob and his reactions and demands due to his encounter with Yhwh. Nonetheless, there is no consensus on the distribution of sources. Von Rad, for instance, identifies 28:10 with E (1972, 283). The following reading acknowledges the fluidity of the sources (cf. Cassuto 1972).

[10] Compare with the gift of death: "Because I cannot take death away from the other who can no more take it from me in return, it remains for everyone to take his own death *upon himself*. Everyone must assume his own death, that is to say the one thing in the world that no one else can *either give or take*: therein resides freedom and responsibility. . . . In order to put oneself to death, to give oneself death in the sense that every relation to death is an interpretative apprehension and a representative approach to death, death must be taken upon oneself. One has to *give it to oneself by taking it upon oneself*, for it can only be mine alone, irre-

problematic, arresting the exchange at the stage of language at which gifts may be rejected and vows may not be fulfilled.[11] He transforms an event of gifts into an event of words.

After making the vow, Jacob continues on his flight as if he had not just made Yhwh responsible for his safety. On the other hand, J makes Yhwh responsible before Jacob asks (Gen 28:13–16). After leaving Yhwh, Jacob shows off before Rachel. He does not wait for the remaining flock to be rounded up, as was customary at the well (Gen 29:1–2 [J]), but rolls the stone from the mouth of the well in order to water only Laban's flock. Yhwh reenters the story to open the womb of unloved Leah, but leaves Rachel barren (29:31–32 [J]; cf. 1 Sam 1–2 [see ch. 5]). Yhwh appears to understand the trickster's moves, leaving unopened the womb of she for whom Jacob had opened the well.

While in the house of Laban, Jacob appears to have forgotten his vow. But Yhwh has not forgotten Jacob's vow, and the reference to it in Gen 31:13 (E) brings it to closure, insofar as Jacob's safe return to his father's house will fulfill his vow: "I am the God of Beth-el, where you anointed a pillar and where you made a vow to Me. Now, arise and leave this land and return to your native land" (Tanakh).

I do not imagine that Yhwh is taking over the vow, as if it has been transferred, nor do I imagine that failing to fulfill the vow will hurt Jacob. On the other hand, Yhwh has something to gain when the vow is fulfilled, and I imagine that it is also for his own interests that he urges Jacob to return home. If Jacob does not come through and make Yhwh his God, and even if he fails to give the house and tithe he vowed, Yhwh will at least be free of the extra responsibilities (care and protection) Jacob had demanded from him.

It would have been helpful if there had been a regulation that warrants the fulfillment of vows, to which Yhwh could have appealed when he urges Jacob to return home. In this regard, Deut 23:22–24 provides what was lacking in Jacob's story world. The Deuteronomist may not be responding to the JE story, but I imagine that s/he had a similar situation in mind. This regulation targets those who are not inclined to fulfill their vows, who do not think that words are binding—the types of Jacob (cf. Gen 28:10–11)—obliging them with the same commitment that Yhwh makes in Gen 28:15b: ". . . for I will not abandon [cf. Gen 2:24] you until I have done what I have spoken to you."

According to this reading, Deut 23:22–24 scrutinizes the JE account. The JE narrator does not associate guilt with hesitation to fulfill one's vow,

---

placeably. That is so even if, as we just said, *death can neither be taken nor given*" (Derrida 1995, 44–45).

[11] Cf. Derrida (1995, 60) concerning language: "Just as no one can die in my place, no one can make a decision, what we call a 'decision,' in my place. But as soon as one speaks, as soon as one enters the medium of language, one looses that very singularity."

implying that the system of retribution in effect at the time of the Deuteronomist was not known in the world of JE (cf. Gammie 1970; Frymer-Kensky 1980). And stylistic differences suggest that Num 30:3 is a later construction than Deut 23:22–24. Two factors in particular underwrite this proposal.

First, the firm resolution of Num 30:3 implies that it is the product of a more rigorous legal process. While Deut 23:22–24 discourages "delaying" to fulfill a vow and requires "keeping" (*šmr*) what crosses one's lips, Num 30:3 speaks against "breaking" one's word and demands "doing" all that come out of one's mouth. Numbers 30:3 is more assertive in its demands. Numbers 30:3 leaves no chance for nonfulfillment of vows, and it erases the distinction that Deut 23:24b makes between "spoken words" and "vows." One must do as one has spoken.

Second, the Deuteronomist uses one term (*ndr*) in referring to a commitment to Yhwh, whereas three terms (*ndr*, *šb'*, and *'sr*) are used in Num 30:3, with a clear distinction between commitments to Yhwh and those upon oneself. This distinction is blurred in Jacob's vow and is ignored in the Deuteronomist's regulation. On the other hand, traces of the Deuteronomist's references to "guilt" and the threat of Yhwh's inquisition (*drš*) are left out of Num 30:3.

I ventured to circumread these texts because of their shared interests and linguistic components, and I established their interrelations on the basis of their differences. The encounter of these texts, these "strangers to each other," takes place at the moment of transtextuality. Four faces of the repressed in Num 30 emerge as a consequence:

First, one may argue that Num 30 challenges the tendency to delay and/or not fulfill one's vows. I identified this tendency in the JE and Deuteronomic texts above. Read in this light, insofar as it is first in the Num 30 order of rules, Num 30:3 sets the standard for the regulation of vows. If this standard is observed, no vow should be left unfulfilled. However, this standard is made problematic by later regulations in Num 30 that endorse the disposition that 30:3 resists. This gender-blind reading takes the permission of fathers and husbands to annul vows (30:4–9 and 30:11–16) as the privilege to repress the demands in 30:3 and 30:10 (to do all that each has spoken). As such, Num 30 "represses" itself by unraveling what it seeks to establish.

This first reading entertains the possibility that the accumulation of rules in Num 30 may be the outcome of an elaborate legal system in which the later additions (double laws) challenge and repress existing (basic) laws. In Num 30, the later regulations that sanction the annulment of vows (30:4–9, 11–16) repress the attempt of basic laws (30:3, 10) to assure that vows are fulfilled. Even if we imagine 30:3 and 30:10 at the end of the process, so that they now challenge and repress the sanctions in 30:4–9 and 30:11–16, they still have a double-law effect (see below). They resist each other, but neither one erases the other. This reading does not determine the development of Num 30, but shows that there are repressed laws in the text, no matter how one reconstructs its growth. Of course, what one reader takes to be "the repressed" (basic laws) another may view as "repressors" (double laws): the repressed are in the eyes of the reader!

A *second* way to read for the repressed in Num 30 takes into account its subjects and complex gendered makeup. According to this reading, basic and double laws do not repress each other because they regulate four different subjects: man (30:3), young unmarried woman (30:4–6), married woman (30:7–9 and 30:11–16), widow and divorcée (30:10). Even the regulations over a "married woman" do not oppose each other because of the different loci of the vow-events (father's house [30:7–9] and husband's house [30:11–16]). The permissions to annul vows (30:4–9, 11–16) do not affect regulations requiring that all vows be fulfilled (30:3, 10), because the former is concerned with vows by daughters and wives while the latter is concerned with vows by a man ('îš), a widow, and divorcée. The regulations may repress each other in principle, but they pass over each other in actuality. Nonetheless, by focusing on the "subjects of the law" I undermine the concern of Num 30 for the "subject of vows." In light of the foregoing reading, I imagine such a shift in between JE's retelling the story of a human subject and the Deuteronomist's turn to regulate the practice of vows. This shift invites a metacritical observation: my second reading correlates the *content of the form* of Num 30 with the "double-law" drive to sanction the annulment of vows.

By focusing on Num 30's "subjects of the law," I repress the "subject of its regulations," the vow, so these first two ways of reading for the repressed resist but do not erase each other. I maintain both of them out of respect for the coexistence of basic and double laws in Num 30; juxtaposing them gives the impression that the subjectification of one agent or agenda may result in the dis-subjectification of another.

A *third* reading for the repressed imagines 30:3 and 30:10 at the end, rather than at the beginning, of the development of Num 30. According to this reconstruction, Num 30 does not dismantle itself by closing with permissions to annul vows but drives to assure that all vows are fulfilled. The integrity of vow-events is maintained, and Num 30 is represented as an ingenious legal construction that drives toward closure. This reading imagines a late date for Num 30 insofar as female persons, the human subjects of the regulations in 30:4–16, were not subjects of the law until late in biblical history (cf. Fewell and Gunn 1993, 94–116). By turning the tables over the issues of redaction and date, I beg the chance to shift attention over the subject matter of Num 30. With a transoceanic move, I turn to Yhwh (as subject) and explore how Num 30 does more than it says.

I have thus far read 30:3 and 30:10 as regulations upon human subjects. Everyone ('*îš*) is obliged to do all that has come out of their mouths, because their words stand upon them.[12] The juxtaposition of 30:3 and 30:10 reminds us that "it takes two" to make a vow, obligating both oneself (30:3b and 30:10) and Yhwh (30:3a). Since human subjects may make more demands on Yhwh than on themselves, as in Jacob's vow, the fulfillment of vows should also involve Yhwh. Yhwh is responsible both for the vows that humans make as well as for his own promises. Yhwh too should not break his words (cf. 30:3b) because all to which and against which he obliges himself shall stand upon him (cf. 30:10b).

This third reading would make sense in situations in which Yhwh delays or reverses his promises. The question here is not only whether Israel jeopardizes Yhwh's promises (Power 1992, 29–30), but also whether Yhwh withholds his promises from Israel. I imagine such a question arising during times of displacement, when the powers of Yhwh are not apparent—the kinds of situations Israel experienced during the wilderness and exilic periods. In those situations, the regulations "he must not break his word; according to all that come out of his mouth, he must do" (Num 30:3b) and "all that she obliges upon herself shall stand upon her" (30:10b) should also be addressed to Yhwh.

By limiting its regulated subjects to human subjects only, Num 30 represses Yhwh's involvement in vow-events. This act of textual repression is indicative of the drive in 30:4–9 and 30:11–16 to legalize the annulment of vows, in other words, to discontinue Yhwh's involvement in vows by unmarried and married women. By reading for the repressed, on the other hand, I bring the regulations to bear on Yhwh. He should be bound to the terms of Num 30, especially since the regulations are linked to him (30:1–2, 17). The upshot of this reading is the exposure of Yhwh's passive role in the making and annulment of vows. Yhwh urges Jacob to return home in the JE story, implying that the fulfillment of vows is necessary. So the Deuteronomist insists. And in Num 30, Yhwh may release a daughter or wife whose vows have been annulled, but he cannot make a vow for either woman. Nor can a father or husband.

Hence, a *fourth* reading. The foregoing readings intend not to repress the obvious, that vows by women, that the Words of Women, are troubling. Numbers 30 stipulates that (male) authorities cannot control women's ability to make and break their commitments. In giving fathers and husbands the right to annul vows, Num 30 implies that those vows should not have been made. But the *making* of vows is beyond the control of Num 30 and of fathers and husbands. In the end, the making of annullable vows is repressed but not erased from Num 30. It is because of these vows that we have Num 30.

---

[12] References to Israel as a divorcée (Isa 50:1; cf. Hos 2:2) and to Jerusalem as a widow (Lam 1:1; cf. Ps 109:9) advocate this generalization.

3.3 The Repressed of Numbers 30

Seeking to determine the repressed of Num 30 is made problematic by the dynamic nature of Hebrew Bible traditions:

> Tradition normally has a leveling effect: early recollections are smoothed out, the tradition is accommodated to the later developments, the more revolutionary understandings are tempered and made to support the successive changes in the social and political life of the community. (Harrelson 1990, 25; cf. Fishbane 1985, 9)

Moreover, it will become evident that "the repressed of Num 30" are not independent of "the repressed in Num 30"; in other words, I am exploring an elusive subject.

3.3.1 *Behind Numbers 30*

There are several theories concerning the *Sitz im Leben* of Hebrew Bible laws, which I briefly revisit to locate *possible* settings behind Num 30. The first theory sets Hebrew Bible laws in the context of ancient Near Eastern treaties, most likely from Mesopotamia, because the (non-Semitic) Hittites used such Semitic terms as *riksu,* covenant, and *mamitu,* oath (Ringgren 1990). The treaties on the "Stele of the Vultures" (Sumer, before 2500 B.C.E.) and of Naram-Sin (Akkad, ca. 2280) display recognizable types in Hebrew Bible legal texts: "parity treaty"—between partners on equal footing— and "suzerain treaty"—between a suzerain and a vassal (Barré 1992, 655). Levenson explains:

> The theology of the Pentateuch is deeply imbued with the idiom of the Near Eastern suzerain treaty: Yhwh . . . elicits from [Israel] a sworn commitment to observe the stipulations he imposes. . . . Much the same pattern can be detected in mythic literature, such as the *Enuna Elish.* . . . the gods willingly and gladly accept the kingship of their heroic savior. (1988, 140–41)

A "curious dialectic of autonomy and heteronomy" (Levenson 1988, 143) is involved in the relation between Yhwh and Israel. Israel (the vassal) may freely enter into a relationship with Yhwh (the suzerain). Failure to do so would be suicidal for Israel. There is no alternative, yet the suzerain must still woo the vassal (LaCocque 1998, 73). In short, "[T]hose who stand under covenantal obligation by nature and necessity are continually called upon to adopt that relationship by free decision" (Levenson 1988, 148).

The second theory is represented by Gerstenberger's opposition to the treaty theory. He argues that treaties express mutual dependence and obligation between partners against a common enemy (third party), while case laws are concerned with crimes that individuals commit against each other. Hebrew Bible laws reflect civil bodies: "The commandments point to an order given to man, not created by contract. . . . The commandments presuppose a social order which antedates all historical beginnings and therefore is not made a subject of reflection. . . . They are universal and timeless" (1965, 49).

Gerstenberger's challenge leads to a third theory that locates Hebrew Bible laws within family and clan traditions (cf. McCarthy 1963; Weinfeld 1967). Hebrew Bible laws are moral prescriptions decreed by fathers, tribal leaders, and sages, for the purpose of protecting and adjudicating society (cf. W Malcolm Clark 1974, 103). These laws were not guarded by oath or curse, as in a treaty formula, but given to (male) members of the society. Some of the prescriptions entered cultic settings later, endorsed as standards of good social conduct demanded by entrance liturgies, but that was not a general condition (Gerstenberger 1965, 45). This theory sets Hebrew Bible laws in a sapiential-didactic milieu: "They freed Israelite faith from its mythical character, religious worship from its ritual stress, and the laws of the Torah from their strict legalistic character" (Weinfeld 1967, 262).

Numbers 30 preserves what appear to be shades of these settings. The commands to fulfill one's vows presuppose the treaty paradigm. The subject is assumed to be in a relationship (friendship, brotherhood) that the stipulations protect by demanding that one must do "according to all that come out of one's mouth" (30:3). And in the case of the widow and divorcée—"[vows and obligations] shall stand upon her" (30:10)—the presumed agreements are revered as if they possess forces that will rise against those who transgress the relationship, the breach of which is seen as an act of pollution. Though directed at different subjects, Num 30:3 and 30:10 shelter the kind of agreements and bonds that treaties establish.

Nonetheless, in the suzerain-vassal treaty paradigm (cf. Barré 1992, 655), Num 30 also has voices which repress (release) bonds. The privileges to annul vows in 30:4–9 and 30:11–16 work against the treaty paradigm, presenting fathers and husbands with the status of suzerains, set in control of the confirmation or annulment of vows made by their vassals. The suzerains are named and their domains are identified ("house of her father" [30:4] and "house of her man" [30:11]), corresponding to the characteristic "preamble" and "historical prologue" of the suzerain-treaty form.[13] In that regard, Num 30:4–9 and 30:11–16 document the terms of agreement which are told from the point of view of the suzerains. Moreover, elements of curses and blessings may be read in the daughter's or wife's release from (30:6, 9, 13) or obligation to (30:5, 8, 12) her vows and oaths. In this reading, the attempts in 30:4–9 and 30:11–16 to undo existing agreements spawn new (different) suzerain-vassal relations. These repressing voices coexist in the received form of Num 30.

---

[13] The standard form of the suzerain-vassal treaty includes (1) a preamble that names the suzerain; (2) a historical prologue with past deeds of the suzerain; (3) the terms of agreement; (4) a notice of deposit in the sanctuary and of regular readings; (5) the invocation of witnesses; and (6) the demand for blessings and curses (cf. Mendenhall 1954 and 1955; McCarthy 1963; W. Malcolm Clark 1974). Lacking from Num 30, however, are (4) and (5).

Clan-family wisdom is also a possible *Sitz im Leben* behind Num 30 (see also Pressler 1993, 5). It reflects the life of civil bodies, which Gerstenberger calls "clan ethic" (*Sippenethos*). From this perspective, Num 30 prescribes correct social behavior. The prescriptions allow annulment of vows for the sake of protecting family order, testifying to the "curious dialectic of autonomy and heteronomy" (Levenson) in Hebrew Bible laws. Nevertheless, the text's ambiguity concerning the point of transition from the house of the father to the house of the husband (30:7) jeopardizes family order. In this case, female subjects lose their autonomy to a male-defined heteronomy. It is not clear if vows that a father approves in his house (30:4–5) are protected against annulment when his daughter enters a husband's house (30:9). Nor is it clear whether the husband, if he approves (30:7–8), may reestablish the vows that the father annulled. Tensions, therefore, may arise between a husband and his father-in-law if the former annuls a vow approved by the latter, or vice versa (see §3.3.2). Disorder between families, contrary to the concern of the clan-family wisdom settings, is a possible outcome of the enforcement of Num 30:4–9.

Whether one reads Num 30 as the product of the treaty paradigm or of the clan-family wisdom circles, attempts to repress are evident "behind" the text. The reason for this is in the nature of tradition itself:

> In different ways, then, the older *traditum* is dependent upon the *traditio* for its ongoing life. This matter is paradoxical, for while the *traditio* culturally revitalizes the *traditum*, and gives new strength to the original revelation, it also potentially undermines it. (Fishbane 1985, 15; cf. Knight 1990, 2)

But tradition is not fixed, and one expects attempts to repress in Hebrew Bible traditions, corresponding to what Crenshaw calls the phenomenon of dissent (1990, 235 n. 2). This is the case in Num 30 also. Numbers 30 works against Israelite institutions concerning agreements and bonds between parties, which are made at all stages of life, both personal and communal. In the religious stage, bonds manifest as covenant relationships (cf. Mendenhall and Herion 1992, 1201).

The theological implications of the treaties theory set the stage for another theory: Hebrew Bible laws are derived from the covenant, and are embedded in liturgical celebration (Zimmerli 1965; Greengus 1992, 245). Covenant is not the *Mitte* of the Hebrew Bible, but one of its basic themes (so Eichrodt 1961, 36–69) and the unmistakable textual setting (*Sitz im Wort*) of Hebrew Bible laws (LaCocque 1998, 76). According to this view, Hebrew Bible laws protect the covenant (cf. LaCocque 1998, 74).

This theory has not gone unchallenged (cf. McCarthy 1963; Gerstenberger 1965), on linguistic and historical grounds (W. Malcolm Clark 1974, 111–12; Crüsemann 1996, 9–10). Nonetheless, referring to Exod 34:27–28, which bases the decalogue on the covenant, and Josh 24, which associates covenant with law, Zimmerli rejects Gerstenberger's (1965) objection that covenant and law are fundamentally separate concepts (1978, 55). This theory prevailed mainly because of the religious functions of the Hebrew Bible and of its laws, as if they were from and for the Israelite religion (cf. Greengus 1992, 250):[14]

> The basic notion that Israelite law is direct divine utterance is not at all common in the ancient world. The idea that a character from the distant past mediated the law is equally unusual. . . . As in the ancient Near East, our laws are a function of the state, but in Israel the function preceded the state and thus is above the state. (Crüsemann 1996, 15)

Z. Falk adds that the unique character of Hebrew law "is shown in its relationship towards religion. Israel's social, economic and cultural structures, were deeply impressed by monotheism, which, consequently, also shaped law and custom" (1964, 34; cf. Berman 1974, 21–47, 77–105; Morden 1984, 8–9). The law-covenant theory thus shifts our attention from the subjects of genre and form to the realm of practice and functions.[15]

I pose the question, at my own risk, if and how it is still possible to speak of Num 30 as a divine commandment enjoined by God (cf. 30:1–2, 17). My concern aims not only to challenge the attribution of Num 30 to God, but also to expose tensions in the covenantal relationships between God and God's people. As Bal, by transference, has stated:

> The law, the institutions in relation to which the subject establishes itself (Lacan), is at the same time the paradoxical institution that both sets the limits to subjectivity and, by its fundamentally *intersubjective* nature, *subject* to interpretation by *subjects* who are *subjected* to it, designs the limits of its own (pseudo-)objectivity. It represents the performative acts of interdiction (of transgression) and of promise (of social intersubjectivity), both turned toward the future; it also represents the constative act of *stating* (transgression in the past). (1987, 79; cf. LaCocque 1998, 79)

If the regulations in Num 30 are fulfilled, assuming that a woman's vow may include her commitment to be in covenant relationship with Yhwh, then they also threaten the institution of the covenant. When vows are violated, covenants too may be broken. Why should one cut a covenant if it may be broken later? Why would God demand commitments, then allow some of them to be annulled? Why annul vows if one cannot make vows for another?

In this brief look behind Num 30, I identified ideologies that may have stirred Num 30. Reading in this manner allows Num 30 to do what it stipulates—to restrain, ignore, break, and annul words. Form and func-

---

[14] "The relation of law to religion is two-fold: the sanctions of the legal system provide for and organize the institutions of religion; and, on the other hand, religion undergirds the system of law" (Sibley 1984, 45, in contrast to Samuel Thompson).

[15] We will be well served to recall Rosenzweig's clarification: "Judaism is *not* law; it creates law, but it is *not* identical with it; Judaism is *being* a Jew" (1935, 762).

tion reproduce content. Metacritically speaking, this exercise reminds us that biblical texts are not "original" records of the events or teachings that they exhibit, as if they were located at "zero degree" (Barthes), or at "ground zero," but the reworking of existing "texts" (so Carmichael 1985, 1992; see also Levinson 1997).

3.3.2 *In Front of Numbers 30*

This subsection looks in the other direction, still taking the MT as my point of departure, toward early interpretations of Num 30. The focus shifts from "behind" to "in front" of Num 30, and I address these "frontal" idiosyncrasies on the premise that "translation belongs to the history of reading, itself governed by the 'history of effects'—the *Wirkungsgeschichte*—of the words themselves" (Ricoeur 1998, 337; so Bal 1991b, 17):[16]

> *There is no innocent translation;* I mean one that could escape the history of reception of our text, a history that itself is immediately a history of interpretation. *To translate is already to interpret.* The scholarly work of exegetes . . . do not escape this constraint. They all belong to this long history of reading and interpretation. . . . Modern exegetes are like us. They work and think at the end of a history. In this sense, the one thing that would be criticizable would be the naive claim of an exegesis that held itself to be without a history, as though it were possible to coincide, without the mediation of a tradition of reading, with the original signification of a text, even with the presumed intention of its author. (Ricoeur 1998, 332; my italics)

I turn to two interpretations of Num 30: tractate *Nedarîm* (consisting of several interpretations) and John Calvin's "harmony" to Exodus–Deuteronomy. They disclose the interests in/of the synagogue-church.

The Talmud is characterized by what Steinsaltz calls the *Talmudic dialectic:* "This dialectic is unique in taking nothing for granted. It is only satisfied with proofs that approach absolute certainty. It constantly tries to sharpen the proofs, cull the evidence, and reach the very essence of the problems, with the greatest possible precision" (1989, 3). Debates and dissension characterize this dialectic, similar to what we read in the Gemara over Num 30:10:

> It was taught: If a widow or a divorced woman declares, "Behold! I will be a nazirite when I marry," and she marries—R. Ishmael said: He [the husband] can annul. R. Akiba ruled: He cannot annul. . . .
> R. Hisda said: Our Mishnah agrees with R. Akiba. Abaye said: It may agree even with R. Ishmael: in the Mishnah she made herself de-

---

[16] So Burke Long's critique of the Albrighteans' (Albright and the "Baltimore School") production of knowledge about the Bible: "I view it not as innocently objective learning, conforming to the master paradigm of scientific rationality, but as aggregates of interested actions that sustained various personal and institutional relations" (1997, 2).

pendent upon a time factor; the period may end without her being divorced or the period may end without her being married; but in the
Baraitha [a Tannaim tradition excluded from the Mishnah] she made the
vow dependent upon marriage. (*Ned* 89a)[17]

R. Ishmael and R. Akiba take contrasting positions, but neither one had to
be wrong. Abaye claims that the Mishnah may agree with R. Ishmael,
without rejecting R. Hisda's support for R. Akiba (cf. Steinsaltz 1989, 4).
Upon these voices, the Mishnah transcends Num 30:10.

Though based on Num 30:3–16 and Deut 23:22–24 (cf. Blackman 1963,
205), tractate *Nedarîm* (*Ned*) also addresses other subjects like sacrifice (*Ned*
6a), *harem* (*Ned* 18b), adultery (*Ned* 20a), and circumcision (*Ned* 31b–32b).
In good Talmudic fashion (cf. Steinsaltz 1989, 7), these subjects are associated with the making and annulment of vows in Num 30. The following
reading focuses on *Ned* chapters 10 and 11, which focus on vows made by
women.

When *Ned* chapter 10 opens with a debate on who between a father
and a husband has more authority over the vows of his daughter or wife,
we find the crucial issue for the Tannaim: Who has (more) authority?
Depending on the circumstances, a father and a husband both have authority over each other:

> If the father died the right [to annul vows] does not pass on to the hus-
> band, but if the husband died the right is vested in the father. In this
> respect the father's power surpasses the husband's power. In another
> matter the husband's power exceeds the father's power in that the hus-
> band can nullify in the case of a girl who has reached the age of majority
> [*bogereth:* around thirteen years old], whereas the father can not annul
> after she has reached the age of majority. (*Ned* 67a)

The debate goes on in the Gemara, posing different circumstances, all the
while ignoring the subjects, the daughters, whose vows are the issue.
R. Ishmael's cry then, "The daughters of Israel are beautiful but poverty
renders them ugly" (*Ned* 66b), tells only part of the story. The daughters
of Israel are beautiful but lack of authority renders them weak. We find
the same scheme in *Ned* chapter 9, where the sages concede that the
vows of a son may be absolved for the honor due his father and mother
or for some unexpected circumstance (*Ned* 64a–66a). The upshot is the reversal of Num 30:3, and the suspension of a son's desires in order to
privilege his father and mother. At the underside of the talk about vows
in *Ned* chapters 9–10 is a drive to establish authority. In this case, the
"younger children of Israel" are beautiful, but tractate *Nedarîm* robs them

---

[17] Translators too attempt to control texts (cf. Havea 2000, 174–87). I cited
Freedman's translation, but Neusner's translations (1995a; 1996) left out Abaye's
defense of R. Ishmael's position. Whether this shows a bias towards Rabbi Akiba's
position is not clear, but it is curious that R. Ishmael's justification appeared in
Neusner 1995b.

of authority.[18] In addition to the gender issue, we also have generational bias here.

To avoid conflicts between a father and a future husband, the Mishnah introduces the following "scholarly" practice:

> It was a custom among disciples of the Sages, before the daughter of any one of them passed out of his control, to say to her, "All the vows that you vowed in my house are annulled." Likewise the husband, before she enters into his control would say to her, "All vows which you vowed before you entered into my control are annulled"; because once she enters into his control he can not nullify. (*Ned* 72b)

Whereas the condition for annulling vows in Num 30 is hearing them on the same day (cf. *Ned* 76a–79a), the Mishnah allows the father and the husband to categorically annul vows before they hear them. This is a double move to repress. While the Mishnah rewrites Num 30, the Gemara brings the stipulations of Num 30 to bear on the circumstances imagined in the Mishnah without rejecting the latter. The working of the Talmudic dialectic does not endorse total rejection, but fences its authorized subjects as if R. Jochanan's words apply: "One may seek absolution from confirmation, but not from annulment!" One must protect what is confirmed but not what is rejected.

The Mishnah takes a different turn in *Ned* chapter 11, limiting vows that "he" (husband [Freedman] and father [Blackman]) can annul to ones that involve self-denial ("against the soul," cf. Num 30:13; Blackman and Neusner use "self-affliction") (79b–80). The Mishnah appears to have the interests of women in mind, seeking to protect them from themselves. But as the terms are refined and new circumstances are considered, the interests of the father and husband take over. Should the women injure themselves on account of vows of self-denial/affliction, fathers or husbands bear the burden of caring for them. So the Mishnah goes further to protect male authorities from their women:

> [If she vows] "Konam! that I do not work for the benefit of my father; your father; my brother; your brother"—he cannot annul. "That I do not work for your benefit"—he does not need to annul. R. Akiba says, "He ought to revoke it lest she produce more than is due from him." R. Jochanan b. Nuri says, "He must absolve it, lest he divorces her and she will then be forbidden to him." (*Ned* 85a)

Both R. Akiba and R. Jochanan b. Nuri protect the man. But tractate *Ned* finds more reasons to protect a father, even if in opposition to his son-in-law. A daughter under the authority of a husband is still expected to honor her father:

---

[18] In Neusner's rehash (1998) of the Division of Women titled *How the Rabbis Liberated Women*, he examines texts from the other four tractates but leaves out tractate *Nedarim*. This gives the impression that the rabbis did not liberate women in the *Nedarim*, as the forthcoming reading argues.

> If a man is under a vow that his son-in-law shall not benefit from him, and he desires to give money to his daughter, he must say to her, "This money is given to you as a gift, providing that your husband has no rights over it, and that you alone shall put it to your personal use." (*Ned* 88a)

The Mishnah protects the father from his son-in-law, but not the husband from his father-in-law, giving further evidence of a generation bias in the text.

The Mishnah also limits a man's right to annul vows according to the kind of woman who utters them. As in Num 30:10, neither a father nor a husband can annul vows by a widow or divorcée. The general rule is that "if any woman has entered for even one hour into her own independence [by divorce or widowhood], he [husband] can not cancel her vow" (*Ned* 88a). According to this principle, if a woman makes a vow just before being divorced and her (ex-)husband takes her back that same day, he cannot revoke her vow (cf. *Ned* 71a). Being a divorcée that same day, he cannot annul her vows. Tractate *Nedarim* also names other women, beyond Num 30, whose vows cannot be annulled:

> There are nine maidens [*na'arah*] whose vows stand: [1] one who was an adult [*bogereth*] and as it were *an orphan* [during father's lifetime, compare with 4–5]; [2] one that was still a maiden, then became adult and as it were also *an orphan;* [3] a maiden who has not yet become adult and she was as it were *an orphan;* [4] an adult *whose father died;* [5] a maiden and is now adult *whose father died;* [6] a maiden who is not yet adult and *whose father died;* [7] a maiden *whose father died,* then she becomes adult; [8] an adult *whose father is alive;* [9] a maiden who becomes adult and *whose father is alive.* R. Judah says, "Also one who married his daughter who was a minor, and she became a widow or divorcée and returned to him, and she was still a maiden." (*Ned* 89a–b; my italics)

In response to R. Judah's supplement one may ask, Why don't fathers take back all of their widowed and divorced daughters, along with their orphaned granddaughters? This question shifts the focus from authority to responsibility.

The Talmud to this section is peculiar because of the silence of the Tannaim and Amoraim, implying approval on their part (cf. *Ned* 71b), as if they have exhausted the Talmudic dialectic:

Babylonian Talmud	Palestinian Talmud
Said R. Judah said Rab, "These are the words of R. Judah. But the Sages say: 'The vows of three maidens stand: a *bogereth, an orphan,* and *an orphan* during her father's lifetime.'" (my italics)	Said R. Yochanan, "They are two [not nine (or three)]. [The orphan makes one category, the other maidens the second category.] Why then do we learn, Nine? In order to sharpen the wits of the disciples."

Two observations need to be made: First, the foregoing analysis uncovers two further criteria for categorizing subjects: (1) age/generation differences and (2) the marital status of one's mother. The father is given more authority than his son-in-law (*Ned* 67a), parents (the father is the privileged parent) keep their authority over their children (cf. C. J. H. Wright 1992, 766–69), and daughters of widows and divorcées are distinguished from their mothers and "the rest" (*Ned* 89a–b). In this regard, the Talmuds reflect the common theological drive in ancient Near Eastern societies for respect toward the elderly (J. Gordon Harris 1987, 18–40). The Talmuds reinforce the authority of the elderly by denying younger generations the chance to assume authority for/over themselves. This double move is necessary, because authorizing one constituent requires deauthorizing the other (who is experienced as a threat).[19] *Control is sought by repressing the other.*

The Talmuds fail to account for the connectedness of the generations. And prejudices against widows and divorcées blind the Tannaim to the fact that daughters become orphans when their fathers die/leave; in other words, mothers do not make orphans on their own. The biases of the Tannaim and Amoraim are repressed, but not erased.

Second, the foregoing review discloses double repressions in the interpretive process. The Mishnah takes the stipulations of Num 30:10 one step further by binding the children of widows and divorcées to their vows and oaths, and the two Talmuds restrict the articles of the Mishnah to two or three categories. The Babylonian Talmud attributes the Mishnah section to R. Judah and addresses three categories: the *bogereth*, and two types of orphan. The Palestinian Talmud (R. Yochanan) goes further, constricting the three categories to two, orphans and the others, suggesting that they were presented as nine categories "in order to sharpen the wits of the disciples." Both readings disclose the tendency of the Talmudic dialectic to restrict the text which, according to this review, is a form of control present in all readings.

R. Judah's departure from Num 30:10 points us to the underside of the list in *Ned* 89a–b, where I detect anxieties with children of both the divorcée (1–3, 8–9) and the widow (4–7). R. Judah shows that the widow or divorcée may return to her father's house (see ch. 6), a privilege not offered to the nine maidens identified earlier. This alternative reading assumes that the last two maidens (8–9) are orphans also (the children of divorcées), like the first three, whose fathers are still alive. Internal evidences fence this reading. First, the next Mishnah section (no. 11) addresses the issue of a wife who benefits from, or works for the benefits of, her father or father-in-law (*Ned* 89b). This begs the question of whether

---

[19] J. Gordon Harris distinguishes Israel from its neighbors by proposing that the respect and honor of parents and the elderly according to Israel's literature went beyond fear of their authority. Younger persons were urged to honor the "signs of aging" (cf. Lev 19:32) out of respect for God (1987, 32).

the children named in the previous section benefit from their fathers (cf. C. J. H. Wright 1992, 762, 763–66). Second, the subject of the last section of tractate *Ned* (no. 12) is the three kinds of divorced women who may receive their Kethubah (settlement owed a divorcée, according to her marriage contract). Benefit is the concern in *Ned* 89a–b also. These two sections urge us to reexamine the previous section in light of the subjects of both the divorcée and the benefit of/from one's father. I read the last two subjects in the Mishnah list (89a–b) accordingly, as daughters of a divorcée who do not benefit from their (still-living) fathers. In that regard, the nine women are all orphans; hence, only one subject is repressed in the Mishnah list: orphans.

I identified the repressed in the Talmuds by using the Talmudic dialectic to imagine what a critical Gemara of Mishnah section no. 10 might look like. Such a practice can be beneficial to (post)modern critics, as Neusner explains:

> What the second-century sages of the Mishnah have to teach the generations of the last decades of the twentieth century and the first of the twenty-first, is how to make use of imagination and fantasy to confront, defy, and overcome chaos and disorder. (1992, 7; cf. 1991, 137–58; see n. 6 above)

Calvin's *Commentaries on the Four Last Books of Moses Arranged in the Form of a Harmony* (1564) emerged from a different setting, against the church and the papacy, but he shares similar strategies with the Tannaim. Together, they draw attention to two types of extrabiblical "texts": Mishnaic and Talmudic "literary accounts," on the one hand, and (oral) "traditions" such as rabbinical teachings and church institutions and authorities on the other.

Calvin's work was ideologically motivated, opposing readings that sought out discrepancies in biblical texts and consequently dismantled the text. Bingham claims that "[t]he fancies of the Rabbins and of the Allegorists were his aversion; and it may be that he sometimes ran into the opposite extreme, and cleaved too rigidly to the literal interpretation" (1950, xi). This assessment is taunting because the tendency to untangle biblical texts is preserved by higher critics, most of whom would find Calvin's harmonies too doctrinal. Calvin was aware of the controversial nature of his harmonizing study, for it rearranges and offers *to improve* the organization of the Bible. Nevertheless, he believed that his cause was noble, aiming to free the Bible from the church's control and to give the "common man" an opportunity to read and interpret it (1950a, xv). Calvin was controlling in practice. His harmony sets "unpractised readers" in particular directions, which may differ in substance from what the church set, but both influence (coerce) the reader.

Calvin assigns the laws in the Pentateuch to the Decalogue under two subcategories: (1) "exposition" of each commandment; and (2) a "supplement" containing prescriptions of ritual exercises or political laws presupposed or produced by each commandment. The Decalogue is the deciding factor for "nothing can be wanted as the rule of a good and upright life beyond the Ten Commandments" (1950a, xvii). He takes Num 30, along with Lev 19:12 (together with Exod 23:13; Deut 6:13; 10:20), Deut 23:21–23, and Lev 27:1–29, as "exposition" texts of the third commandment (Exod 20:7; Deut 5:11). His treatment of Num 30 comes last, guided toward his understanding of the third commandment and the other "exposition" texts.

The third commandment is straightforward: one must not take the name of Yhwh in vain. So is the consequence: Yhwh will not hold that person guiltless. But what it means to take a name in vain is unclear. Calvin proposes to read it as a synecdoche: "[I]n order that God may procure for His name its due reverence, He forbids its being taken in vain, especially in oaths" (1950b, 408). Calvin transforms the third commandment into a regulation on oaths, even though "oath" is not used in either of the two versions of the commandment, the violation of which signifies taking God's name in vain. In other words, God's *name* fuses with God's *essence*, like putting the *species* for the *genus,* so that an oath given in God's name acknowledges that *He is God;* one *honors God* by making an oath *in the name of God.* An oath made in God's name but which is unfulfilled, and an oath that was made improperly, accordingly, profanes (the name of) God. "God's name, then, is taken in vain, not only when any one abuses it by perjury, but when it is lightly and disrespectfully adduced in proof of frivolous and trifling matters: I speak with respect to oaths" (1950b, 409).

The texts that Calvin read as "expositions" of the third commandment are not just interpretations "which the Lawgiver has added unconnectedly!" (1950a, xvi). They also give us an idea as to why he read the third commandment in conjunction with oaths. The first series of texts, Lev 19:12, Exod 23:13, Deut 6:13, and Deut 10:20, links the act of making an oath (*šb'*) to the name of God. To swear by the name of another god (Exod 23:13) is to take God's name in vain, "for it is not lawful to refer the judgment of things unknown to any other than the one true God" (1950b, 411–12). Assuming that one recognizes as "God" he by whose name one swears, Calvin argues that to swear by the name of another god is to give him the honor due to God. That act also profanes (the name of) God (cf. Deut 6:13; 10:20).

With Deut 23:21–23, Calvin inserts the "event of the vow" into his construction. "The rule of vowing also pertains to the keeping of the Third Commandment, since, by vowing, men exercise themselves in the sanctification of God's name, and to promise anything to God is a kind of swearing" (1950b, 413). As with the oath, one dishonors the name of God by failing to fulfill his vow. "On this point, then, God justly rescues His name from contempt, and to this end demands that what has been promised to Him should be paid" (1950b, 414). It is equally important to safeguard oneself against "ungodly" vows, so it is wise to be sparing of vows: "[A] a mutual agreement is required between the heart and the tongue" (1950b, 417). Calvin turns against the papacy with a definition which shows that not all vows are lawful and godly: "[N]othing can be properly vowed to God, except what we know to be pleasing to Him; for if 'to obey is better than sacrifice,' (1 Sam. xv. 22), nothing surely can be more absurd than to indulge ourselves in the liberty of serving God, each according to his own fancy" (1950b, 414):

> Assuredly it is more than blind arrogance, nay diabolical madness, that a mortal man should wish to present as if it were his, what he has not received. . . . No gift, then, can be acceptable to God, except what He in His goodness has conferred upon us. But what is done in the Papacy? Monks, and nuns, and priests, bind themselves to perpetual celibacy, and do not consider that *continency is a special gift;* and thus whilst none of them has regard to the measures of his ability, they wretchedly abandon themselves to ruin, or envelop themselves in deadly snares. . . . Hence it appears, that *whether a vow should be kept or not, is to be estimated from the character of him that vows.* But a more gross and more common error is committed in respect to the object of vows. I said above that the godly never made vows to God, except in testimony of gratitude; whereas almost all the vows of the superstitious are so many fictitious acts of worship, having no other aim than to propitiate God by the expiation of sin, or to acquire favour meritoriously. (1950b, 415; my italics)

In light of his definition, celibacy should be an honorable vow because it offers back to God the special gift of continency. And insofar as the *character* of the one who makes the vow determines whether the vow should be kept or not, monks, nuns, and priests are not ungodly by default for their vows of abstinence. One may thus turn Calvin's critique of the pope on himself: Calvin too did "not hesitate to heap together directly contradictory sentences" (1950b, 425).

Calvin continues his charge against the papacy with his reading of Lev 27:1–29, the text that stipulates the price and manner by which a person may redeem vows he cannot fulfill.[20] He turns on the papist's authority to announce restitution for, and/or nullification of, a person's vow. "Now, since people have improperly and in foolish mimicry imitated the vows which God permitted to the Jews under the Law, so the Pope, in providing for their redemption, has dared in his diabolical arrogance to rival God" (1950b, 424). Calvin's spirited criticism indicates both that the

---

[20] Concerning Lev 27:4–5: "A woman he estimates at thirty shekels; since for the most part less profit is made by a woman than a man; and although it might occur that some women would be much more valuable than men, since sometimes women are found to be industrious, prudent, discreet, and strong to labour, whilst men are idle, dull, lazy, and weak, still a general law must needs be given, for the examination would have been too difficult if each individual was to be estimated according to their good qualities" (1950b, 421).

texts gave him an opportunity to speak against the papacy, and that his hostility toward the papist and the church determined his reading of these texts. This curious dialectic of connection (of different texts) and disconnection (from church authorities) is the (unconscious) setting of his reading of Num 30, which echoes his resistance to church authorities:

> Moses teaches in this chapter that the vows which were made by *persons who were not free* [my italics], were not held good before God; and although no mention is made of male children, still, as their condition was the same, it seems that by *synecdoche* they must be included with the daughters and wives, unless perhaps God chose to pay regard to the weaker sex. (1950b, 428)

The defining factor in his understanding of Num 30 is status. Calvin was aware of the difference that gender makes,[21] and he even refers to a weaker sex, but contends that authority is the object of Num 30.

Lawful and godly vows by people who are their own masters must stand, but vows by women and children, who are not their own masters, "do not hold good." In this regard, Calvin uses Num 30 to disqualify vows by monks, nuns, and priests, who are not their own masters. Calvin's fudging with the gender issue suggests an (unconscious) attempt to set the stage for a reading that is critical of both males and females. If my suspicions maintain, Calvin's contempt toward the authority of the papacy is the repressed factor in his reading of Num 30. It does not surface in his analysis of Num 30, but it backgrounds his harmony of the Third Commandment.

●

The foregoing analyses uncover two possible paths for transtextual readers. First, one reads the text *and* the world "in front of" her, as in the cases of Talmud tractate *Nedarim* and Calvin's harmony. The rabbis were concerned with the authorities in family and societal settings while Calvin charged against church authorities and papal practices. It is impossible (irresponsible?) to read without accounting for what is "in front of" the reader and the text, and I address this concern further in part 2.

Second, appealing to the Italian proverb *Traduttore traditore* ("the translator is a traitor") I add that the interpreter, too, whether she counterreads or not, is a traitor. Something is lost in the reading process, from the text and from the worlds in front of the reader. The challenge is for the reader to be a responsible traitor!

We saw in tractate *Nedarim* how uneasiness with orphans may have

---

[21] He elected not to address the gender enigma, explaining that he "will not pertinaciously contend about this, because it is better to leave undecided whatever is doubtful, and *disputable*, as it is commonly called, on either side" (1950b, 428).

caused the Amoraim to extend Num 30:10 to the children of widows and divorcées. And Calvin's opposition to vows by nuns, priests, and monks influenced the gender-blind placement of boys and girls under the category of "children who were not their own masters," which violates the distinctions made in Num 30. Interpreters betray the text in order to sustain privileged views and positions. Lacking is the betrayal of the text for the sake of repressed privileges, to which part 2 will also be devoted.

3.4 The Many Faces of the Repressed

I discovered that "the repressed" in/of Num 30 has many faces: female and male, human and divine, ideological and real. The face that readers find is conditioned by the texts (literary or otherwise) we read, the repressed in/of those texts, the worldview we bring, and the world in front of us. In the end, the faces of the repressed may just be strangers within oneself. What we repress can rise through the "violation" (transgression) of our words.

I circumread Num 30 with other biblical texts (§3.2) and traditions presumed to lie behind Hebrew Bible laws (§3.3.1), with the assumption that Num 30 counters existing (traditional) stories and principles (laws), and I also posed Num 30 as a text that interpreters counter (§3.3.2). I allowed dissenting readings to coexist, similar to what Steinsaltz calls the "Talmudic dialectic."

I arrived at conclusions reached in previous chapters: *gender* and *authority* are central concerns in Num 30 and strong influences upon its readers. Now and then readers try to repress these concerns (as in Calvin's dispute with the church), or repress one in favor of the other (as in Calvin's gender-blind affirmation of the authority of the masters), but they resurface through their re-presentations of the text. As if to imitate the text, readers may repress but they cannot erase the interests of the text and/or of themselves.

I also discovered other (but not "new") concerns repressed in Num 30 and/or its interpretations. Lurking over Num 30 is an uneasiness with the interactions between different generations, to which the law extends better protection to the older generation (as in tractate *Nedarim*), and resistance against the rest. The foregoing readings image two forms of "the rest": the character of Yhwh, who should also be obliged to fulfill his promises (§3.2.2), and the orphans (i.e., children of widows and divorcées), whom the Talmuds also bind to their words (§3.3.2).

Yhwh and the orphans are linked to the regulations of Num 30 in different ways. Vows are made to Yhwh and he releases the subjects whose vows are annulled, so he is involved from beginning to end. As a participant in vow-events, I subjected Yhwh to the stipulations of Num 30. On the other hand, orphans are linked to Yhwh through their mothers, who are limited in Num 30, and the Tannaim extend the stipulation over a widow or divorcée to her children, the orphans. Yhwh and orphans represent, at the moment of reception, the strangers within both text and readers.

The price of reading for the repressed is the chance to uncover readings that unsettle—in other words, to face troubling faces of the repressed. I identified such instances in tractate *Ned* and in Calvin's "harmony," who did to the text as it stipulates. They "hold their peace" when they approve of the text, but "restrain" it when they object. If they, and we, have the courage to "hold our peace" when we disapprove, in order to assist the rising of the repressed, we face the strangers within ourselves.[22]

---

[22] Part 2 will account for this concern. I examine vow-stories in which a young woman in her father's house (ch. 4), a wife in her husband's house (ch. 5), and a widow and divorcée (ch. 6) claim their vow-events in ways that unsettle the regulations of Num 30.

Part II
Elusion of control

At the risk of labouring the point, I begin by reiterating the three fundamental tenets of Derrida's case: all *texts resist totalisation;* no *text is absolutely free from a context or a centre; and* some *texts seem to totalise other texts.* (Hart 1989, 42)

1. The deconstructibility of law (for example) or of legitimacy makes deconstruction possible. 2. The undeconstructibility of justice also makes deconstruction possible, indeed is inseparable from it. 3. The result: deconstruction takes place in the interval that separates the undeconstructibility of justice from the deconstructibility of law (authority, legitimacy, and so on). (Derrida 1990, 945)

The aim of deconstructing the law is not to level the law, to bring down the wall—because it is the strong arm of the law that holds oppressive, unjust forces in place—but to give the law flexibility and "give." To deconstruct something is not to wreck it but to rewrite it, reformulate it, redo it, remake it; better still, it deconstructs itself, auto-deconstructively [cf. Derrida 1990, 981]. Deconstruction thus is essentially positive, an affirmation of everything that we want to dig out from under the constructions under which it labors, in order to prevent the distinction between justice and law from becoming hard and fast. (Caputo 1993, 194)

4

A Daughter No Man Knew

*True, the academic practice of interpretation, linked with journalism
and other more popular forms of interpretation through a common ideology and often even through shared personnel, can be a form of
censorship in itself.* (Bal 1991c, 13)

4.0 Navel-Reading

In *Lethal Love* (1987), Mieke Bal presents difference as a site where literary,
feminist, and narrative theories engage. This engagement releases patriarchy's hold over readings and truth claims: "[T]he point of literary
analysis is that there is no truth, and that this contention can be reason-
ably argued. And where the truth is absent,[1] women can creep in, and
rewrite themselves back into the history of ideology" (Bal 1987, 132; cf.
Penchansky 1990, 17–18; Fewell 1995, 121–24).[2]

Reading for differences does not deny the domination of patriarchy
but shifts it from the center, thus undermining it (Bal 1991c, 23). This deconstructive practice provides a hole, a gap, a point of entry for repressed

---

[1] "'Truth' is a way of colonizing the text, of occupying it and posing as its
owner. No method whatsoever can provide the true meaning of a text, because
semiosis is not dealing in truth. 'Truth,' in interpretation is, as in other semiotic
practices, a matter of carrying conviction. And conviction is sought, by formalist
discourse, through the presentation of contextual and co-textual evidence for its
results, as well as through the intersubjective accessibility . . . of its terms" (Bal
1991b, 12).

[2] So Fuchs, concerning Judg 11: "Literary strategies work here in the interests
of patriarchal ideology, the ideology of male supremacy. This understanding calls
for a resistant reading of the biblical text, a reading attuned to the political implications of omissions, elisions and ambiguity. A reader, above all, that resists the
tendency in biblical narrative to focus on the father at the daughter's expense"
(1993, 130).

subjects. Bal uses "navel" to refer to this hole, which she presents as an alternative to the gender-blind phallus of psychoanalysis (which dichotomizes subjects on the basis of the haves and have-nots [castration]) and to Derrida's destabilizing concept of *dissemination* (which appeals to the hymen as a surface on which meaning circulates without fixity; cf. Bal 1991a, 15; Penchansky 1990, 23). The navel preserves the curious dialectic of autonomy and heteronomy, being a trace of one's mother and a sign of the autonomy of male and female subjects:

> The navel . . . is a metaphor for an element, often a tiny detail, that hits the viewer [and reader], is processed by her or him, and textualizes the image [and text] on its own terms. . . . the textualizing navel is an emptiness, a little surface which the work leaves unfilled. (Bal 1991c, 22–23)

> The navel, in contrast [to phallus and hymen], is fundamentally gender specific—the navel is the scar of dependence on the mother—but it is also democratic in that both men and women have it. (Bal 1991c, 23)

Bal adds a semiotic twist in *Murder and Difference* (1988b). She uses the semiotic concept of *codes*, to which scholars appeal in resolving the meaning of texts, to differentiate dominant readings (i.e., academic disciplines; 1988b, 3–5, 15ff.). Bal concludes that no code on its own is satisfactory. "Codes control interpretation; they are assisted in this by institutions, which propagate certain codes while discrediting or silencing others" (1988b, 7; so Penchansky 1990, 9). In this regard, reading the navel in texts requires crossing the boundaries of dominant disciplines toward a transdisciplinary code (1988b, 137–38):

> The concept of code, flexible when necessary, more tightly delineated when it was profitable, proved to be useful as a critical approach. Criticizing the current hermeneutic practice, it helps us to *differentiate*, undermining the cultural homogenization that impoverishes our dominant culture as much as its subcultures. (1988b, 138)

The complexity of the texts that Bal studies in *Murder and Difference*, Judg 4–5, containing a story and a song by gendered subjects, and her focalization on difference, make a transdisciplinary approach necessary. And insofar as she, too, is a gendered reader, it is not fortuitous that she prefers a transdisciplinary code. Transdisciplinarity and difference are characteristics of her gender code:

> This should not surprise us: the gender code, which is transdisciplinary, depends upon the integration of disciplinary codes. (1988b, 111)

In the concluding volume of her trilogy, *Death and Dissymmetry* (1988a), Bal supplements her gender code with a countercoherence that embraces the reality of gender-bound violence in biblical texts (1988a, 5; see also Exum 1993), and that challenges readings that impose a political coherence over the book of Judges. Bal writes against two claims in particular: that Judges is a collection of literary sources, which is undermined

when critics privilege one cultural text (e.g., MT), and that Judges is a coherent theological and historical account (1988a, 10ff.). Focalizing on
subjects left out by the politics of coherence, she claims that history and
theology intertwine in dominant readings of Judges in response "to a
need so deeply rooted in the interaction between the book and its modern, committed readers" (1988a, 5). Bal's countercoherence seeks to
explain why the political coherence is a tool—or should I say weapon?—
in "politics of coherence" (see, e.g., Soggin 1981, 212–13). What the politics
of coherence represses in the process of reading is interwoven with political events (1988a, 16–17; Fuchs 1993, 128); in other words, the personal is
political (cf. George Foot Moore 1901, 290; Slotki 1959, 256).

In *Death and Dissymmetry*, Bal examines ideo-stories (three stories of
the murder of women and three stories of lethal women) in which political violence gives way to violence in the domestic realm,[3] aiming

> to show how we can see ancient narratives, not as sources for knowledge
> that lie outside them, but as the materialization of a social reality that
> they do not simply and passively reflect, but which they are a part and
> to which they respond [cf. J. I. Miller 1967, 75]. My hypothesis will be that
> the murders of young women in the book are caused by uncertainty
> about fatherhood. . . . (1988a, 6)

The present chapter creeps in Bal's footsteps, focalizing on the story of
a nameless young woman in the book of Judges, Jephthah's daughter (Judg
11). I first present Bal's reading of this story (§4.1), then, taking her reading
as a new moment in the politics of coherence, offer an alternative reading
(§4.2). I close by extending my reading of this story toward Num 30, bringing *circumreading* to meet *countercoherence* (§4.3). Eventually, here and there,
my reading takes its place as another moment in the politics of coherence,
indicating the coherence of counter- and in-coherence (cf. Bal 1988a, 20).

4.1 The Narrator's Navel

Similar to Samson's wife (Judg 14–15) and the Levite's concubine (Judg
19), Jephthah's daughter is nameless and victimized by a *gibbor* (a hero; cf.
Bal 1988a, 26–27).[4] For Bal, what sets Jephthah's daughter apart is that she
has "known no man" (11:40), which dominant readers take to mean that

---

[3] "An ideo-story is a narrative whose structure lends itself to be the receptacle
of different ideologies. Its representational makeup promotes concreteness and
visualization. Its characters are strongly opposed so that dichotomies can be established. And its fabula [cf. Bal 1985, 11–12] is open enough to allow for any
ideological position to be projected onto it. Ideo-stories, then, are not closed but
extremely open; however, they seem to be closed, and this appearance of closure
encourages the illusion of stability of meaning" (Bal 1988a, 11; see also Exum
1993).

[4] Bal associates namelessness with powerlessness (1988a, 23; cf. Trible 1984,
65–66), used in the politics of coherence to promote the development of the nar-

she was a virgin. She belongs to nobody. She is in between the positions of daughter and wife, the archetypal position of danger and uncertainty (1988a, 80–81), hence the negative formulation of "virginity" in the book of Judges (1988a, 41–42).

Bal resists the violence of the text by giving Jephthah's daughter a name, *Bath*-Jephthah ("daughter of Jephthah"), a name that preserves her dependent status. Her story evolves around her father's vow:

> And Jephthah vowed a vow unto Yahweh and said: If you will indeed/ fully deliver the sons of Ammon into my hand, then the goer-out who/ that will go out of the doors of my house to meet me in my returning in peace from the sons of Ammon will be to Yahweh and I will offer as a burnt offering. (11:30–31 [translation in Bal 1988a, 43])

Jephthah needs Yhwh's help, hence the vow, even though the spirit of Yhwh overtook him earlier (11:29). Being bestowed with Yhwh's spirit should have assured Jephthah of Yhwh's support, making the vow unnecessary.[5] He nonetheless utters a vow, a speech-act that later will kill. The intention of the vow is questionable.[6] It seems unlikely that Jephthah expected an animal to go out of the doors of his house and to be first to meet him upon his return (George Foot Moore 1901, 299; cf. Boling 1975, 209; Soggin 1981, 215).[7] On the other hand, Bal argues, the ritual in which young women come to meet the victor (cf. 2 Sam 6) seems more likely (so Pseudo-Philo; cf. Kramer 1999, 69). "The vow ends with a difference: the daughter will not be given away as a bride but as a burnt offering. Object

---

rative (1988a, 33). But namelessness does not automatically identify a victim, since one of the lethal women in Judges, the woman who killed Abimelech (9:51–54; cf. Bal 1988a, 217–24), also was nameless. Some men, too, are both nameless and victimized, like the "Levite" in Judg 19 who also was victimized by the townspeople (but his lot was not as grave as his concubine's; cf. Müllner 1999, 134–35).

[5] So Trible, who suggests that Jephthah's vow shows his desire "to bind God rather than embrace the gift of the spirit" (1984, 97). Along the same line, Hamlin argues that Jephthah's deep sense of personal insecurity was the reason behind his vow (1990, 118).

[6] Bal reads Jephthah's vow as retaliation against his rejection from the virilocal house because he was the son of a harlot (1988a, 199–200). Appealing to Nancy Jay, one may also argue that Bath was sacrificed as "remedy for having been born of women" (Bal 1988a, 96): "As a patrilocal son expelled from a virilocal father-house, Jephthah is torn between the two institutions and the two possible figurations of fatherhood they entail. . . . To sacrifice her [Bath] is to escape the need to give her away in virilocal marriage. . . . To prevent her from becoming a 'harlot,' Jephthah has to keep her a 'virgin' " (1988a, 179).

[7] In *Genesis Rabbah*, Jephthah's vow is improper because he might have had to offer an impure animal, or a slave, to Yhwh. "Said the Holy One, Blessed be He, to him: 'Then had a camel or an ass or a dog come forth, thou wouldst offer it up for a burnt-offering!' What did the Lord do? He answered him unfittingly and prepared his daughter for him. . . ." (*Gen. R.* 60:3). Jephthah's vow "affected God directly, insulting him and calling forth his wrath" (Valler 1999, 53).

of promise, of trade, of gift, and of offering by fire, Bath's position is already delineated before she is even mentioned" (Bal 1988a, 44; cf. Boling 1975, 208). Instead of a marriage bed, Bath will be laid on an altar.

Readers who uphold the politics of coherence see Bath as a submissive character, devoted to the cause of the nation (cf. Boling 1975, 207; Slotki 1959, 258). Bal argues, on the other hand, that Bath did not totally submit, for she asks for an opportunity to lament her condition. Her request indicates someone going through a period of transition, characterized by danger and insecurity. The mountains to which she goes and the companions she takes along, who were probably of the same age and state, suggest rites of passage (cf. van Gennep 1960; Day 1989, 58; Exum 1993, 140–41). These young friends, Bal claims, expect to be given away to men. Bath's case, however, is different because she is due to be given away in a burnt-offering:

> Knowing that her father owns her, and owes the victor his daughter, she will, in any case, have to go through the transition that awaits all *bethuloth*. She cannot protest, neither can Achsah, nor Bath's friends. But she can lament, and that is what she intends to do. . . . (1988a, 50)

Bath presents herself with respect to her future—as a *bethulah* who expects marriage. But the narrator portrays her in relation to her past—as one who has "not known a man." Both characterizations, reflecting male concerns, have to do with Bath's value as a possible wife. She is "marriageable, and doubly so: physically nubile—her status as a subject—and morally pure—her value as an object" (Bal 1988a, 51). Both characterizations are entangled, (con)fused, in the narrator's rhetoric.

Bal claims that the narrator's account was influenced by the value his society placed on virginity. The father of a virgin faces two threats: defloration of his daughter and, in the event of her marriage, release of his possession to another man who shall take his place of ownership (1988a, 52–53):

> Defloration entails a whole series of changes in the woman's life. Her subjectivity is systematically denied; her love is claimed by two men who compete for her, over her; the moment of givenness is the beginning of a state where her subjectivity will be constantly undermined by male fear. (1988a, 59)

Bath's value to Jephthah is underscored by the fact that she is alone, his only child; "beside *her* [i.e., *from him*] he has no son nor daughter" (11:34b). The narrator portrays her relation to Jephthah as one of dependence: "The absolute property of the father, the virgin daughter does not only belong to him, as a metonymical extension of him; she is part of him, as a synecdochical integration, which causes her loss to be the loss of himself. His wholeness rather than hers is threatened with loss" (Bal 1988a, 61; cf. 72–73; so Fuchs 1993, 119; Exum 1993, 142).[8]

---

[8] A similar loss occurs in 2 Kgs 3, involving the king of Moab. Moab was under attack from a joint campaign by Israel, Judah, and Edom, and upon offering his

Jephthah's vow (11:30–31) places Bath at the center of our focalization, and we follow the narrator's direction toward the doors of Jephthah's house. When Bath comes out to meet Jephthah with timbrel and dancing (11:34), the narrator puts us at the place of the focalizer, Jephthah, looking at Bath as an object of vision instead of as a subject of actions. The meeting of the father and daughter is described as a spectacle (11:35), shifting our attention from a joyous ritual to a ritual of mourning and anticipation of separation:

> [I]t becomes consistent that Jephthah blame his daughter, not, of course, for celebrating his victory but for being prepared to marry the real victor, for being ready to leave him, in other words: for reaching *bethulah*. The meeting between father and daughter becomes a confrontation in time: the confrontation with the transition, with the impossibility of postponing the gift of the daughter that will destroy the identity of the father. (Bal 1988a, 63)

In Jephthah's censuring cry, "you have caused me to kneel [brought me low]" (11:35), the "castration anxiety" (Freud), fear of separation, comes into play. When he opened his mouth to make the vow he promised death and when he reopens his mouth to blame his daughter he sees himself as the victim (cf. Fuchs 1993, 121). In this regard, Jephthah mimics the Freudian phallic mother who dreads having to deflower a virgin (Bal 1988a, 55–56). He dreads having to lose his daughter and what her death means to his memory. What Bath does next, distancing herself from her father's dying memory, allows her memory to stay alive. The irony here, subverting Bal's understanding of namelessness, is that the memory of the nameless character has a chance to survive.

The account of Bath's departure with her companions for the mountains is revealing: "And she departed, she and her companions, and lamented in confrontation with ['al] her nubility in confrontation with ['al] the mountains" (11:38; cf. 11:37). Bal's translation takes into account the elusive Hebrew 'al-preposition, which signifies both *direction* (in spatial terms) and *confrontation* ("against"). In this regard, the narrator directs us to Bath's "future rather than on the past, on her subject-status rather than on her value as an object, on the female life-cycle rather than on male possession" (Bal 1988a, 65). Her separation to the mountains is a form of transition and resistance, a passing on/against, a rite of passage, which sets Bath apart from her father. The aftermath is a custom, a *ḥoq*, which allows two translations: (1) *ḥoq* as law, rule, prescription, and (2) *ḥoq* as obligation, task, duty: "And it was a *ḥoq* [rule? duty?] in Israel, that the daughters of Israel went every year to lament [*tnh*] the daughter of Jephthah the Gileadite four days in a year" (11:39b–40).

---

eldest son upon the wall "there came great wrath on Israel; and they withdrew from him and returned to their own land" (3:27). "This king is not just sacrificing his child; he is publicly imperiling the destiny of his dynasty" (Auld 1984, 201). That this son was not spared, like Isaac in Gen 22, suggests ethnic biases.

Bal reads the verb *tnh* ("to lament") as a speech-act that recounts in order not to forget.[9] *Tnh* is the F(emale)-term for memorialization: "Memorialization, a form of afterlife, replaces the life that she has been denied" (1988a, 67). This F-term stands in contrast to the Hebrew (M-)verb *zkr*, "to remember," which is present in the modifier "male" (also *zkr* in Hebrew). The F-concept looks to the future, while the M-concept is rooted in the past.

> If writing history has become a male property, oral history can still be a female prerogative. . . . If the sons of Israel make history by fighting wars and going astray, the daughters of Israel recount the price that such a history requires. What has happened must not be forgotten. (Bal 1988a, 67)

In requesting to go to the mountains Bath breaks from the M-past and develops into a full narrative subject, taking advantage of available opportunities (1988a, 71).

> Using oral history as a cultural means of memorialization, she makes her fellow virgins feel that solidarity between daughters is a task, an urgent one, that alone can save them from total oblivion. Although she can only be remembered as what she never was allowed to overcome, as Bath-Jephthah, it is she and not the man who does have a proper name who is remembered. She is remembered as she was, in submission to the power of her father, a power over life and death, exclusive possession, which he decided to exercise until death did them part. (Bal 1988a, 68)

Bath's death fulfills Jephthah's vow of a specific kind of sacrifice, burnt-offering (*'olah*), in which the entire victim is burned to ashes (cinders). The victim is offered in its entirety in a fire, implying a purification rite and/or excessive cooking. The latter desacralizes the rite and excludes the chance for a communal fellowship meal.

In Bal's countercoherence, Jephthah's vow is a radical speech-act. It sounds like a riddle, which is characterized by its deficit of meanings, insofar as the vow denotes an unknown human victim. And the vow is also lethal, resulting in the death of a human subject, rendering its meaning excessive (1988a, 131; 142–43). The vow has the potential to be both deficient and excessive, depending on the s/words of the reader. In that regard, the powers of narrativity work: "Narrativity is the force that motivates the ever-dynamic meaning both to occur and to present itself as fixed.[10] It is on the basis of that illusion that the dialogue of speech can take place" (Bal 1988a, 134). On the other hand, at once, readers may use the force of narrativity to battle the illusion of stability.

---

[9] "Unfortunately she has been forgotten by Scripture, which praises the father but makes no mention of the daughter (1 Sam. 12:11; Heb. 11:32)" (Hamlin 1990, 120).

[10] "It is through attempts to fix the fluidity of language that a new form of speech-act has been invented—the written word. *Writing* is a revolutionary materialization of speech, one that can cut and kill at a distance. Writing has, from its early days on, worked to support, to become, *law*" (Bal 1988a, 243).

The contrast between the sacrifice of Bath and the binding of Isaac (Ben-Abraham) is revealing. Both subjects went to the mountains, the place of transition, but Yhwh is silent in the story of Bath. Bath is accompanied by her companions but Isaac is accompanied by Abraham, who has power over his life. Abraham binds Isaac out of submission (love) to the divine father, an act that externalizes his belief structure (Scarry 1994), while Jephthah reverses the structure of belief. "This is yet another sense in which Jephthah's is an improper sacrifice, not because sacrifice has to be initiated by God, but because the speech-act, the conditional vow, presupposes the predominance of the voice over the body that is reserved to the deity" (Bal 1988a, 110).

The narrator tells Isaac's binding with details, but summarizes the sacrifice of Bath with "he did the vow that he had vowed," and no divine voice stops the narrative. The virgin vanishes into ashes, cinders, as the consequence of Jephthah's vow, and the narrator adds, "she had not known man," which brings to mind another rite that initiates the separation of a father from his child—when a groom lays his bride on the marriage bed (Bal 1988a, 111).

Bath's death testifies to the power of words. Words, s/words, cut and kill. Moreover, s/words are seductive, evident in Jephthah's negotiation with his kinsmen (11:4–11). Jephthah's stake is his sword and he requires total control, to be the head ($ro'\check{s}$) over his people, after he gains victory over the Ammonites (11:9). Jephthah uses the language of power:

> But negotiation is not only about or *for* power, it is also based on power. Thus Jephthah negotiates for his own status as leader over the people who had expelled him as the son of "another woman," a "harlot" or patrilocal wife, on the basis of his power as a master of the sword. (Bal 1988a, 161)

> Negotiation is based on power, the one who has none has nothing to negotiate with. But it is also a recognition of the limits of power; the negotiator both has something and lacks something. Jephthah, the head of the people to be, hero of might, has the power of his s/word, but he lacks some other power, the power that would give him security, certainty about his victory. (1988a, 162)

The problem with negotiation is that the negotiator risks losing what he already possesses, and it can become addictive. Jephthah is accordingly swept by both waves of the speech-act *of* and *for* power. "Jephthah vowed to sacrifice, not his daughter as a person, but his house. House and daughter are one and the same. The house as an institution—as patrilocy—is to be sacrificed for the public good" (Bal 1988a, 172; see §4.2.1). Jephthah's desire to reenter his father's house will cost him his identity, and Bath her life.

Jephthah continues to negotiate even after Bath's sacrifice. In the *shibboleth* affair (12:5–6), negotiation involves the speaking mouth instead of the mouth of the sword. The latter takes over when the former fails.

Judgment is passed on the Ephraimites, the enemy, who are their brothers, for not speaking properly.

Bal's countercoherence exposes violent acts that anchor the narratives of Judges. By focusing on characters rather than on story lines, on practices rather than on events, on domestic rather than on national interests, which are motifs that dominant readings ignore, Bal shows how women and daughters are victims of the institutional violence of the social order. The upshot of her readings is the destabilization of dominant readings, the politics of coherence, which traditionally represent the book of Judges as military histories with national interests (1988a, 232–33). Bal also shows the power of s/words at work in interpretation. Her gender code undermines the exegetical traditions of dominant readings and the delusive stability of the status of meaning; in other words, Bal works against the illusion that meanings can be determined, and fixed, and the interests that motivate such an illusion. "The attempt to deconstruct the traditional meanings attributed to words rests, in its turn, on a suspicion of the abuse of that power to attribute meaning" (Bal 1988a, 129).

> This mode of reading rests on a view of language and of narrative that is not uncommon, yet has hardly been applied to biblical narrative. In this view, language is seen as action; as material, bodily, physical, historical, and social action. As soon as such a view is adopted, we are almost overwhelmed by the penetrating importance of characters' speech as motors of the narrative. What I called the cutting speech-act turned out to be a central narrative event. . . . Actual sacrifice, that other founding event in the book, is in a sense but the insistently material realization of the cutting speech-act. It is called for when the *gibborim* begin to feel insecure about the material reality of their acts: *their cutting speech-acts, as well as the sacrifice of their daughters, are nothing else than the obstinately material proof of what in their experience is not material enough:* fatherhood, the construction of a *house*, as a spatial, material possession *as well as* a historical, chronologically acknowledged position. . . . If this view is convincing, then "spatial" reading becomes an urgent task [cf. Jobling 1980; 1986, 88–134, 142–47]; it alone can truly account for the book on its own terms; it alone can bring out the book's obsessions and its stakes. Narrative becomes a warp onto which the stories are woven, not a thread that leads only through chronology. (Bal 1988a, 232–33; my italics)

The foregoing account focuses on Bal's reading, which exposes the "navel," the scar, the hole, in the narrator's account of Bath's story. I presented Bal's reading in the spatial order she followed, which diverts from the narrative sequence (temporal coherence) of the MT narrator (which dominant readings prefer). Bal focalizes upon Bath, weaving Jephthah into her story while keeping a curious dialectic of autonomy and heteronomy between the two characters. Bath demands separation from Jephthah, the navel of her identity, Bath-Jephthah, in order to assure her own future. Nevertheless, it is the narrator who allows Bath's memory to survive.

I was selective in my sketch, focusing on one particular character, in order to materialize Bal's theory. In the process, I unraveled Bal's inter-weaving of characters from Judges and beyond. As a cutting speech-act, the transdisciplinary nature of her countercoherence encourages entan-glement in *jouissance:*

> Bal is an acrobatic reader, never content to view a text from one place or code. Her readings remind us that feminist critics can settle too compla-cently on the sturdy rock of their gender code. Bal's reading makes it clear that no discipline or view-point, even one's own, acting alone can possibly account for the impact of a text. (Bach 1991, 336)

To identify Bal's repressed ideologies is beyond the scope of this chap-ter, though I recovered some of them above, but it is evident from the foregoing that the politics of countercoherence also has navels. In other words, we materialize our navels in our readings (so Bal 1988a, 239–40).

In the next section I extend Bal's reading to Jephthah's navel, the scar that anchors the identity of Bath-Jephthah, by focusing on three speech-act motifs that Bal identified: *house, vow,* and *sacrifice.* I share with Bal an interest in spatial reading, but I place more emphasis on crossing textual space, on transtextuality. In what follows I, as surfer, join Bal's acrobatic performance. That is a fair way, I believe, to honor this, Bal, "giant" (Robbins 1994, 386).[11] My reading refocalizes on the spatial "final form" of the narrator's account and retells the story differently, yet the same, at once, one more time.

4.2 Jephthah's Navel

Jephthah is inserted into the account of a face-off between Ammonites and Israelites, as the Gileadites were looking for a leader. He is a capable warrior who is also an "outsider," son of a prostitute (*zonah*), rejected by his brothers (11:2). He lives outside his family and his people, in the land of Tob (good) among "outsiders" (empty men) (11:3). He is also an out-sider to the circle of judges, insofar as he is Transjordanian (cf. Jobling 1986, 125).

Cut from home and people, Jephthah is a threat to Gilead. It is thus understandable why the Gilead elders want to bring him under their con-trol, to woo this outcast back into his father's house (11:7). This is the "verbal combat preliminary to the military combat" (Jobling 1986, 128).

When Jephthah enters the story, he grabs the narrative center, and the narrator directs our focalization to him. As the story unfolds, other outsiders come into the picture, to claim their "houses."

---

[11] The significance of Bal's works is acknowledged by Fewell and Gunn (1990), Bach (1991), Detweiler, Jobling (1991a and 1991b), Beal (1992) and Robbins, and the foregoing account presents a Balian reading of Bal. I offered another narrative that performs the speech-act of *countercoherence*—the s/words of the gender code.

4.2.1 *Claims on His House*

The stake that the elders of Gilead offer Jephthah is the opportunity both to reenter his "father's house," Gilead, and to become their chief (*qaṣîn*) (11:6). They offer a place and power (see also Timothy M. Willis 1997). Since the elders are his father's house, hence, Jephthah's house, they were literally offering themselves to Jephthah. But a miscommunication occurs between the elders and Jephthah, a moment of countercoherence, turning Jephthah's house into a bargain. In this case, also, the narrator steps in to set the records straight.

The initial desire of the Gileadites is to make "the first to fight the Ammonites be leader [*ro'š*] over all the inhabitants of Gilead" (10:18). But they compromise when they approach Jephthah, asking him to be their chief (*qaṣîn*) (11:6). Jephthah is not "first to fight the Ammonites," and the elders do not invite him to "be *ro'š* over all the inhabitants of Gilead." Nonetheless, becoming their *ro'š* appears to be just what Jephthah wants. He rebukes the elders for courting him after having rejected him (11:7),[12] and the elders raise the stakes: "We have truly returned to you. If you come with us to fight the Ammonites you shall be our *ro'š* over all the inhabitants of Gilead" (11:8). If he goes along, he shall become *ro'š* after they fight the Ammonites (11:9). The elders compromise their initial desire (cf. Boling 1975, 198) by presenting the opportunity to be their *ro'š* to a figure whom they have to woo into fighting for them. And Jephthah compromises his opportunity by making Yhwh a part of the bargain. "If you bring me back to fight the Ammonites and *Yhwh gives* them to my face, I will be your [elders? Gilead?] *ro'š*" (11:9). The elders offer Gilead to Jephthah, who in turn offers Yhwh a place in his campaign. Jephthah and the elders of Gilead, his "[father's] house," risk themselves in the bargain.

The narrator settles the bargain in a narrative compromise: "Jephthah went with the elders of Gilead, and the people placed him over/against them to be leader [*ro'š*] and chief [*qaṣîn*]" (11:11). The narrator expedites Jephthah's transition; Jephthah is, without delay, their leader and chief. The outsider and the insiders are (con)fused, so that the danger associated with their separation is no longer. The narrator unites Gilead, and identifies the real danger as the Ammonites.

The elders get from Jephthah something they could not get from Yhwh: assistance. In the previous episode, Yhwh rejects the Israelites: "I shall not deliver you again" (10:13b). And although the people repent, remove their alien gods, and serve Yhwh, the narrator declares that Yhwh "could not bear the miseries of Israel" (10:16).[13] In the end, the Gileadites

---

[12] For Slotki, Jephthah "reproaches them, not so much for coming to him when they needed his aid, but for not coming to his help when he needed them" (1959, 251).

[13] Whether this means pity or disgust is not clear (cf. Polzin 1980, 177; Fewell 1992, 71–72), but the narrator is certain that Yhwh commends what the Ammon-

convince Jephthah to fight the people who were carrying out Yhwh's will (10:7), and Jephthah expects Yhwh to help him out. Jephthah pitches Yhwh against himself. I sense a storm brewing over the horizon.

The bargain between the elders and Jephthah intertwines with the bargain between Jephthah and God, over a piece of land that the Ammonites want to take back. The shift from the bargains between Jephthah and the elders (11:4–11) to the bargains between Jephthah and the Ammonite king (11:12–33) also shifts focalization from *house* to *land*. Both realms signify placement and power. Jephthah returns to become the leader and chief of the house from which he was rejected, and the Ammonite king comes to claim the land from which he was rejected.[14] House and land (con)fuse in the bargain Jephthah offers on behalf of his house.

The transition from house to land figures in Jephthah's message (11:12) to the Ammonite king: "What have you against me that you come to make war with me in my land?" He speaks as a leader and chief, addressing another leader and chief. As characters of power from different ethnic backgrounds, one is a threat to the other. The narrative intensifies the danger in their exchange by sustaining a distance between them. They communicate through messengers, who may cause miscommunication as they uphold the separation, the place of insecurity and danger, and of transtextuality, between the parties involved (cf. Slotki 1959, 252). Read in light of the bargain between Jephthah and the elders of Gilead, the Ammonite king is bound to lose. The narrator does not allow him the privilege of bargaining face-to-face. The Ammonite king, nonetheless, states his case: "When Israel came from Egypt, they seized my land from the Arnon to the Jabbok as far as the Jordan. Now, then, restore it peaceably" (11:13). His demand is radical. The king does not offer anything in exchange, neither a condition nor a reward, but demands that his land be returned in peace. Unlike Gilead, the foreign king does not come to compromise his land. Rather, like Jephthah, he comes to take all or nothing.

Jephthah does not deny the king's legitimate claim to the land (so Exum 1993, 134). Rather, he explains how Israel passed through the land and in the process affirms that Israel is occupying a land that is not theirs (11:15–22; cf. Jobling 1986, 130; Hamlin 1990, 114; Boling 1975, 203); thus, Jephthah shifts the blame to Yhwh:

> Now, then, Yhwh, the God of Israel, dispossessed the Amorites from before his people Israel; and should you possess [their land]? Do you not hold what Chemosh your god gives you to possess? So we will hold on to all that Yhwh our God has given us to possess. Besides, are you any

---

ites were doing: "And Yhwh, incensed with Israel, surrendered them to the Philistines [cis-Jordanian] and the Ammonites [Transjordanian]" (10:7; cf. Jobling 1986, 124).

[14] My concern is with the difference ethnicity makes, which, evident in the following reading, makes problematic the unity of Israel (cf. Jobling 1986, 120).

better than Balak son of Zippor, king of Moab? Did he start a quarrel
with Israel or go to war with them? (Judg 11:23–25)

Jephthah's response is insulting. Yhwh took the territory between the
Arnon and the Jordan from the Amorites (cf. Mendenhall 1992) and gave
it to Israel, thus making the Ammonites late inhabitants of this territory
(de Tarragon 1992). He adds fuel to the fire by naming Chemosh, the deity
of the Moabites (Mattingly 1992), as the deity of the Ammonites, who is
Milcom (John Gray 1986, 316). He (con)fuses the Ammonites with the
Moabites, both of whom trace their roots to Lot and his daughters (Gen 19;
cf. Brenner 1994, 124–25; Heard 2001, 60–61). The crux of Jephthah's cutting speech-act is the reminder that Ammonites are bastards who have no
rights to the land. In Jephthah's eyes, the Ammonite king is no better than
the Moabite king Balak (see §2.2; cf. Slotki 1959, 255). His charge sounds
like his own story; it materializes something that was not material enough
in his own life: the right to his house. Jephthah is also suspicious of the
Ammonite king's claim because of the three hundred years that have
passed since Israel inhabited the land (11:26). The war that the Ammonites
now wage against Israel is thus gratuitous, and insulting (11:27).

The irony in the story is that "house," for Jephthah, and "land," for
the Ammonites, are places of unrest that merge in the narrator's account.
The outcasts of both places believe that they were unjustly rejected, and
they return to claim the house-land that is no longer theirs.

A similar story is in 2 Sam 7. After the narrator, David, and Nathan acknowledge that the king was settled safely in his own house, rested from
all his enemies around him (2 Sam 7:1–3), Yhwh enters the story and disturbs David's rest (7:4–16). Yhwh declares that David's "house" (son?
throne?) will be built in the future; in other words, David rests in a house
that is not a house. David's son, who will become Yhwh's son (7:14), will
build a house for Yhwh. There shall be a "house" for David, who will build
a "house" for Yhwh. In response, David comes to sit before Yhwh and demands that Yhwh does as he has said (7:17–29). David echoes (anticipates?)
the concern in Num 30:3, bringing the stipulation to bear on Yhwh himself:

Num 30:3	2 Sam 7:25
If a man makes a vow to the LORD or takes an oath imposing an obligation on himself, he shall not break his pledge; he must carry out all that has crossed his lips. (Tanakh)	And now, O LORD God, fulfill Your promise to Your servant and his house forever; and do as You have promised. (Tanakh)

Yhwh threatens to displace David from his house as Jephthah was
ousted from his house. But both are later allowed to keep/return to their
"houses."

Taking into account the difference that ethnicity makes, we see that the Ammonite king does not share the privileges granted to Jephthah and David. This foreign king is not given the chance to return and retake his house-land, even though the ethnic difference between him and Jephthah is only as removed as the "separation" between Abraham and his nephew Lot. The ideological complexity of this story is emphasized by the narrative suggestion that the son of a harlot, Jephthah, does not heed the demand from descendants of incest, the Ammonites. Both Jephthah and the Ammonites are troubling because their mothers do not fit the mother-of-a-hero paradigm (Brenner 1993a, 205). The troubling issue of ethnicity covers over the deeper ideological pains of family matters. Ethnicity materializes what is not material enough, namely, the uneasiness with unacceptable mother-figures. It is revealing that the dispute between Jephthah and the Ammonite king involves "land," a place of (difficult) sustenance (cf. Meyers 1988, 47–71), and a figure, a "metaphor" (cf. Weems 1995, 15–34), for motherhood (cf. Keefe 1995). Put simply, descendants of problematic mothers engage over their mother-figures.

Endowed with the spirit of Yhwh, affirmed by a vow, Jephthah marches against the Ammonites and Yhwh delivers them into his hands. The masculine-singular perspective from which the story is narrated (see 11:29–33) is curious. This implies a narrator who supports Jephthah's narrative position, implying that Jephthah is the only one who has right to the land, his house. Jephthah's bargaining earlier had shifted focalization from "house" to "land" (11:12), and his vow returns focalization to "house" (see Gunn 1987, 116–17). He vows to offer as sacrifice whatever comes out of his house to meet him upon his return.

The narrator's account of Jephthah's victorious return sounds like a birth narrative, in which Jephthah's house plays the role of a mother giving birth to a child. The child who comes forth from Jephthah's house to meet him is not yet named, and she has no other sister or brother (11:33). The encounter between father and daughter, their first meeting in the story, is not an accommodating occasion. Jephthah meets his daughter's "timbrel and dance" with reproach: "Alas my daughter. You have caused me to kneel and you have become my troubler [cf. Gen 34:30].[15] For I have opened my mouth to Yhwh and I cannot retract" (11:35). A character who was rejected then restored to his father's house is troubled by a daughter who comes from his house, as if his house is his burden. The text reverses the situation. Instead of explaining how Jephthah causes his daughter's demise, it focuses on how the daughter causes her father's demise. "Rather than exposing Jephthah as a selfish coward, the text depicts him as a victim; a victim through his own wrongheaded actions, but

---

[15] I imagine that this response would be common from fathers whose first child turns out to be a daughter, in a society in which sons were valued more.

a victim nonetheless" (Fuchs 1993, 124; cf. Exum 1993, 140; Valler 1999, 48–49). In this regard, Jephthah's daughter materializes what has not been material enough in Jephthah's experience: that his house is a troubler to him!

The house for which Jephthah bargained issues his daughter; his (paternal) "house" takes a(n) F(emale)-turn. The troubling daughter functions as the navel, the scar, that points back to her absent mother. She figures her mother, whom the narrator represents as Jephthah's house, and substitutes for Jephthah's harlot mother. The charge "you have brought me low and you have become my troubler" may also apply to Jephthah's mother. Jephthah's daughter is condemned to the burdens solicited by his loose mouth and for the troubles his mother brought upon him. The daughter is the navel, the hole, in Jephthah's "mother's house." According to this transtextual reading, the narrative materializes the trouble that Jephthah's own mother brought upon him.

The F-turn of the narrative is told from a(n) M(ale)-point of view, evident in the androcentric biases of the story. While the father's house is sought with passion, the navel of the mother's house is castigated. The former is valued and grasped, but the latter is dispensable (castrated). Yhwh is invited to be involved in the former, but he is absent in the latter. The narrator is involved in securing the former for Jephthah and Gilead, but he is impartial toward the latter. The mother's house is up for grabs, and soon to be offered to Yhwh in ashes.

This reading traces a coherent picture of Jephthah's house from the "father's house" that he desires, through the "land" he denies the Ammonites, to the doorsteps of his own family ("mother's house"). By focusing on the shifts in the representations of Jephthah's house, while maintaining the interconnectedness of these different houses, I loosen the impression of fixity that the narrator paints. Jephthah's house and Gilead's land are not as secure as one is led to believe, because the house that in the end troubled Jephthah is a part of his "father's house." To undo one representation of Jephthah's house also affects the others. I, therefore, divert from Bal's reading in two ways.

First, I maintain the national implications of the story even though I do not read it as a historical account per se (see also Fuchs 1993, 117). I extend her gender code to account for the difference that ethnicity makes, seeking to uncover the narrative repressions in the narrator's account. By extending the reading of "Jephthah's house" to his own family I extend the gender and ethnic codes, located in the public domain, to the private realm, as if to materialize the interpenetration of private and public realms. The public is private and the private is public; together, these claims materialize the Freudian entanglement and Balian countercoherence (cf. Detweiler 1991).

Second, I leave Jephthah's daughter nameless, even though I do not favor the narrator's voice. Naming her gives her character substance, but it also gives an elusive sense of stability. As the capitalized transliteration of the Hebrew word for "daughter," Bath "cannot but transfix the textual daughter precisely within the confines of her relational figuration" (Brenner 1993b, 11). *The act of naming is a speech-act that brings the character under control.* I resist that tendency for this particular character, whom I read as the navel, the hole, in Jephthah's house. I refer to her with metaphors so that she eludes my interpretive grasps, to be a troubler in both Jephthah's house and in my reading. I transform the narrator's negligence into the daughter's freedom.[16]

This reading crosses the gender and ethnic interests of the narrative, and cuts across biblical history by bringing Jephthah's house to bear on David's house (2 Sam 7). I presented a picture of a house that is not secured (cf. Gunn 1989), a house with a hole, a navel, a house with many "faces" that resist inside-versus-outside portrayals. To "cover" this hole will dismantle the house.

4.2.2 S/words in His Vow

Jephthah's vow drives to unify his house. He is successful in bargaining with the Gileadites, but he is still in a land dispute with the Ammonites, the event in which he entices Yhwh with a vow. Jephthah earlier appealed to Yhwh to be his aide and witness against the elders of Gilead (11:9–10) and the Ammonites (11:27), but Yhwh does not respond in either case. He neither affirms nor rejects Jephthah's program. The narrator, on the other hand, gives the impression that Jephthah wins Yhwh's approval: "Then the spirit of Yhwh came upon Jephthah" (11:29). The narrator prefigures Nathan's endorsement of David, "Go and do whatever is in your heart because Yhwh is with you" (2 Sam 7:3). He leads Jephthah across two boundaries, physically to the Ammonites and psychologically to Yhwh. But what if Jephthah does not want to go where the narrator wants to take him (cf. Bal 1991a, 14)?

To assure Yhwh's participation in his campaign, Jephthah vows something from his own house (11:30b–31), thereby bringing the nation's interest to bear on his family, his house, and urges Yhwh to deliver the foreigners into his hands. In the cutting s/words of this speech-act, a vow, Jephthah brings the figures of his house under his authority. His own family, his father's house Gilead, and the national interests of Israel entangle ([con]fuse) in his vow.

---

[16] No matter how liberating this position may appear, it binds and confines: "The limit of freedom is thy neighbour's freedom. The same holds for language. Language is slippery, to be sure, and therefore, interpretation cannot be objective. But language is also embedded in power relations, and therefore, interpretation cannot be neutral. This locks us into an aporetic position: we are caught between pluralism and positivism, two ways of keeping power where it is. There is no innocence in freedom" (Bal 1991a, 13).

We see the concern with "house" more clearly in Jephthah's vow when we juxtapose it with Jacob's vow in Gen 28:[17]

Judg 11:30–31	Gen 28:20–22
And Jephthah made the following vow to the LORD: "If you deliver the Ammonites into my hands, then whatever comes out of the door of my house to meet me on my safe return from the Ammonites shall be the LORD's and shall be offered by me as a burnt offering." (Tanakh)	Jacob then made a vow, saying, "If God remains with me, if He protects me on this journey that I am making, and gives me bread to eat and clothing to wear, and if I return safe to my father's house—the LORD shall be my God. And this stone, which I have set up as a pillar, shall be God's abode; and of all that You give me, I will set aside a tithe for You." (Tanakh)

Both subjects utter their vows while away from home. Their mothers have had something to do with their troubles, which influences their placement in their father's houses (cf. Gen 28:4). Both vows are made during a period of resistance against mixing with foreign subjects: against the Ammonites for Jephthah, and the Hittite and Canaanite women for Jacob (Gen 27:46–28:1). Both subjects seek to secure their "houses": Jephthah seeks to defeat a foreign nation to fulfill his bargain with his people, but Jacob flees for his life in order to protect his father's blessing. Both subjects are insecure in their campaigns, and they beseech Yhwh's protection until they safely return each to his "father's house." And both subjects expect something from Yhwh.

In spite of the similarities between Jephthah and Jacob, there are crucial differences between the contents of their vows. Jacob expects safety and material goods, part of which he vows to give back to Yhwh, while Jephthah expects safety and authority. The vow of one materializes what is lacking in the experience of the other. In Jacob's case, he has his father's blessing (Gen 27:26–29) but lacks control over his house. On the other hand, Jephthah has been given his father's house but he lacks authority over it, as well as over the land. According to this transtextual reading, the vows signify the subjects' attempts to grasp what they lack, their desires (cf. Jobling 1994).

Both subjects vow an offering to Yhwh, but one is more ominous than the other. Jacob vows to set up a stone, a pillar, as a house for Yhwh, and to set aside a tithe out of all the things that Yhwh will give him. He vows something he does not have, a gift he has not received. And Jephthah

---

[17] That Jacob fled to the mountains of Gilead when he escaped from Laban (Gen 31:23), then renamed the place as Gal-ed (31:47), anchors this transtextual reading.

vows something that he does not determine—whatever will come forth through the doors of his house. Jacob's pillar materializes what is lacking in Jephthah's vow, an altar for his burnt-offering. Offered in its entirety, an altar would be the remainder, the evidence, the alibi (Derrida) of the burnt-offering. Without an altar, the ashes would be scattered together with the signs of the burnt-offering. Jephthah's vow offers to efface all signs of his victim (read: text) in the fire, and without an altar he omits any external sign (read: context) of the ritual. While Jacob is intentional about building the signs of his vow, a pillar as a house for Yhwh, Jephthah focuses not on the performance of the vow but on its victim. Jacob provides points of focalization beyond himself, while Jephthah draws attention to himself—to his victory, his safety, his house, his burnt-offering. The vow concerns Jephthah in person.

Both subjects make their vows to Yhwh, but Jephthah does not vow to make Yhwh his God as Jacob does (Gen 28:21). Jacob offers Yhwh a place in his "house," whereas Jephthah does not invite Yhwh into his house, nor offer to build him a house. Rather, he offers whatever comes out of the doors of his house. According to the cutting assertion of Jephthah's vow, then, Yhwh's reward will be taken from "outside his house." For Jephthah, a subject concerned with securing his authority over his house, the one who comes forth is expendable. In this reading, the burnt-offering will both fulfill Jephthah's vow and keep Yhwh outside his house. The vow that gets Yhwh involved also keeps him at a distance: "Yahweh, like Jephthah, has been cast out and is only recalled when there is fighting to be done. Yahweh is merely another party to be bargained with and, once the victory is granted, to be dispensed with, like the daughter" (Fewell 1992, 72). In this sense, the vow materializes a desire for disentanglement from Yhwh.

A similar preference for disentanglement is implied in David's declaration, "Look here, I am dwelling in a house of cedar, but the ark of Yhwh is dwelling in a tent" (2 Sam 7:2b). David distinguishes his house from the dwelling of the ark, as if to say that his house is better, and indicates that his house is separate from the tent of Yhwh's ark, just as Jephthah's cutting speech-act keeps Yhwh outside. Jephthah does not bring Yhwh to his house nor bring his house to Yhwh. Rather, he offers whatever will leave his house on its own accord. It would not be pushed outside of his house, like Jephthah himself and the Levite's concubine (Judg 19:25), but it will "come forth from the doors" of his house (11:31). According to this reading, Jephthah's vow will push an unsuspecting subject into the fire in order to maintain his separation from Yhwh.

When Jephthah "did to her his vow which he vowed" (11:39) soon after, in narrative time and space, he materializes a lack in Jacob's case. Jacob is in no hurry to fulfill his vow, and Yhwh has to urge him on (Gen 21:3). Leaving Laban behind, Jacob faces Esau (Gen 33). But instead of continuing to his "father's house" at Beersheba, and thus bringing closure to his vow, Jacob turns toward Succoth on the east side of the Jordan, close to where it meets the Jabbok (cf. Seely 1992, 218). The narrator shifts focalization to Dinah and Shechem (Gen 34), delaying the fulfillment of the vow. In return, Yhwh takes matters into his own hands with the command, "Arise. Go up to Bethel and remain there; and build an altar there to the God who appeared to you when you were fleeing from the face of your brother Esau" (35:1). Yhwh demands what Jacob offered, and he sets up a pillar and offers a libation anointed with oil (35:14). For the narrator, presenting the offering "upon his arrival from Paddan-aram" (cf. 35:9) fulfills the vow he had uttered on the way (28:5). The vow is finally fulfilled, after several marriages and the birth of many children while he was in flight from many faces and places. Jephthah, on the other hand, appears eager to fulfill his vow. He turns neither to the left nor to the right, but waits at home for his daughter's return from the mountains.

If the foregoing transtextual reading holds, we have reasons to assume that Jephthah's eagerness to perform his vow is in the interest of "his house." He utters his vow while in the process of unifying "his house" (family, tribe, nation), making Yhwh his accomplice. The fulfillment of the vow, its closure, will terminate Yhwh's agency. The performance of the vow is both in gratitude for Yhwh's deliverance of the Ammonites as well as for the event that marks Yhwh's release. Like the Balian s/words, the vow charges and discharges. Both cutting effects are in the interest of Jephthah's house.

The luxury—or should I say trouble?—of Jephthah's house are its doors: it is a house with openings, a structure with holes. No matter how much Jephthah wants to secure his house, to close it off, its doors keep it open. Jephthah's vow opens the confines of his house, and draws readers to its openings/doors. In this sense, Jephthah's vow undermines his drive to secure his house.

The vow opens up the doors (womb) of his house, and through them we expect children to come forth (born) into the narrative. The vow presents Yhwh in a midwife role, delivering the child to her father. An exchange is inscribed. Yhwh will deliver into Jephthah's hands the "sons of Ammon," who are also children from "Jephthah's house" ("land"), and Jephthah will give Yhwh whatever comes forth from his actual house. This is a tragic exchange, however, because "Jephthah's house" is torn apart on both sides of the bargain. The father will utterly abolish the "sons of Ammon," and offer whatever comes out the doors of his house in its entirety. Appealing to birth imageries, the vow cuts the umbilical cord and sets both subjects (daughter of Jephthah and sons of Ammon) loose to face the danger of separation from their mothers. They are not nursed into maturity; they die in the mouth of the vow.

The drama of Jephthah's vow unfolds as his speech *acts*. His daughter comes to him, born into the story, and I anticipate the cutting edge of the vow. She comes as the product of the cut of his vow, whose fulfillment will undermine the goal for which he had returned to Gilead.

By reading Jephthah's vow in relation to his house I offer a space-oriented reading that presents Jephthah as a victim of his own agenda. Like the elders of Gilead, he offers the house he wants to keep. And by presenting a reading with nuances of a birth narrative, instead of the marriage ritual that Bal prefers, I emphasize the entanglements of the story. I find death at the place where I expect life and security, and bitterness in the embrace that I associate with happiness. Such is the stuff of Jephthah's vow. It binds, and it cuts, both the subject who is offered and the subject who makes the offering.

4.2.3 *Rem(a)inder of His Sacrifice*

When Jephthah's daughter comes out to meet Jephthah upon his safe return, she walks into the mouth of the vow and she is rebuked before being consumed by the fire. Jephthah turns bitter, rends his clothes, and condemns his daughter (11:35). Jephthah, so to speak, places his finger over the hole (navel) in his house. On the one hand, he blames his daughter for something she did not initiate, as if he were the real victim (cf. Fewell 1992, 71). On the other hand, one may read Jephthah's reaction as an acknowledgment of the way things are.[18] His daughter will bring him low because his house will be brought down if he does to her as he vowed. His rejoinder both shifts the blame to his daughter and indicates his resignation to the circumstance (Fuchs 1993, 116): "Alas my daughter . . . you have become my troubler!"

Though Jephthah is bitter, he intends to fulfill his vow (in contrast to Fuchs 1993, 127–28). He does not question the legitimacy of the vow, but states that he cannot retract what he has already said. The die is cast. What his words cut cannot be restored. His daughter holds the same idea, and her response both sustains and undermines the regulation in Num 30:3 concerning the vow of a man:

Judg 11:36–37	*Num 30:3*
"Father," she said, "you have uttered a vow to the LORD; do to me as you have vowed, seeing that the LORD has vindicated you against your enemies, the Ammonites." (Tanakh)	If a man makes a vow to the LORD or takes an oath imposing an obligation on himself, he shall not break his pledge; he must carry out all that has crossed his lips. (Tanakh)

One may view the daughter as a self-sacrificing subject who begs her father to carry out his vow since Yhwh has already fulfilled his part of the agreement (Fuchs 1993, 121). In her unselfishness she urges her father to

---

[18] This is not to say that Jephthah is therefore blameless, as Auld puts it: "There is of course a particular poignancy that the victim was his only daughter; but we cannot seek to absolve Jephthah of full responsibility by any suggestion that he simply blurted out a rash vow" (1984, 201).

do "all that has come out of his mouth" (Num 30:3b). Another may read her as a wise woman, like other women in Israel's popular history such as Jael and Deborah (Boling 1975, 209), or as a courageous and tragic heroine (George Foot Moore 1901, 302). But the doors of her response are still open.

Another may read the daughter turning her father's rebuke, his s/words, against him (Fewell 1992, 71). She who *came through* the doors of his house calls upon him to do according to the words that *came through* his mouth. But she asks her father to do one thing for her first: "[L]et me alone for two months, and I will go down against the mountains and bewail against my maidenhood [*bethulah*], I and my companions" (11:37b). She delays the fulfillment of the vow, in time, and she leaves the vicinity of her father's house, in space. Bal discusses the similarities and differences between this story and the binding of Isaac (so Fewell 1992), and I stress only one other difference between these stories. Both Isaac and Jephthah's daughter go to the mountains accompanied by subjects of their kind,[19] anticipating a burnt-offering, and both come down from the mountains alive. But the story of Jephthah's daughter involves a vow, a cutting speech-act, which the subjects in the story believe must be fulfilled. Since Yhwh changes his mind in Isaac's story, I imagine Jephthah's daughter also giving her father time and space to change his mind. He made the vow on his own, and he has the final say whether to fulfill it or not. She gives him two months, enough time for him to long for her and maybe to reconsider the situation.

But the narrator leaves no room for error (Boling 1975, 207). He assures the reader that Yhwh delivered the Ammonites to Jephthah and Israel, in an act that the daughter sees as vengeance against the enemy, cornering Jephthah to reward Yhwh as he had vowed. In this regard, the daughter's request for time and space, which delays the reward of Yhwh, is sublime. There are two transtextual readings that one may pursue.

First, the daughter demonstrates that *her sacrifice can be delayed.* Yhwh has yet to ask Jephthah for his offering, nor has he told him to return to Mizpeh, where he probably uttered his vow, as he had told Jacob, in Gen 35:1, to go to Bethel. We do not even know if Yhwh approves of Jephthah's vow. If silence indicates his approval, then I assume, for the same "silent" reason, that Yhwh also approves of delaying her sacrifice. In this reading, the daughter gives Jephthah a chance to say something like, "Father, if thou art willing, remove this cup from me; nevertheless not my will, but thine, be done" (Luke 22:42 RSV).

Isaac's story also shows that *the victim of the sacrifice may be replaced,* substituted. So in the case of Jacob, who vows a tithe (Gen 28:22) but offers a libation (Gen 35:14). I assume that two months is sufficient time for

---

[19] The two servants who accompanied Abraham and Isaac are referred to as "lads," and so is Isaac (Gen 22:3, 5, 12). They share the same "lad" status, similar to the way that Jephthah's daughter shares the status of her *bethulah* companions.

Jephthah to consider replacing his daughter, and there are guidelines for doing so:

> Yhwh spoke to Moses, saying: Speak to the sons of Israel and say to them: If anyone explicitly vows to Yhwh the equivalent for a life, the following scale shall apply: If it is a male between twenty and sixty years of age, the equivalent is fifty shekels of silver by the sanctuary weight; if it is a female, the equivalent is thirty shekels. If the age is between five years and twenty years, the equivalent is twenty shekels for a male and ten shekels for a female. . . . But if one cannot afford the equivalent, he shall be presented before the priest, and the priest shall assess him; the priest shall assess him according to what the vower can afford. (Lev 27:1–5, 8)

The life of Jephthah's daughter could have been redeemed. On the other hand, one may rule out this option on the basis that the regulations in Lev 27:1–8 were probably not in effect during Jephthah's days. They are nonetheless available for this reading to open the doors of the narrative with the possibility that the daughter could have been replaced, substituted, released from the burnt-offering (cf. Valler 1999, 56; Kramer 1999, 73).[20]

In a story in which characters bargain with, and compromise, one another, substitution holds the story together. The story materializes substitutions, and there is no reason why the daughter too should not have been replaced from the altar of the *'olah*. On the flip side, this turns out to be the lot of this daughter: excessive substitution results in displacement.

Second, the daughter's request *reopens the possibility for bargain*. She accepts the fate to which her father has committed her, and bargains for some time so that she may be alone with her companions. She turns the table. Jephthah is now on the other side of the bargaining table. This time he accepts: "He said, Go! And he sent her for two months. And she went, she and her companions, and she bewailed [fem. sing.] against her maidenhood and against the mountains" (11:38). The daughter is a successful negotiator; like father, like daughter.

The daughter's request may be read as an attempt to reignite her father's bargaining tendencies. He bargained successfully with the elders of Gilead and with Yhwh, both times concerning "his house." He refused the terms of the Ammonite king because of the interest, again, of "his house." When his daughter approaches with her request, the table turns on him, for "his house" now bargains with him. The daughter is a figure

---

[20] This is not exactly a daring reading. It was also proposed by Richard Rogers (1615, 579, sermon 68), who also raised the possibility that Jephthah may have been pushed to the vow by Yhwh's spirit (571, sermon 67; so Exum 1992, 49–50). Rogers also warns that one must be careful with what he swears because it may be violated in order to avoid evil. It is a double evil to keep a vow that is intended to accomplish evil (553–54, sermon 65).

of the Ammonite king, both of whom are from "his house" (§4.2.2). By accepting his daughter's terms, but not the Ammonite king's, we get the impression that Jephthah is capable of granting special favors. He may not be willing to replace his daughter on the altar, but he can at least go back to the bargaining table with Yhwh on his daughter's account. Yhwh may even change his mind and annul his vow.

The story world of Jephthah contains instances of Yhwh changing his mind. Incensed with their offenses, Yhwh decides not to deliver Israel from the Philistines and Ammonites (10:13b–14). Later, he delivers the Ammonites into Jephthah's hands. Jephthah's daughter refers to this change of heart when she tells Jephthah that he must do what he has said, "seeing what Yhwh did for you to vindicate you from your enemies, the Ammonites." Does she also hope for divine repentance on her account? Does she buy time so that Jephthah may go back and bargain with Yhwh over the vow, for the sake of "his house"? Does she request the delay of her sacrifice so that her father may be himself again, a negotiator? It is what Jephthah could have done, but did not, that is bothersome in this reading.

The narrator is quite a negotiator himself, seeing that the subject of the verb "bewail" in his account is feminine singular. The daughter went up with her companions to the mountains, but she bewails her maidenhood alone. She takes her father's vow upon herself but does not choose his company (cf. Fewell 1992, 71), and the narrator does not let her company participate in her ritual. The narrator distances the daughter from her company, and cuts off her maidenhood from everyone else. Bewailing her maidenhood is her own affair. For his part, the narrator bewails that no man had known her. Reiterating the foregoing reading, the narrator bewails that "her doors" were not opened, thus closing off "Jephthah's house" (so John Gray 1986, 319). For the narrator, it is not so much the loss of a maiden that matters but the loss of the privilege to keep the doors of Jephthah's house open. We can tell from the narrator's closing remarks (11:39b–40) that he is already focalizing on her father:

> So it became a custom in Israel, every year, for the daughters of Israel to go and lament for the *daughter of Jephthah the Gileadite*, four days of the year.

The daughters of Israel memorialize the daughter-of-Jephthah the Gileadite. She is memorialized in relation to (she-as-a-daughter-of) the father who bargains and defines her life (Exum 1993, 139). In this reading, the narrator is disturbing. He identifies the daughter with a father who is willing to get rid of her.

The "sacrifice" of the daughter takes place in the hands of Jephthah (in contrast to Landers 1991) and in the account of the narrator (11:39a). But the "ashes" of her sacrifice "lament" the countering bargain that her father did not make with Yhwh. Thus she is violated by what is done and what is not done.

In the end, Jephthah chooses to materialize his vow at the expense of "his house." Upon the daughter's return from the mountains, Jephthah returns to his former self—an empty man.

4.2.4 *Countering Daughter*

The story of Jephthah's daughter is not her story. She is born into the story of Jephthah's house and vow, a story that illustrates the power of s/words to (pro)create and kill, led out by the words of the narrator. Jephthah, who was rejected on account of his mother, chooses to honor the power of words over the face of his daughter. This is a story about the use and abuse of the power of s/words, in practice and in idleness. As proposed above, this is also a story about the entanglement of stories. I provided a site where text and interpretation engage to expose the need to read biblical texts responsibly.

The daughter's fate was destined when Jephthah opened his mouth, sanctioned when she opened the doors to his house (was she pushed through the doors?), delayed when she opened her mouth to ask for two months, and sealed when Jephthah and Yhwh kept their mouths shut. This "open" and "shut" story is dynamic, with the narrator making the final cut. He cuts off the sacrifice from public eyes (11:39) just as he makes the location where Jephthah made his vow ambiguous (11:29–31). The placement of these events would determine who in the story world knows what, and their intentions in what they do. If the daughter knew of Jephthah's vow, for instance, her "innocent submission" takes a critical turn:

> She *is* one of Jephthah's troublers because, as she steps forth, she takes the place of someone whom he has considered expendable. She thereby passes judgment on her father's willingness to bargain for glory with the life of another. Her action condemns his priorities, and perhaps those of all Israel. (Fewell 1992, 71)[21]

We may yet assume that the daughter did not know of Jephthah's vow, allowing words to act in Jephthah's cry (11:34). This alternative gives her the chance to interpret her father's words on the spot, and to determine that she is a troubler. In this regard, she is critical by stepping forth (Fewell) and by responding to her father. The story, however, does not lean in one direction or the other. To borrow Abigail's rhetoric (1 Sam 25:25), Jephthah's story is about an opening, a hole, for he is just what his name says: His name means "open," and his story is still open.

The narrator separates "inside" from "outside," posing the latter as a threat to the former. He first presents Jephthah as an outsider, an outcast,

---

[21] The sages in *Genesis Rabbah* imagine a similar reaction from Yhwh: "The divine plan seems to have been to frighten Jephthah so he would learn a lesson, that is, to teach the ignoramus by giving him a shock so he would see how foolish his vow was" (Valler 1999, 56).

who needs to be controlled. So, too, the Ammonites. Jephthah is brought inside but the Ammonites are ousted. Jephthah's vow is uttered away from home, at Mizpeh (11:29), but it is fulfilled at home, Mizpah, where he receives his daughter when she returns from the mountains (11:39).[22] Against the narrator's attempt to push the "outside" away from Jephthah, the daughter (re)turns the "outside(r)" home. She penetrates the "separation" that the narrator wants to uphold. She is the hole who is inside and outside Jephthah's house, who comes forth from and returns home. If this reading, which relies on the narrator's account, is possible, the daughter's action also condemns the actions of the narrator. I must admit, however, that the narrator has a better way of representing this nameless daughter: no man has ever known her!

4.3 The Daughter of Numbers 30

Jephthah bemoans his daughter because he believes that what is said cannot be unsaid. He is directed to the past; he must now do to her as he has said. His daughter, on the other hand, focuses on the present and on what needs to be done. These attitudes imitate the regulation of Num 30:3:

A man, when he vows a vow to Yhwh or oaths an oath to oblige an obligation upon himself, he must not break his word;	[Jephthah] "For I have opened my mouth to Yhwh and I cannot retract" (Judg 11:35b).
According to all that come out of his mouth, he must do. (Num 30:3)	[daughter] "Do to me according to what came from your mouth" (Judg 11:36aß).

The account of Jephthah's daughter upholds the principles of the regulation in Num 30:3: (1) a man must *not break* or *retract* his vow but (2) *do* according to all that comes out of his mouth. In their juxtaposition, however, one principle assaults the other. The principles of Num 30:3 are split between a male and a female character in Judg 11. Jephthah's M-voice prohibits, but the daughter's F-voice permits. The two voices in Judg 11 cut Num 30:3 to expose the ideological construction of gender and the gendered construction of ideology. I imagine the story of Jephthah's daughter opening the doors for a critical evaluation of the stipulations in Num 30.

The account of Jephthah's daughter provides two elements lacking from Num 30: (1) a content and subject for the vow and (2) a story world in which the principles of the regulations are honored. Jephthah's daugh-

---

[22] I distinguish the place of the vow (Mizpeh) from the place of the sacrifice (Mizpah), associating the former with the *peh* (mouth, lips) that Jephthah opened (cf. Exum 1993, 133).

ter makes problematic in two ways the content-less vow regulated in Num 30:3.

First, Num 30:3 fails to account for *actual* differences between different vows, oaths, and obligations (see §1.2.2). The legal motivations in Num 30 and Judg 11 fail to realize that vows are not all the same, nor are all oaths or obligations. Because the act of making a vow is binding, Jephthah's lethal vow has to be observed like other, less-lethal vows. Lacking from Num 30:3 and Jephthah's view of his vow is the chance for compromises. When we focus on Jephthah's daughter we open up the regulation of a man's vow for the weightier matters of legal qualifications and revisions.

Jephthah's daughter also shows that the fulfillment of a man's vow *can* be delayed. Delay of fulfillment is a narrative attempt to qualify the principles that necessitate the fulfillment of vows. Failing to consider these openings, in Jephthah's case and in Num 30:3, is the consequence of gender biases. From the standpoint of the gender code, a daughter exposes the androcentric biases of both the M-narrator (Judg 11) and the M-legislator (Num 30). In other words, Jephthah's daughter uncovers the holes of these men.

Whereas Jephthah's daughter is involved in delaying her sacrifice, the daughter of Num 30 has no say in the fulfillment or annulment of her vows. Jephthah's daughter exposes the repressed subjectivity of the daughter of Num 30, while the latter discloses the repressed opportunity for the former. Jephthah himself uses delay as an opportunity for bargain and reconsideration (he delays fighting the Ammonites so that he may bargain with the elders). Likewise, the regulations in Num 30:4–9 recognize the gift of delays by decreeing that a father or husband must decide on the same day, that is, with no delay. A one-day delay is sufficient time for annulling a subject's vows.

The delay that Jephthah's daughter gains from her father also counters the narrator's tendency to rush matters toward closure.[23] The narrator locates her memorialization at the four-day ritual that the daughters of Israel perform every year. On the other hand, I locate her memorialization in the delay she requests. She memorializes herself. For two months, she stays her father's hand. It is tragic that Yhwh does not take advantage of the delay to reconsider Jephthah's vow.[24] By emphasizing the significance of the delay (separation) in this transtextual reading, I resist the narrator's program.

---

[23] The narrator, for instance, makes Jephthah chief and leader over Gilead before he gains victory over the Ammonites (11:11). Like the narrator, the Ammonite king presents a claim and demands immediate fulfillment. Without the opportunity of a delay, his claim is denied.

[24] Simon Patrick adds that a high priest could have absolved Jephthah, and that Jephthah was not bound to separate his daughter from human company nor to burn her in an offering (1702, 505).

Second, turning to the subject of the one making vows, the narrator presents figures according to their characters. Jephthah is praised as an able warrior (11:1), but his mother is slighted for being a harlot (11:1), an outsider (11:2); Jephthah's companions are snubbed as empty men (11:3); Jephthah denounces the elders of Gilead as dispossessors (11:7) and the Ammonites as false claimants (11:14–15) and Israel's enemy (11:36); Yhwh is viewed as a deliverer (11:36); Jephthah's daughter is lamented for having never known a man (11:39); and the daughters of Israel are favorably presented for preserving the custom of memorializing Jephthah's daughter (11:40). The story world of Jephthah's daughter opens up the idea that a vow is fixed to the possibility of legal qualifications and revisions, on the basis of the *character* of the subjects involved.

Most dominant readers, with their politics of coherence, underwrite the narrator's characterization of an able warrior (so Heb 11:32). Boling sees Jephthah as a knight, "like Gideon in 6:11–12, one trained in upper class combat, and who furnished his own equipment as well as a squire and/or unit of soldiers" (1975, 197). Boling's upper-class figure stands in contrast to Patrick's characterization of the "empty men" who gathered around Jephthah as poor and needy "men of no estates" (1702, 488). On the other hand, readers in antiquity did not find Jephthah and his vow so appealing.

> Josephus condemns it [Jephthah's vow]. The Targumist in Pseudo-Jonathan says Jephthah should have redeemed his daughter. Augustine also blames Jephthah. . . . Jephthah was a character commended in the New Testament and not actually condemned in the Old. The author of Judges does not seem to hold that Jephthah should not have made his vow, or that, having made it, he should not have carried it out. (A. T. Hanson 1989, 299)

In recent years, some feminist readers, though troubled by Jephthah's character, embrace the narrative because of the women's ritual to which it gives rise (see Day 1989; Fuchs 1993). They seek something positive in this gruesome story, shifting the focus from the salvation of Israel to a ritual that memorializes a woman (cf. Gunn and Fewell 1993, 117). Other feminist readers, without rejecting the ritual readings, offer critical readings of both Jephthah and God (see, e.g., Fewell 1992; Exum 1992, 45–69).[25] I pursue my analysis of the character of Jephthah, in relation to the legal subjects of Num 30, along this critical path. I proceed from the insecure character that Gunn finds:

> Having risked all for the victory, he is unwilling to risk its undoing by offending YHWH through reneging on the vow; and from Jephthah's

---

[25] Note Exum's query: "If we allow the women's ceremonial remembrance to encourage glorification of the victim, we perpetuate the crime against Bat-jiftah. How, then, do we reject the concept of honoring the victim without also sacrificing the woman?" (1995, 77).

perspective the vow-victory sequence has to be captivating. He is a prisoner of his words ("I have opened my mouth to YHWH, and I am unable to return {repent?}," v. 35 {AT}), as he is a prisoner of his understanding of the immutability of both the vow (see Num. 30:1–2) and YHWH. (1987, 117)

The master of words is imprisoned by his own words. It is only after he sacrifices his daughter in order to fulfill his vow that he stops compromising words, by emphasizing the difference between *shibboleth* and *sibboleth* (12:1–6). A master of compromises, like David (see 1 Chr 22:8; 28:3), Jephthah has blood on his hands. He sheds the blood of foreigners (11:32–33) and kinsmen (12:1–6) both, including his own daughter (11:39). How, then, should we evaluate his character? According to his words? to his deeds? In whose interest?

In Exum's reading, Jephthah's story has the potential for tragedy, but he does not quite fit the composition of a tragic hero, as Saul does (see Gunn 1980): "Unlike Saul, who knows he has lost the kingship yet multiplies his efforts to hold on to it, Jephthah does not grapple to find a way out of a situation for which there is no way out. . . . We pity Jephthah, but we do not at any point admire him" (Exum 1992, 57). The source of tragedy for Exum is the silence of God: "Silent transcendence, if not a form of hostile transcendence, clearly raises questions about divine benevolence. Jephthah does not experience Saul's sense of separation from Yhwh, but, like Saul, he cannot depend on the goodness of Yhwh" (1992, 60; see also Exum 1989). Nevertheless, we should not lay all of the blame on Yhwh's silence, especially since he was called upon as a matter of convenience, and it is to the narrator's credit that Yhwh became involved in the story. If we bracket the narrator's voice, Yhwh still honors his decision in 10:11–16 not to deliver Israel. He does not speak up again until the story of Manoah and Manoah's wife in Judg 13. Yhwh's silence results in the destruction of the Ammonites, the daughter, and the Ephraimites. His silence also kills.

Why, then, does Jephthah, with blood on his hands and negotiation in his mind and tongue, not compromise his vow on behalf of his daughter? The most tragic moment in the story, according to this reading, is when the one who was returned to his house will not return his words (11:11, 35). Jephthah should know what it is like to be returned.[26] Had he gone back on his vow, he would have done as I expect from a character such as his—a killer, a negotiator. The "young woman of Num 30" would have approved had Jephthah not fulfilled his vow, because, in her case, a vow can be compromised. A vow is a bargain, defined by compromises. Yhwh, too, knows that:

---

[26] This sentence is purposefully ambiguous, to employ both positive and negative effects of "being returned." To "be returned" is both to bring back and reinstate, to send away and reject. It may have liberating and/or limiting effects.

I brought you up from Egypt and I took you into the land which I had promised on oath to your fathers. And I said, "I will never break My covenant with you. And you, for your part, you make no covenant with the inhabitants of this land; you must tear down their altars." But you have not obeyed Me—look what you have done! Therefore, I have resolved not to drive them out before you; they shall become your oppressors, and their gods shall be a snare to you. (Judg 2:1b–3; Tanakh)

The foregoing reading inserts a tragedy: While Jephthah and the narrator honor the power of words, this reading also honors the power of deeds (praxis). My preference for the power of deeds undermines the honorable character that the narrator presents.

I turn at this juncture, finally, to the weightier matters of the narrative theory that I employed—Bal's speech-act narratology, which emphasizes the power of words to act and cut. To Bal, they are s/words. The foregoing reading used the opening that Bal's theory allows for circumreading the regulations of Num 30. If words can act and cut bodies, then I assume that words can act and cut words, too; "[I]f words can kill, they can also heal" (Exum 1993, 132). This is the basis for deconstruction[27] and transtextuality. But words do not act and cut bodies or words on their own. Agents initiate the speech-act, and subjects perform and/or are cut as a consequence. Both of these speech-act basics are ignored in Num 30, but exposed by the delay that Jephthah's daughter requested.

The daughter's delay has a metacritical effect. Posed against the speech-act theory, her delay separates the *saying* of the vow from its *doing*. The saying of Jephthah's vow did not kill her; the doing of his vow is what killed her. In that connection, the daughter of Num 30 presents an alternative opening: the undoing of vows is possible, and legal.

---

[27] "Of course, deconstruction is not a- or antipolitical; it demonstrates the politics in the positivism, the emotions in the logic, the exclusions in the formalism" (Bal 1991a, 16).

5

A Wife No Man Controlled

Reading is to follow the text, to trace its workings, even if it turns out that it is undecidable. (Miscall 1983, 2)

Critics can debate what the meaning of a given work is and may never agree on one meaning, but they do not challenge the assumption that the work does have a fixed and determinate meaning. (Miscall 1986, xix)

5.0 Reading Decidedly Undecidable Texts

Peter D. Miscall asserts the possibility that different types of Hebrew Bible texts resist each other (1972, 19–22, 37–38),[1] and that in *overrunning narratives* "one part of the text provides oblique commentary on another" (1978, 28; cf. 1979, 40; 1983, 142).[2] In other words, as Burton Feldman simply but effectively puts it, "The OT is already deconstructed; now read it!" (cited in Miscall 1986, xxiv; cf. Camp 1985, 504).

In *The Workings of Old Testament Narrative* (1983), Miscall illustrates how the Hebrew Bible deconstructs itself with "close readings" of parts of Genesis–2 Kings (which he treats as a unit; cf. Miscall 1992; so Fewell and Gunn 1993). A close reader follows the workings (read: *poesis*) of the text and embraces its undecidability, without trying to control its meanings (1983, 139, 142; 1986, xvi). This mode of reading will not produce a univo-

---

[1] The radical departure Miscall makes in this study has to do with the texts he privileges (law codes) and the lenses (sociological) through which he characterizes the poor.

[2] This dual shift manifests Derrida's notion of *iteration*, which maintains that repetitions alter (cf. Spivak 1980, 36–40): "If it did not, we could never distinguish between an original and a repetition or citation. But if repetition alters, then alteration identifies. Without the repetition, the second, there can be no first, no original" (Miscall 1986, xxv; cf. 1983, 142).

cal, definitive meaning, but it will expose the complex and evasive character of Hebrew Bible narratives (1983, 3–4; 1986, xvi; 1999, 24). In other words, Miscall's readings "deal with the *richness, complexity, and elusiveness* of OT narrative and also with its concreteness and detail," contending "that OT narrative is complex and elusive because of, not in spite of, the concrete details" (1983, 1, my italics; cf. 1986, ix).

This deconstructive mode of reading has been contested. Burke Long, for instance, complains that the open-ended and equivocal nature of the Hebrew Bible that Miscall imagines, in the final analysis, robs readers of the pleasures of reading:

> A reading which settles on one consistent, unified sense to a text may be illusory, or at least put forth provisionally to shut out, temporarily, competing interpretations. *But it is an illusion that satisfies, until one hungers again.* Deconstructionists, M[iscall]'s most radical associates, would rob us of even this amount of nourishment. (Long 1984, 769; my italics)

The consequences of Miscall's deconstructive mode of reading can be very unsettling. First, Miscall leaves an opening for relativism, insofar as he presents undecidability as an ontological aspect of Hebrew Bible narratives. If the meaning of a text is undecidable, infinite meanings are possible. This assaults the hermeneutical task because "an infinity of meaning is the same as no meaning at all" (Camp 1985, 505). An undecidable text cannot control what critics decide as its meanings. And second, Miscall leaves room for tyrannical readings: "[I]f people continue to have blind faith in the authority of the text while being faced with an infinity of undecidable meanings, one can be quite sure that they will find someone to decide for them what it means" (Camp 1985, 505).

Contrary to Miscall's desire, his approach is also an attempt, albeit sublime, to control the text (cf. 1986, xxiii). No reader can decide what a text means except the one who decides that it is undecidable, pointing us to the question, Whose interests does the undecidability of the text serve? Miscall's claim that the text is decidedly undecidable (1983, 140) restricts his program: The workings of language make his text, too, undecidable.

The crux of Miscall's deconstructive approach, notwithstanding the criticism, is directed against the dualistic tendencies of dominant readings (1983, 20; 1986, xx, xxii; so Bal). Concerning the character of David, for instance, Miscall writes:

> This is where I locate the undecidability, the indeterminateness: David is not being portrayed in a definite fashion. David is "good" *and* "bad." The text at the same time supports both and does not support a final decision in favor of only one. (1983, 2)

The text's richness, complexity, and elusiveness deny readers the privilege of drawing a final univocal reading. Although Miscall targets epistemological indeterminacy, he lays the blame at the doors of the text

as if it is ontologically indeterminate, trapping himself in the epistemological net that he sets:[3]

> Miscall consistently confuses undecidability due to the (potentially cor-
> rectable) limitations of one person's view of another person's character,
> with undecidability attributable to the observed person's lack of *any* de-
> terminable character. He is therefore open to the same charge Gunn
> [1984, 116] leveled at Alter, namely, that he confuses a problem of percep-
> tion and epistemology for one of ontology. (Lasine 1986, 54)

To free the text from the grasp of dominating readers and epistemological
tyrants, Miscall exiles it into the wilderness of indeterminacy (cf. Camp
1985, 505). He too falls into the snare of dualistic thinking.

For Miscall, a text or character is undecidable if (1) it can mean *both* A
and B; and (2) the reader cannot decide between A or B, taken to be exclu-
sive of each other. As such, Miscall cannot determine on textual evidences
if David was "good *or* bad," presuming that if David was good then he
cannot also be bad. But claiming that David is both good and bad (Miscall
1983, 2; cf. 60–61) indicates that his character is decidable. And insofar as
David can only be "good and bad" but not also "good or bad," Miscall too
is driven by dualistic biases (see also Walters 1988, 411–12).

If, on the other hand, A penetrates, and crosses, B, so that David is also
good even if he is bad, and vice versa, then it makes no sense to say that the
text is undecidable per se. Miscall claims that the text is undecidable because
he cannot assert an either/or decision (1983, 6; 1986, xx), but he fails to account
for the (ontological) limits of textuality; that is, texts do not capture; texts are
iterations (Derrida). In other words, the richness, complexity, and elusiveness
of texts, their workings, are not just ontological qualities. The reader has a say
in determining the texts' workings (so Miscall 1999, 12, 24; cf. Clines 1998).

In his reading of 1 Samuel, Miscall's point of departure presupposes
the meeting of the ontological and epistemological indeterminacies. "I depart from historical criticism and associated methods and disciplines,
because they do regard and treat the Old Testament as simplistic and primitive" (1986, vii, xviii; cf. 1983, 139–40). The old methods fail to realize the
complexity of the text, its excess of evidence, which makes it undecidable:

> It is not my purpose to overcome ambiguity or equivocation, either by ig-
> noring or explaining away details and repetitions or by filling in gaps
> and missing information. Gaps, details, repetitions, inconsistencies, and
> contradictions are considered to be deliberate, and their impact on the
> reading is assessed. (1986, xvi; cf. 1999, 24)

---

[3] Miscall (con)fuses "undecidability" and "indeterminacy." As I use these la-
bels, "undecidability" is when the text cannot decide which of its alternative
meanings is the "right meaning," whereas "indeterminacy" is when a text cannot
determine what it means and leaves it to the reader to decide (cf. Clines 1998, 126).
There are varieties of both, and they are context-dependent. "The more text, the
more indeterminacy" (Clines 1998, 136). The closer the reading, the harder the
drive for determinacy, the more the indeterminacy.

In the coming sections I explore the implications of Miscall's notion of undecidability for reading Hannah's story, which involves a vow. Many critics have studied this pivotal story, but the significance of her vow has not been considered fully. I first review "pre-critical" characterizations of Hannah and outline the directions of my reading (§5.1). Then, supplementing Miscall's decidedly undecidable characterization of Hannah (§5.2), I offer an *alter*native reading that focuses on Hannah's vow and song (§5.3) and close with its implications for my ongoing circumreading of Num 30 (§5.4).

5.1 Decidable Hannahs

My concern in this section is not with how Hannah prefigures biblical female characters (cf. Jobling 1994), nor with how Hannah is a point of entry for addressing the gender issue in the Hebrew Bible (cf. Jobling 1998, 129ff.), though the analysis will require attention to them. Rather, I review ideologies:

> We shall see hereafter *what points of view control the arrangement of the historical material,* and condition the internal connection of its often seemingly loosely arranged parts. (Erdmann 1877, 9; my italics)

5.1.1 *Mother Grace*

Most critics assume that Philo's allegorical method[4] is derived from the Greek schools, particularly the Stoic tradition of interpretation,[5] "itself eclectic and only fragmentarily attested before Philo's time, but resting primarily on the recognition in texts or myths of three levels of meaning—literal, ethical, and metaphysical" (Lamberton 1986, 47). We catch a glimpse of the working of the allegorical method in Philo's characterization of Hannah.[6]

---

[4] Allegorical expressions say one thing but *mean* another. The commentator's goal is "to *find* the hidden meanings, the correspondences that carry the thrust of the text beyond the explicit" (Lamberton 1986, 20; cf. Winston 1991). Philo inherited this tradition and passed it on to Clement of Alexandria and Origen (cf. Lamberton 1986, 45, 53, 78–79; Sowers 1965).

[5] Seeing himself in a community of exegetes (cf. *Migr.* 89–93; *Abr.* 99; see also Goodenough 1935; 1962, 13–14; Peters 1970, 297–98), Philo fused his Jewish and Greek traditions well: "Out of the two strands he had woven himself a single cloth, warp and woof. He read Plato in terms of Moses, and Moses in terms of Plato, to the point that he was convinced that each had said essentially the same things" (Goodenough 1962, 10; cf. Sandmel 1956, 16).

[6] "A chief purpose of allegorical interpretation is to enable one to continue to bind himself to a textual passage that is both *sacred* and *troubling*. . . . Allegory was Philo's principal way of meeting the difficulties he found in Scripture" (Sandmel 1979, 18–19; my italics). So Origen, as he seeks a "worthy conception of divinity" (*De principiis* 4.2.1; cf. Berchman 1984). So Plutarch's call for allegorical interpretation: "We must not treat the myths as wholly factual accounts, but take *what is*

Samuel is the firstfruit of the divine seed that Hannah ("grace") receives as "the gift of the wisdom of God" (*Quod Deus* 5). Her unselfishness with Samuel equals Abraham's willingness to sacrifice Isaac: Hannah "begat not for herself" and gave the child back "in due payment to the Giver," becoming Abraham's disciple and successor (*Quod Deus* 4). Despite their similarities, Philo does not see Hannah's "Samuel" as a real person, as he views Abraham's Isaac, but as an allegory for an attitude. Hannah's gift to God, therefore, was not "a human being but rather an inspired temper possessed by a God-sent frenzy" (*Somn.* 1, 254). Hannah becomes an allegory for *graciousness*, as she is named *grace* (*Ebr.* 145).[7] This is evident when others oppose her. When "the boy" (following LXX) accused her of being drunk (1 Sam 1:14), her soul was actually filled with grace. Her "soul thereby rejoices and smiles and dances, for it is possessed and inspired, so that to many of the unenlightened it may seem to be drunken, crazy and beside itself" (*Ebr.* 146; cf. Ozick 1994, 89).

Moreover, Philo reads the mention that Hannah did not eat (1 Sam 1:7–9) to mean that she abstained from both wine and the passions (*Ebr.* 151–52). What appeared to be drunkenness with wine was drunkenness with divine grace. Transferring her abstinence from wine to abstinence from sex, Philo finds an explanation for her barrenness. She had "the soul which is sterilized to wickedness and unfruitful of the endless host of passions and vices" (*Mut.* 143). The word "barren" in Hannah's song (1 Sam 2:5b) "applies to the mind which refuses to accept any mortal sowing as fruitful, the mind which makes away with and brings to abortion all the intimacies and the matings of the wicked, but holds fast to the 'seventh' [cf. *Quod Deus* 10–11] and the supreme peace which it gives" (*Mut.* 144). She is barren in body, but filled with the gifts of the mind and spirit; being barren is a blessing in disguise:

> [W]hen she has become barren and ceases to produce these children or indeed has cast them out bodily she is transformed into a pure virgin. Then receiving the divine seed she moulds it into shape and brings forth new life in forms of precious quality and marvelous loveliness, wisdom, courage, temperance, justice, holiness, piety and the other virtues and good emotions. (*Praem.* 159)

Philo thus sidesteps the MT's troubling explanation for Hannah's bar-

---

fitting in each episode according to the principle of likeness" (*De Isis et Osiris* 374E). Dawson rightly suggests that the desire for "a sense of the fitting" allow allegorists (so comedians) to make absurd and embarrassing texts culturally acceptable (1992, 58–70). The texts that they cannot tame face "textual athetization" (67), a phrase in Dawson's book meaning, roughly, "textual death" or "textual murder."

[7] Hannah's antithesis is Onan (Gen 38), Judah's second son, who "through self-love" brought defeat and death upon himself (*Quod Deus* 16). See chapter 6 in the present volume.

renness: that God closed her womb.[8] Her barrenness is God's gift of virginity, a valued condition for Philo's audience. Philo transforms the workings of the story by allegorizing Hannah and her son, creating moral instructions on the basis of the text. His allegorical approach reiterates the narrative.

5.1.2 *Mother of a Prophet*

Josephus also attends to the workings of biblical narratives and rewrites the text. His goals are two: Driven by nationalistic interests, he seeks to present the Jews in a favorable light to the Greco-Roman world (*Ant.* I:5–13), and, driven by theological interests, he urges his readers to conform to God's will (*Ant.* I:14–15). Both goals are exhibited in his characterization of Hannah.

Josephus sees Hannah's story as an aside in the account of the priesthood's demise, intending to "recount the story of the prophet and then proceed to speak of the fate of Eli's sons and the disaster that befell the whole people of the Hebrews" (*Ant.* V:341). Josephus, too, shifts the focus from the situation of a woman to the account of a prophet and of Israel in general, thereby ignoring some of the details of the story.

Josephus does not address the tensions between Hannah and Peninnah, thus transforming "Hannah from a rational human being who responds as would anyone to such constant, cruel harassment, into a silly, frantic woman, who has no control over her emotions and actions. According to Josephus, it is merely the sight of Peninnah and her children that causes Hannah to lose control" (Brown 1992, 164; cf. *Ant.* V:343). Removing explanations for Hannah's outpouring before God (1 Sam 1:10–11), Josephus presents her as a woman obsessed with becoming a mother (*Ant.* V:344)—she wept for her barrenness and lonesome lot (*Ant.* V:345). "To be sure, even according to the biblical version, Hannah desires to have a child. But the story is presented in such a way that we are not completely certain which is the greater source of irritation, anxiety, and unhappiness for Hannah—her barrenness or Peninnah's taunting" (Brown 1992, 166–67).

Josephus also omits Hannah's response to Eli's charge that she was drunk (1 Sam 1:15–16), but quickly moves to Samuel's dedication (*Ant.* V:347). This selective retelling diminishes Hannah's role as nurturer of her

---

[8] Blaikie notices that the story opens with a dilemma, because the God-fearing Hannah did not receive providence while the selfish and cruel Peninnah did, as if God were not in charge. But Blaikie turns this theodic insight into a chance for providence: "If Peninnah had been kind to Hannah, Samuel might never have been born" (1896, 3). Her ordeal, therefore, was part of God's plan to bring her to him because "it is when they become intolerable that men think of God" (10). Hannah's story follows a process that we also find in the Psalter: "First the wail of distress; then the wrestling of the troubled heart with God; then the repose and triumph of faith" (12). Blaikie thereby normalizes Peninnah's taunting of Hannah.

child (Brown 1992, 168–69). Hannah does not get the two years the MT gives her to wean her child, robbing her of the chance to be attached to her son. She is not even a poet in *Jewish Antiquities*. All that Josephus seems to need from Hannah is her uterus and womb, to bear a future prophet and priest, but he finds no value in her actions, words (prayer, vow, and song), and character. He transforms Hannah's story into a man's and a nation's story (so Brown 1992).

However, a slip in Josephus's account indicates that Hannah survives his demotion. When Hannah dedicates Samuel, Josephus suggests that she gave him so that he could *become a prophet* (*Ant.* V:347). She anticipates with words what history alone can (dis)prove. Hannah's gift bears prophetic significance, and Josephus's words cannot fully represent, nor repress or erase, her.

The decisiveness of Josephus's reading is undecidable, for epistemological reasons. As texts fail to capture their subjects, interpretations also fail. And since Josephus's *Jewish Antiquities* is the object of my analysis, I have made problematic the drive to distinguish ontological from epistemological undecidabilities. Josephus's epistemological decidability is the ontological undecidability in this reading. Of course, my interpretation of Josephus's characterization of Hannah does not fully capture "Josephus"!

5.1.3 *Mother of a Leader*

In *Biblical Antiquities,* Pseudo-Philo appears "sympathetic to women, often introducing feminine imagery and significantly upgrading women's status and roles vis-à-vis the biblical account" (Brown 1992, 12). But women are not Pseudo-Philo's central concern:

> Indeed, the most important, overarching theme is God's covenant with Israel, its demands (obedience to the Torah), and its promises (blessings of land and progeny). Within this framework, the author also emphasizes Israel's punishment for failure to live up to covenantal demands, primarily by falling into idolatry and intermarrying with Gentiles, and the sure promise of eventual vindication and restoration, based upon obedience to God's will as revealed in the Jewish scriptures (the Torah).
>
> A further theme concerns Israel's leadership. Israel's leaders cause the people to sin and to disobey the Torah; they are condemned particularly for leading the people astray and for remaining silent in the face of sin or attack by outsiders. (Brown 1992, 27)

These concerns surface in Pseudo-Philo's representation of Hannah. Her story is set during Israel's search for a leader to free them from their distress (*Bib. Ant.* 49:1). Hannah brings hope into a context of desperation (Dyrness 1994).

The Israelites cast lots to determine their leader and the lot falls on Elkanah, who refuses. God responds by extending the leadership role to Elkanah's son: "The one who is born from the sterile woman whom I have given to him as a wife *will be a prophet* before me" (*Bib. Ant.* 49:8; my italics). The transference of leadership "functions to place the birth of Samuel in a larger context; he is the answer to the whole nation's prayer for a leader, not just to Hannah's prayer for a son" (Brown 1992, 144).[9] God promises in *Biblical Antiquities* what Hannah offers in *Jewish Antiquities:* Samuel will be a prophet before God. Viewing these two texts together gives the impression that God's promise is fulfilled by a woman, and the gift of a mother is promised by God (cf. Ruether 1982, 185; Fuchs 1985, 120).

Pseudo-Philo develops the struggles between Hannah (righteousness) and Peninnah (wicked), Hannah and Eli. But he shifts the emphasis "from the *fact of Hannah's barrenness* to the *effect of her barrenness*—she is taunted by her rival" (Brown 1992, 145; my italics). The cause of her barrenness is God's plan "to work a greater miracle among the people of Israel" (Brown 1992, 147).[10]

Hannah's prayer for a son intersected with Israel's prayer for a leader: "You have not asked alone, but the people have prayed for this. This is *not your request alone,* but it was promised previously to the tribes" (*Bib. Ant.* 51:2). Hannah "plays a highly significant, indeed vital, national role" (Brown 1992, 155). Brown thus concludes that Pseudo-Philo

> significantly enhances both Hannah's character and role, and her story becomes paradigmatic of the Israelites' story. Her crisis is their crisis, her longings are their longings, her fulfillment is their fulfillment. . . . His modifications of the story all serve to present Hannah as a model of piety and faithfulness on a personal level, as well as a model of Israel as she moves from barrenness to vindication, when she becomes the source of Wisdom for the nations. (1992, 172, 173)

What is the difference between "Hannah's story is Israel's story" (which is Brown's reading of Pseudo-Philo) and "Hannah's story becomes a man's story" (which is Brown's reading of Josephus)? In both cases, a woman's story is rewritten with national and male interests (cf. Polanski 1995).

•

The readers discussed above have more interests in the history of Israel then Hannah's vow. It is ironic that Philo did not consider her vow, which could have complemented his "spiritualized Hannah." A woman who

---

[9] Brown sees "prophet" as fulfillment of Israel's request for a "leader." Another may find Israel's prayer unanswered if "prophet" and "leader" serve different functions.

[10] Calmet, who argues that Hannah was beloved because she was sterile and without children, emphasizes another effect of Hannah's barrenness but ignores its cause (1730; 1737, II:8). He sees a positive image of God (so Scott L. Harris 1992, 28), but had he addressed the *cause* of Hannah's barrenness he may have seen a different picture of God.

makes a vow, it seems, is a figure of grace. Even Pseudo-Philo, who developed the tensions between Hannah and Peninnah, as part of the reason for Hannah's vow, did not account for her vow. I will return to this ignorance later, but now turn to another category of readers, readers who are invested in the Christian church.

5.1.4 Mother of Piety and Virtue

Church fathers read in the shadows of Jewish readers, whom they did not acknowledge but whose traces can be detected between the lines.[11] There is a simple explanation for this: to fence the Christian church, the fathers severed any links with the Jewish faith. The upshot was the fathers' exclusivist attitude against anything Jewish, with anti-Semitism as the extreme consequence (Barnes 1971, 91–92). For Gregory the Great, "the Jew" represents the dark and blind race that does not see the true working of God in Jesus of Nazareth (*Regula pastoralis* 2.49; cited in Markus 1995, 1–2). Tertullian also, the "first great theologian of the West," wrote his *Adversus Judaeos* treatise as an open rejection of the Jews. These writings suggest that "the Jew" in the church fathers' world of discourse was not formed independently of real Jewish people in their societies.

Two church fathers are relevant for this study, Chrysostom and Gregory I. I preface their readings of Hannah's story with a reference from Tertullian. This is an uncanny entry into the church fathers, given Tertullian's African context and uncertain ties to the Christian church (cf. Havea 2000, 288).

Tertullian used Hannah's story to support the claim, appealing to Luke 6:20–22, that God's kingdom is for the poor. When Hannah praises God in 1 Sam 2:8, she acknowledges that God lifts up *"the poor from the earth, the indigent also, that he may make him to sit with the mighty ones of the people,* evidently in his own kingdom, *and upon thrones of glory,* royal thrones" (*Adversus Marcionem* IV:14; my italics). The barren Hannah is a figure of the poor and indigent, the ones whom God shall deliver. God on the other hand condemns the boastfulness of the rich; God "puts down the mighty from their seat and lifts up the poor from the dunghill" (IV:28, 34). Tertullian directs the biblical teachings to the dunghill and the place of the poor.

For readers who focus on the class divide in human societies (see Ruether 1982; Bellis 1994, 141), Tertullian reveals the navel (read: plight of the poor) in the readings by Chrysostom and Gregory I. Neither of these church fathers found Hannah's story a fitting place to address the situation of the poor.

---

[11] As they were well-read in Greek philosophy and Roman law (cf. Sider 1971, 1–10), I imagine that the fathers knew something about their Jewish neighbors and their view of Scripture. That most fathers did not mention Jewish/rabbinic literature does not mean that they did not know (of) these writings.

•

John Chrysostom offers typological readings in his five sermons on Hannah. He stays closer to the biblical text in sermons I–III, but his thematic-typological tendencies take over in sermons IV–V (compare with Philo's allegorical approach). He was concerned for the plight of the poor and slaves in other writings, but that concern did not surface in his reading of Hannah.[12]

Chrysostom appeals to Hannah as an example of patience and "endurance in faith." His intention in these sermons was to "create piety of spirit" (III:1) because he felt that Hannah's life was worth imitating: *imitatio Anna!* Hannah was a pious woman who held her tongue even though Peninnah taunted her, and Eli called her a madwoman, but she became the "mother of piety" to many generations (I:4). Hannah's faith and wisdom set her among great figures of faith like Moses (II:3), Paul, and Christ (IV–V). These sermons show that "John was not primarily a theologian. He was a pastor, concerned with the preservation of faith and morals in his flock" (van Ommeslaeghe 1987, 466). Chrysostom's pious reading may appeal to some critics, but if we read his sermons within their supposed historical contexts we may react differently.

Baur suggests that Chrysostom delivered the five sermons right after Pentecost 387, after a series of martyr's feasts and the observance of Lent (1959, 285). The Christian calendar, therefore, influenced his focus on piety.

The political situation in Antioch during Lent 387 may also have played a role in determining the content of the sermons, in which case the call for *imitatio Anna* sounds restrictive. Emperor Theodosius imposed a tax upon the citizens of Antioch toward the end of February 387, against which "common people" rebelled, led by low-class actors and foreigners who had nothing to lose but who hoped to gain something in every tumult. The dissidents pulled down the golden statues of the emperor and his family, and dragged them through the streets. "That was open rioting, a public insult and mockery of the highest authority of the kingdom, the commission of high treason, which from the time of the ancient Roman Empire was punishable only by death" (Baur 1959, 260). The city prefect, Tisamenus, retaliated by ordering his soldiers under a sort of martial law to arrest whomever came their way, adult and children, guilty and innocent both. The captives were sentenced soon thereafter to death by the sword, by burning on funeral pyres, and some were thrown to wild

---

[12] Van Ommeslaeghe explains that Chrysostom's "early popularity as bishop and orator was soon adversely affected by the simplicity of his life, his endeavors to repress abuses in the clergy, his defense of the poor, and his criticisms of injustices and the display of wealth" (1987, 466). The concern for the poor testifies to the influences of his rhetoric master Libanius, who, though critical of Christianity and its clerics, willingly helped poor students on several occasions (Baur 1959, 20).

beasts. A mighty anguish and terror seized the citizens of Antioch, and no one dared to step out of their homes for fear of arrest and persecution. Chrysostom did not step into the pulpit for a week after the riot, even though it was the season of Lent (Baur 1959, 264). Only after Bishop Flavian approached the emperor in Constantinople were the Antiochenes pardoned, and people came out of their houses to celebrate Easter 387. That was the assumed atmosphere in which Chrysostom delivered his sermons on Hannah around Pentecost 387.

A diachronic reading finds Chrysostom urging the citizens to endure their persecution, to submit to the Roman authorities, to face persecution with "piety of spirit," in the way that Hannah tolerated ridicules by Peninnah and Eli. Piety therefore is *passivity*. Such a message assumes that the citizens had to accept their victimization, because of the grave outcome if they had resisted the Roman authorities. To borrow from Koheleth, Chrysostom appears to prefer pious "live dogs" rather than "dead lions" (Eccl 9:4).

A metacritical reader may also find Chrysostom justifying his passivity during the rebellion and persecution of the Antiochenes. He focused on one aspect of Hannah's character, that she absorbed the ridicules given by her rivals, but ignored how Hannah challenged Yhwh to open her womb so that she may have a son. Hannah does not passively (and piously?) accept her barrenness but confronts (with her vow in 1 Sam 1:11) the one responsible for her lot. I imagine that Chrysostom would have had a different characterization of Hannah had he taken part in the rebellion against the emperor with Bishop Flavian. In other words, Chrysostom did not fully account for the *workings* of Hannah's story.

•

About one and a half centuries later, Gregory (the Great) I offered two typological readings of Hannah's story. In the first reading (I:1–60), Gregory argues that Elkanah represents the unique man, Christ, and that his wives represent two religions. Peninnah signifies the synagogue, and Hannah stands for the Christian church. The conflict between Peninnah and Hannah represents the persecution of the church by Jews. Hannah is the sign (*res*) of Jesus' preference of Christians over Jews: as Elkanah favored Hannah, Gregory argues, so did Jesus favor the Christian church.[13]

---

[13] Gregory's thought moves within a thoroughly Augustinian groove, in which exegesis proceeds in two levels: the level of signs (*res*, the words written by the authors) and the signs that those words signify (the *signa divinitus data*). The exegete aims to transcend the "miserable slavery of the soul" to the *res* toward the *res* of the *res*. "Captivity to the sign is inability, or refusal, to pierce its opacity; not knowing, or not seeking, the range of potential further meaning it can have in a larger discourse. So the Jews who refused to understand the Old Testament as interpreted in the New remained captive to the closed world of its (nonetheless useful) signs" (Markus 1995, 4).

In the second reading (I:61–84), Gregory presents life as if it were the site of a spiritual battle. Elkanah signifies the virtuous man who renounces the world and wholeheartedly seeks God.[14] At home, the virtuous Elkanah faces the tension between the contemplative (Hannah) and the active (Peninnah) ways of life. The active way of life is easier, for its primary concern is with surviving the needs of daily life, while the contemplative life involves steadfast reading of Scriptures and continuous prayer. In Gregory's judgment, Elkanah chooses wisely by favoring Hannah even though the contemplative way of life is more difficult (so Philo's portrayal of Abraham as one who seeks *sophia*). The shift in this second reading is from belief to behavior.

In both readings, Gregory extends the workings of the biblical narrative to the interests of the Christian church. He focuses on Elkanah, with Hannah playing a secondary role. Concerning Hannah's prayer in 1 Sam 2:1–10, Gregory suggests that the church celebrates the triumph of Christ over the Jews through Hannah's mouth. Hannah signifies the soul that loves God and the heart that resists the attempt of evil (Jews) to establish itself (II:1–28). This review exposes two navels in Gregory's reading, one conscious (hostility toward the Jews) and the other unconscious (preference for the "male-type").

As in the readings by Tertullian and Chrysostom, Hannah's vow does not figure into Gregory's reading. Its absence is curious because it would have complemented his religious interests. On the other hand, its absence may have to do with the fact that it was a vow *by a woman*.

•

The readers above read the story of Hannah intertextually with concerns in other texts, literary and/or social, to which they find parts of Hannah's story applicable. The shortfall of their reading practice is the tendency to ignore parts of the story, such as Hannah's vow, the primary concern of my study, and even to rob Hannah of her story.[15] Moreover, they put the

---

[14] Simon Patrick (1703) also directs attention to Elkanah, seeing Hannah as the "example of an excellent wife; sensible of her Husband's Kindness, endeavour'd to please him, by complying with his Desires, and avoiding all things that might be gravies." Although Hannah's grief for her barrenness turned a festival into a fast (cf. Esther), Patrick explains that fasting was an appropriate religious response to her situation. Hannah's excellent character is also exhibited in the respect she showed Eli, primarily because of the "Office which Eli held in the Church." And the prayer she offers in response to the gift of a son, at Eli's bidding, also testifies to her character.

[15] For Henry Preserved Smith, Hannah's vow was unnecessary because "the ancient regulation that every male that opens the womb is already the property of Yhwh" (1902, 9) means that her son already belonged to Yhwh (12). And finding no references to Hannah's situation in the song, Smith argued that it must be the work of an editor.

female characters in the service of male figures and Israel's history. They did not explore the burden of female figures (e.g., Hannah's barrenness[16] and Peninnah's ridicules), possibly because of the unsettling image it would have connected to God.

I exposed the selectivity of these readings in order to interject the view that readers who argue for undecidability read the text more closely. In the next section, I turn to Miscall's close yet selective reading of 1 Sam 1–3.

5.2 Hannah, a Lure

Miscall shifts the focus from the "history" of Israel to the literary setting of 1 Sam 1–3, as part of the radical departure from historical criticism that he favors. In the birth story of Samuel, Miscall argues, the text sets narrative lures (by means of wordplays, themes, character and place names) that point the reader to other stories in the Hebrew Bible.[17] These lures suggest ways of interpreting the text, but they do not provide enough evidence so that the reader may assure herself of her reading (Miscall 1986, 9). In this regard, Miscall argues, the text is undecidable.

Miscall reads Elkanah's wives, one of whom was barren, as lures toward the stories of Sarah and Hagar, Rachel and Leah. But there are differences among these characters. Rachel and Leah were sisters while Sarah and Hagar were set apart by class (master–slave) and ethnicity (Israelite–Egyptian), so Hannah and Peninnah cannot be "hooked" to their stories. The reader is lured toward Genesis, but she cannot firmly anchor the reading.

Moreover, this birth story lures the reader to other characters like Moses and Samson (Exod 2:1–10 and Judg 13). Both figures "delivered" Israel from foreign enemies. This lures the reader to expect that Samuel will deliver his people. But Samuel cannot be hooked to either Moses or Samson, both of whom were born into situations of distress (Miscall 1986, 2–3). "Based only on Samuel's birth story, it cannot be confidently stated that Samuel will, or will not, have something to do with salvation from the hand of the Philistines" (1986, 3).

The name of one of Eli's sons, Phinehas, links Eli to Aaron, whose grandson also was named Phinehas (Judg 20:27–28). Has the house of Aaron been figuratively transferred to Eli? "We can ask of the house of Eli what another will ask of the band of prophets, 'Who is their father?'

---

[16] "As a wife, Hannah has only one justification for her existence—to bear a son and male heir for her husband. Lacking that honor, she is accounted worthless. It is not simply that she is childless. If she had only girl children, she would still be accounted unfortunate. Only male children can redeem woman's existence. The idea that she might have a girl rather than a boy is, in fact, not even considered in the text" (Ruether 1982, 182; see also Ozick 1994, 89).

[17] The metaphor of narrative lures is refreshing, especially for islanders, because it depicts the reader as the fished and not just the fisher.

(1 Sam 10:12). The question is unanswerable. The lack of a clinching genealogy for Eli is emphasized by the presence of one for Elkanah" (Miscall
1986, 9).

These examples of the workings of lures indicate that Miscall's mode
of reading does *not* entail that "anything goes." He identifies narrative
lures that point readers to other stories, then explains how the text does
not hook these stories together. Critics who decisively link these stories,
or deny that they may be linked, ignore the undecidability of the text. The
relation between 1 Samuel and the book of Judges is a case in point:

> The question cannot be definitely decided in favor of just one alterna-
> tive. All three, and probably more, hold. 1 Samuel *continues* the narrative
> of Judges; it *marks a break*, since something new is to happen; it *repeats*
> Judges, particularly from chapter 13 on, since Samuel's birth story "re-
> peats" Samson's. (Miscall 1986, 8; my italics)

Miscall releases the text from the "imaginary authors" and "linear readings" of modern readers in order that it may bear (bare) more than one
meaning.[18]

Miscall's approach is both text-initiated (lures) and reader-responsive
(undecidability). Tracing narrative lures requires imagination, and it may
lead the reader away from the text under examination. One may consequently ask, Why bother with narrative lures if, in the end, one will not
be able to disentangle (decide, clinch) what they mean? Miscall's characterization of Hannah offers interesting solutions to this utilitarian critique.

Miscall rightly reads 1 Sam 1–3 as a birth story, but he does not include the most crucial character in a birth story, a mother, in his list of
"main characters" (1986, 1; cf. Fuchs 1985; Meyers 1994, 94–95). He jumps
out of the canoe to fish for lures! He now and then turns back to Hannah
(canoe) to note her barrenness and conflict with Peninnah, her distress
and request from Yhwh, her face-off with Eli and dedication of Samuel,
as openings for exploring the dissemination of words (lures) in the story,
a process he calls *metonymic dispersion*. But for Miscall, the reader is as
blind as Eli:

> We are then in Eli's position and have to accept the possibility that we
> can misjudge what we are seeing, but, unlike Eli, we are not then pro-
> vided with the means to decide whether we have judged correctly or
> incorrectly. We are akin to Eli in his later condition—blind, unable to

---

[18] Miscall's distinction between *words* (text) and *meanings* (interpretation)
points to the constraint that he sets: "In the concern for 'words,' at one stage I treat
them as material entities on the page with little or no regard for their primary and
explicit meanings. There is wordplay, dissemination, dispersal of the words. The
text is not to be reduced finally to a set of meanings. However, I do not remain always at that stage of reading but also talk of themes and meanings. The text is not
to be reduced finally to just the words on the page. The two approaches, 'words'
and 'meanings,' undermine each other and prevent each other from producing
the true reading or interpretation of the text" (1986, 23–24).

see—in the sense that we are unable to decide exactly what we are seeing. (1986, 13)

Saying that the text is undecidable, therefore, in this regard, is a form of
control.

Nonetheless, Miscall did not trace all the lures in this birth story. I
track two of those lures here, one that he ignored and one he dismissed;
in other words, I am lured to Miscall's blind spots. Attending to these
lures will not ease the blindness that Miscall revealed, but it will extend
the workings of Miscall's reading in order to clear a path for my analysis
in the next section.

Miscall agrees that the primary concern of Samuel's birth story (1 Sam
1:1–2:26) is not Samuel but Hannah's distress and request from Yhwh
(1986, 10; so Alter 1981, 81–86). Her distress is a reflex of the bitterness of
Israel in Egypt. The situations of Hannah and Israel, one personal and the
other national, coincide in Miscall's reading:

> They [Israel] cry to God; he hears their cry and remembers his covenant.
> Moses is sent to bring them out of the house of slavery. The Lord remem-
> bers Hannah, and Samuel comes to relieve her misery, to blunt her rival's
> provocations. (1986, 11)

Miscall does not pursue this intertextual relation because "1 Samuel does
not begin with a specific problem or crisis that is to be addressed and cor-
rected" (1986, 11). He jumps to another theme of the story, eating and
drinking, on which he attempts everyday and ritual readings (see also
John T. Willis 1972; Meyers 1994). He anchors his double reading on 1 Sam
1:7b, which can be translated as (1) Hannah "wept and would not eat"
(*everyday* option) or (2) Hannah "lamented and fasted" (*ritual* reading). As
expected, Miscall argues that the text does not endorse one translation
while rejecting the other. Both readings are possible, together. If we bring
this "everyday-ritual" complex to bear on the beginning of 1 Samuel, we
find "a specific problem or crisis" that the birth of Samuel resolves.
Miscall's analysis of 1 Sam 1:7b is, here, the lure that reopens a reading
that he has already rejected, namely, that there is no crisis that the birth
of Samuel resolves (cf. Brueggemann 1990, 34–35).

Whereas Israel faced an international crisis in Egypt, Hannah faces a
personal crisis at home (so Doody 1994, 113). The everyday and ritual coincide in the narrator's claim that Hannah's barrenness was worsened by
her rival's taunts "that Yhwh had closed her womb" (1 Sam 1:6b). Her crisis consists of (everyday) taunting by Peninnah and (ritual) closure of her
womb by Yhwh. Such is the setting of Hannah's vow, the string of words
that breaks Yhwh's grip over her womb. The birth of Samuel will free
Hannah from the crisis (thanks to Peninnah) brought by her barrenness
(thanks to Yhwh). Nonetheless, Hannah must still labor before she is re-
lieved of her crisis. This lure points me to Hannah's vow, as a step toward
her relief (see §5.3).

The foregoing suggests that a double reading does not always make the reader choose between alternatives. Alternatives supplement each other. In other words, the text is determinate as a complex. This points us to the underside of Miscall's approach: *a concealed expectation that texts are decidable.* The problem is not the decidability of the text, because the text suggests (i.e., decides) more than one alternative reading, but the tendency to privilege one reading over the other. Miscall's challenge, therefore, is against critics who easily dismiss an alternative reading that does not fit their "larger picture" (politics of coherence), but, in light of the foregoing review, Miscall too is a victim of this inhibiting way of reading.

•

The link between the birth story and the Song of Hannah (1 Sam 2:1–10) is the second lure I wish to address. Miscall finds no parallels between these two texts:

> Hannah praises the Lord, but the praise is general and universal and does not include his specific action on her behalf. . . . [M]any of Hannah's statements in the Song have the flavor of platitudes with no predictable relevance to the context. There is no proportion, direct or inverse. (1986, 15)

> [T]he Song has no simple, mechanical relation to the narrative. . . . The Song as a whole is a lure; it offers much but produces little. (1986, 16)

It is ironic that Miscall, who thrives on exploring narrative lures, reaches a point of impasse. There are ways out of this impasse, but Miscall does not pursue them because they do not fit his larger picture. One way to link the narrative with the song comes from his explanation of the link between promise/judgment and fulfillment/dissemination: "Judgments, prophecies, etc., are not fulfilled *in an exact, proportional manner, i.e., literally. Yet they are fulfilled 'literally,'* taking 'literal' as meaning 'letters,' 'words,' and 'written'" (1986, 22; my italics). A text may disseminate into another text by means of the "letters, words, and written." In other words, the critic may find literal lures of the narrative in Hannah's song even if the "explicit and primary" meaning of the song has nothing to do with the narrative.

The reading I propose below, supplementing previous readings, presupposes a literal (Miscall) link between the story and Song of Hannah. The lure that releases this reading is Hannah's vow, which she uttered in response to a crisis in her life. That helps me make sense of the opening remarks in the song:

> And Hannah prayed:
> My heart exults in the LORD;
> I have triumphed ["My horn is high"] through the LORD.
> I gloat ["My mouth is wide"] over my enemies;
> I rejoice in Your deliverance. (1 Sam 2:1)

Owing to Yhwh's deliverance, the song marks the end of her crisis. Hannah exults that Yhwh delivered her from her enemies, but (in her story) Yhwh played a part in her troubles. She thanks Yhwh for delivering her from himself, as if she is a character who is both pious and precarious.

I owe my transtextual reading to the workings of Miscall's reading. In his analysis of Hannah's song, for instance, he presents Hannah as a knowledgeable woman who "knows to whom to pray in her distress— Yahweh, not just Elohim" (1986, 15). I add that Hannah is also a brave woman who knows whom to thank for her deliverance—Yhwh—even if Yhwh was also her troubler. My reading transfers Jephthah's reproach to Hannah:[19] "Alas, Yhwh! You have brought me low; you have become my troubler!" The song will take a critical turn in my transtextual reading (in contrast to Ruether 1982, 184; Walters 1994, 76).

The next section revisits two lures in Miscall's reading—the first (Hannah's vow) he passes over and the second (Hannah's song) he dismisses. Both lures fit the "larger picture" that I have been exploring in this book. In that respect, I use Miscall's reading to lure me to issues that interest me already. In other words, the critic's interests determine what and how she reads, even if she thinks that the text is both decidable and undecidable, and indeterminate.[20]

5.3 Hannah's Decisive Words

Hannah's vow and song lure me to the regulations of a wife's vow in Num 30 (see §5.4), and vice versa, providing me with another opportunity to revisit the relationship between law and narrative. The following transtextual reading of different literary types also creeps in the footsteps of Miscall.

I offer an alternative to Jobling's "too positive" reading of Hannah's vow and song (1998, 129), which portrays her as an ambitious woman who desired a son in the service of Yhwh. Her desire comes in response to her experience of a rotten priestly regime (1998, 132–34; so Silber 1988, 66). "Hannah is a woman of powerful initiative who does not live under

---

[19] There is a difference between the birth story of Hannah's son and the account of the sacrifice of Jephthah's daughter, for Yhwh delivered Hannah from her enemies whereas Jephthah delivered his daughter to Yhwh in ashes. The Song of Hannah, therefore, exposes something that is ignored in the story of Jephthah's daughter—the deliverance of a female character and the courage to thank and/or critique Yhwh. Such are the workings of narrative lures, suggesting alternative readings without preferring one in particular.

[20] When one reads a text across other texts, many texts, as in this transoceanic event, the text becomes indeterminate. I do not locate the cause of indeterminacy in the text alone, or upon the reader alone, but at the "crossing point" of transtextuality. In other words, if it was possible to read a text on its own accord, without the coercion of other "texts," literally or otherwise, it would have been easier to make the text determinate.

monarchy, yet monarchy has co-opted her services too—in the Deuteronomic text, in the process of canonization, and in the tradition of biblical
interpretation" (Jobling 1998, 165; cf. Cook 1999, 37). I follow Jobling's lead
with another reading that resists the narrator's desire, and I co-opt his
forward (to the monarchy) and backward (to the women of Judges) approach into circumreading Num 30 with the story of Hannah (see also
Silber 1988, 66; Cook 1999, 34–35).[21] Moreover, I co-opt Cook's two-part
reading (Hannah "finds" and "uses" her voice) by making Hannah also
use her voice against Yhwh (1999, 35–49).

The birth story is introduced as an everyday affair. It begins at the
home of Elkanah, who is presented as the product of his paternal lineage,
traced back to his great-great-grandfather (1 Sam 1:1), but his two wives
are distinguished between the have (Peninnah) and have-not (Hannah).
Whereas the male subject is firmly anchored, the female characters are
adrift on something over which they do not have complete control. Their
subject (non)positions involve the fruitful cooperation of Elkanah and, in
Hannah's case, Yhwh. Moreover, the narrator influences how they are
perceived.

The narrator reverses the subject position of the wives. Hannah
(have-not) is named first, which does not necessarily mean that she was
the first wife (in contrast to Patrick 1703), but Peninnah's ability to produce is acknowledged first:

> He had two wives,
>   The first named Hannah
>   And the second Peninnah
>   Peninnah had children
>   But Hannah was childless (1:2)

The narrator is not troubled by Elkanah's marriage to two women (so
Kirkpatrick 1886), but with Hannah's nonproductivity. Having two wives,
one of whom bore children, proves that Elkanah is not responsible for
Hannah's childlessness. He is productive. So is Peninnah. But Peninnah's
fertility, hence the opportunity to preserve Elkanah's lineage, is ignored.
The children that Peninnah *has*, who are not named, are no different from
the children that Hannah *has not*. In that regard, Peninnah is *literally*
(Miscall) barren. She bears children that do not interest the narrator, who
shifts the focus from the story's family (everyday) backdrop to a public
(ritual) setting (Meyers 1994, 103).

Elkanah usually takes his two wives every year to Shiloh for worship
and sacrifice. New characters are introduced, the two priests at Shiloh,

---

[21] "One advantage of a synchronic analysis is that the reader can move forward or backward through time. Foucault is correct that 'the lateral connections
across different forms of knowledge and from one focus of politicization to another (makes it possible) to rearticulate categories which were previously kept
separate' [Foucault 1980, 127]" (Bach 1999, 146).

Hophni and Phinehas, and their father, Eli (1:3). Eli is identified in relation to (i.e., anchored by) his sons, but he plays a more significant role in the narrative. He is the "priest" whom Hannah encounters at the temple (1:9–10, 24–25), and the one to whom Samuel turns for guidance (1 Sam 3). The characters who are introduced as priests at Shiloh, Hophni and Phinehas, are not associated with the temple at this point of the narrative. Similar to the way he treats Peninnah's children, the narrator literally (Miscall) dismisses Hophni and Phinehas early in his account (cf. 2:12–17).

During one of the visits to Shiloh, Elkanah's two literally (Miscall) barren wives quarrel, for he treats them differently. He favors Hannah (have-not), and jealousy on the part of Peninnah (have) is both implied and justified (Klein 1994, 78–79). The everyday and ritual cross in Hannah's childlessness, acknowledged by the narrator (1:5) and underscored by Peninnah's taunts (1:6). Unable to comfort Hannah with food and words (1:4–8), Elkanah also fails to give her the "seed of men." His rhetorical question, "Am I not more devoted to you than ten sons?" is insulting (cf. Doody 1994, 109; Amit 1994, 75).[22] How can a childless woman know what the devotion of ten sons is like? She does not even know if Elkanah is as devoted as one son![23] In response, Hannah approaches the house of Yhwh with her double miseries of being childless and being ridiculed by Peninnah and Elkanah.

Hannah does not direct words toward her mockers but takes her anguish directly to Yhwh, who is blamed for her barrenness, with a vow (*neder*):

> And she vowed a vow and said, "Yhwh of hosts, if you would indeed look on the affliction of your maidservant and remember [*zkr*] me, and not forget your maidservant, but give [*ntn*] to your maidservant a seed [*zr'*] of men, then I will give [*ntn*] him to Yhwh all the days of his life and a razor shall not come upon his head." (1:11)

Her vow is not rash (so Brueggemann 1990, 36). A woman who feels afflicted asks for deliverance, and she does not give Yhwh a chance to decide how he should deliver her. Hannah decides for him: she wants

---

[22] Klein offers a *mimetic* alternative: "[I]s not your love for me greater than your desire for ten sons?" (1994, 87). This resonates with Ozick's feminist reading: "Hannah, cries Elkanah, with or without sons *you have value in yourself!* What Elkanah—a feminist hero—has discovered in himself is the first principle of feminism: the ethical passion that expresses itself against instrumentality, against woman-as-instrument, against woman-as-the-instrument-of-societal-policy" (1994, 90; cf. Doody 1994, 108–9; Jobling 1998, 131).

[23] Marcia Falk sees Hannah as a doubly misunderstood woman, "as she weeps—in her sorrow—by Elkanah, her husband; as she prays—in her yearning—by Eli, the high priest. Yet Hannah has a voice; she means to be heard" (1994, 96). She did not respond to Elkanah's rhetorical question about "ten sons" because he would still not understand her answer.

Yhwh to remember (*zkr*) her with a seed (*zr'*) of men. She also decides what will become of the gift that she requires: she will give (*ntn*) him to Yhwh all the days of his life, and a razor shall not come upon his head. Yhwh closed her womb; she puts a demand upon Yhwh. As a consequence, Yhwh is put in a position where he has to respond, not with words but with deeds. Hannah is a decisive character who puts Yhwh in the position of responsibility, where he can accept or reject her demand.

Still, the vow may also be read as a pejorative response against the taunting by both Peninnah and Elkanah (cf. Klein 1994, 83–86). The vow implies that Hannah was barren because no one gave her the "seed of men." It blames Elkanah, who has given his "seed of men" to Peninnah. Moreover, neither Elkanah nor Peninnah shall reap the "seed of men" that Hannah expects from Yhwh because the child-to-be will be given to Yhwh, who is depicted as a seed-giver. This is the *everyday* reading. In the *ritual* reading, on the other hand, Hannah vows to dedicate her child to Yhwh by submitting him to a Nazirite lifestyle, implied in the avowal that no razor shall touch the child's hair. This ritual reading, however, is made problematic by the chance that Nazirites must cut their hair (cf. Num 6:18–19). But the text does not allow me to reject the ritual alternative because Hannah's vow is made at a ritual space. This text presents alternative readings, so it is decidable. But it does not allow me to affirm or reject one alternative over the other, so it is also undecidable.

Eli witnesses Hannah's vow but he cannot hear her words, and he confronts Hannah before Yhwh can respond. Thinking that Hannah is drunk, he rebukes her: "How long will you make a drunken spectacle of yourself? Sober up!" (1:14). Eli aims to nullify whatever Hannah is praying for, perceived as the rash words of a drunkard, but her reply indicates that her words cannot be silenced:[24]

> No, my lord! I am a very unhappy [*qᵉšat-ruaḥ*] woman. I have drunk no wine or strong drink, but I have been pouring out my life [*nfš*] to Yhwh. Do not take your maidservant for a worthless woman; I have only been speaking all this time out of my great anguish and distress. (1:15–16).

Eli cannot annul her vow, and he sends her away: "Go in peace, and may the God of Israel grant you what you have asked [*š'l*] of him" (1:17). Eli decides not to restrain Hannah, thereby assuming the subject position which Num 30 reserves for the husband (cf. Scott L. Harris 1992, 30), that is, the position of annulling or confirming his wife's vow. According to this transtextual view, two other characters play the husband-role for

---

[24] "In the words of the feminist theologian Nelle Morton, we need 'to hear each other into speech,' so that listening becomes the stimulus for expression instead of—as we are more accustomed to having it—speech being the stimulus for our hearing" (Marcia Falk 1994, 101). In this regard, Eli fails the feminist test. Moreover, as in the story of Jephthah's daughter, so does Yhwh.

Hannah: Yhwh is asked for the "seed of men" and Eli ignores (as if to confirm) her vow.

Hannah departs with the perception that another man endorses her request, even though he does not know what she asks for. After the encounter with Eli, Hannah's disposition begins to change. She eats and is no longer downcast (1:18). I imagine that her "anguish and distress" are beginning to be resolved.

The story continues as if Elkanah does not know of Hannah's vow, so he has no chance to pass judgment on it.[25] Hannah's fate changes in a short narrative space. The combination of being known by Elkanah and remembered by Yhwh leads to the realization of her request, a son whom she names Samuel. Hannah bypasses Elkanah earlier to ask for the "seed of men" from Yhwh, but the narrator is not ready to let Elkanah go. Elkanah "knows" Hannah before he exits.[26] On the other hand, Peninnah's criticisms are no longer applicable, and she disappears into the rest of the family. The productive Peninnah loses her edge. No longer named or heard, she disappears into Elkanah's household (cf. 1:21).

While the face of one wife fades into the household, the other sets herself apart (so Fuchs 1985, 125–26). With a son in her arms, Hannah decides not to accompany Elkanah and his family during their yearly journey to the house of God. It is not clear how many years she stays home, but it is long enough to wean her child. This is the *everyday* reading. A *ritual* reading is also possible. The reason Hannah gives for not taking part in the annual sacrifice suggests that she is also keeping distance from the face of God (cf. Silber 1988, 69; Amit 1994, 75–76): "Hannah did not go up. She said to her husband, 'When the child is weaned, I will bring him. For when he has appeared before Yhwh, he must remain there for good'" (1:22). Based on her response alone, one may think that Hannah had vowed to bring the child to Yhwh *after he was weaned*. Multiple readings are possible. On the one hand, we find a dedicated woman who convinces her husband that she wants time to make sure that she fulfills her vow properly. She is being considerate, not wanting to burden Yhwh and his attendants with a nursing child. And for the sake of her child, Hannah does not want to give him up during a fragile stage of his life. Hannah is a considerate worshiper and a caring mother.

On the other hand, we also hear a mother who is not ready to let go of her child. She was ridiculed for not bearing any children and, now that she is no longer childless, she is not ready to give up the child who brings peace to her life. To give up her child may bring more scoffs upon her as

---

[25] It is only after Samuel is born that Elkanah endorses her vow (if we follow LXX and 4QSam): "Do as you think best. Stay home until you have weaned him. May Yhwh fulfill the utterance of your mouth [MT: his word]" (1 Sam 1:23). See also Walters 1988.

[26] Just as Hannah's barrenness is not her responsibility alone, so is her fertility not just the responsibility of Yhwh.

"child abandoner" (cf. Klein 1994, 83) or "child abuser" (cf. Jobling 1998, 306). She is not quite ready to be made barren again, so keeping the child until he is weaned is her way of looking out for herself. On this count also, Hannah is a considerate character.

A third reading is possible, reading Hannah's response to Elkanah in light of her vow to Yhwh and presentation of the child to Eli:

1 Sam 1:11	1 Sam 1:22	1 Sam 1:26–28
And she vowed a vow saying, "Yhwh of hosts, if you would indeed look on the affliction of your maidservant and remember me, and not forget your maidservant, but give [ntn] to your maidservant a seed of men, then *I will give [ntn] him to Yhwh all the days of his life* and a razor shall not come upon his head."	Hannah did not go up. She said to her husband, "When the child is weaned, *I will bring [bô']* him. For when he has appeared before Yhwh, he must remain there for good."	She said, "Please, my lord! As you live, my lord, I am the woman who stood here beside you and prayed to Yhwh. It was for this boy that I prayed; and Yhwh has granted [ntn] my petition [š'l]. So *I lend [š'l] him to Yhwh; for all his days, he is lent to Yhwh."*

Things have changed since Hannah made her vow. In the first place, she had vowed to give the child to Yhwh all the days of his life, but she now delays bringing the child to Yhwh. She compromises her vow by keeping the child until he is weaned. She will give the child to Yhwh for all the days of his life *minus* the weaning period. In the literal (Miscall) sense, Hannah breaks her vow.

In the second place, Hannah's response in 1 Sam 1:22 gives the impression that she is bringing the child to Yhwh not because of the vow but because she decides to do so. She decides on her own; Elkanah has no say. Her subject position has changed from that of the anguished and distressed woman who asked that she may be given a male seed, to the nursing mother who decides that it is not time to bring her son to Yhwh. When Hannah made her vow, she was willing to risk what she did not have (a child). But now that she holds a child in her arms, she has second thoughts about giving the child to Yhwh, as if she is a reluctant giver (Walters 1988, 399–400). With a wordplay that overlooks her vow, Hannah decides to lend (š'l) the child to Yhwh because he granted her petition (š'l). She does not acknowledge that her vow was what set the š'l-process in motion. In other words, she literally (Miscall) erases the vow from her exchanges with Eli and Elkanah. This vow-maker is a vow-breaker!

From a metacritical point of view, I also read Hannah's excuse for holding on to her child as a critique of the way that characters are quickly cast off from the narrative. She was not ousted by Peninnah's taunts (words), because she uttered a vow, and now, in a narrative in which Peninnah is quickly dismissed, Hannah opts to hold on to another character, her child. When she has to choose between keeping her vow to Yhwh and keeping her child to herself, Hannah decides literally (Miscall) to break her vow. Like Jephthah's daughter, she demands a delay, which means that she fails to give her child to Yhwh all the days of his life. In this transgressive reading, Hannah's delay cries against the sacrifice of Jephthah's daughter by exposing the fragility of vows. Hannah offers a critique of the way that human and/or literary characters are easily cast off, as if to say that characters should not be broken, as vows are.

Taking the gender code into account, this reading represents Hannah as a determined and courageous character (so Jobling). She both stirs up Yhwh's memory, moving him to issue the "seed of men," and literally (Miscall) breaks the vow she had given to Yhwh. Hannah realizes the limits of words, the undecidability of texts, and the ability of characters to transcend them. She transcends the taunts of Peninnah, the rebuke of Eli, the control of Yhwh over her womb, the annual rituals of Elkanah's household, and the vow she set on herself. She then adds a song (1 Sam 2:1–10), a form of expression that is also performative. The anguished and distressed character again bursts into words.

The placement of the song has been questioned because it lacks historical links to the narrative. The song sounds more like the gaiety of a victorious hero, upon deliverance from his enemies, than the delight of a woman. Even the textual lures that point the song to the narrative are fragile. The barren woman in the song bears seven children (1 Sam 2:5), whereas Hannah bears (after Samuel) three sons and two daughters (1 Sam 2:21). Historical and literary critics, therefore, reject any effort to relate the song and the narrative: They are strangers that meet in the text of 1 Sam 1–2.

I propose, on the other hand, to read them transtextually. They may have no historical links, but they share the same space (cf. Cook 1999, 40–49). I propose to read the song as an interrupting voice. Hannah is in the process of lending her son to Yhwh, through Eli, and before she returns home she prays a song.[27] The song is the next moment in Hannah's critical (mis)conduct, and I assume that it is the reflection of the "Hannah" character in the narrative.[28]

---

[27] The singular male subject in 1 Sam 2:11 ("Then he went home to Ramah . . .") implies that Hannah stays with Samuel for a while. She binds to Samuel but breaks from Elkanah.

[28] I read Hannah as if she is both "a hard, obstinate or stubborn woman" (Ahlström cited in Muraoka 1996, 98) and a "persistent" (McCarter) and "ambitious" (Jobling) character. She is a heroine (Ozick) who is both ordinary and extraordinary (Marcia Falk 1994, 98).

The song marks the end of Hannah's distress. She has survived the taunting of Peninnah and Yhwh's hold over her womb (cf. Fuchs 1985, 129).[29] The song is personal and, in this first reading, its tone is complimentary (cf. Doody 1994; Cook 1998). She exults in Yhwh, who gave her victory (1 Sam 2:1), acknowledging his unique reputation as the most holy and steadfast God (2:2). She demands her listeners not to talk with lofty pride and arrogance, because Yhwh is all-knowing and he will judge each person according to his actions (2:3). She focuses on the double effects of Yhwh's actions: Yhwh breaks the power of the mighty but girds the weak, he "deals death and gives life, casts down into Sheol (*š'l*) and raises up, . . . [he] makes poor and makes rich, he casts down, he also lifts high" (2:6–7). The hungry shall hunger no more (cf. Lewis 1985) while the once-sated shall hire for food, and the barren shall bear children while the mother of many shall be forlorn, all because of Yhwh's actions (2:4–5, 8–9). In the context of Hannah's experiences, the song portrays a grateful mother who rejoices in Yhwh's deliverance and protection.

But by closing with a different subject, the song invites a second reading. Whereas 2:1–9 focuses on Hannah's enemies, 2:10 turns to Yhwh's enemies:

> The foes of Yhwh shall be shattered;
> He will thunder against them in the heavens.
> Yhwh will judge the ends of the earth.
> He will give power to his king,
> And triumph to his anointed one.

The change of subject literally (Miscall) entangles Hannah's dilemma with Yhwh's actions. Yhwh will shatter both of their enemies, and give power and victory to his king. Yhwh is both a deliverer (2:1–9) and one who empowers those whom he favors. This concluding affirmation anticipates the Israelite monarchy,[30] which is portrayed as Yhwh's instrument for "judging the ends of the earth" (Brueggemann 1990, 43–44). It also lures us back to Hannah's situation and how she received power and triumph (from Yhwh) over her enemies. According to this transgressive reading, Hannah is "the king"!

Looking back at Hannah's situation produces another reading. The praise of Yhwh for the future empowerment and protection of his anointed, his favored one, recalls the way Yhwh initially ignored

---

[29] For Doody, Hannah's song substitutes for her son. "Hannah becomes poetical and powerfully verbal, giving voice at the moment of intense pain, the loss of her son. Her canticle, her voicing, is a substitution for the child she is in the process of losing" (1994, 110).

[30] On the other hand, in light of the "extended book of Judges," Jobling suggests that "[w]hat Hannah celebrates is the social revolution that *gets rid of* kings, and the positive reference to the king in the final verse seems to have no business being there" (1998, 173).

Hannah. What Yhwh will do for his favored king, a male character, he did not do for Hannah. She who is named *favor, ḥannah,* did not receive deliverance until she uttered her vow. Strictly speaking, her deliverance was not due to the gratuitous actions of an "all-knowing God" (2:3) but in response to her demands. In this reading, the song takes a stab at Yhwh. The vow made Yhwh remember Hannah, and her song exposes the androcentric nature of the story-world. In both cases, Hannah literally re-members herself! The song both praises (from an M-/Israelite perspective) and sentences (from an F-perspective) Yhwh. This double reading accounts for the (un)decidability of the text, for it invites alternative readings and unfastens the hold of decisive critics, especially the ritual type of readers.

The birth story of Samuel ends when he enters the service of Yhwh under the guidance of the priest Eli (1 Sam 2:11), but Hannah does not yet exit the story. She does not totally let go of her son. When she makes the yearly pilgrimage with her husband to offer the annual sacrifices, Hannah brings a robe for Samuel (2:19; see also Silber 1988, 73). The child of the vow is on loan to Yhwh, and each year the child is clothed with a robe that reminds him of his mother. The vow is further compromised. Unlike Yhwh, who appears to suffer a bad case of memory loss when it comes to women, Hannah does not forget her son (cf. Fuchs 1985, 133). To adopt Klein's conclusion, "Victim and redeemer, Hannah reinforces the patriarchal image of women" (1994, 92).

As far as Hannah is concerned, her child is not given (*ntn*) totally to Yhwh. Eli, on the other hand, drives to make the transference of the child final by praying for offspring to take Samuel's place in Hannah's life:

> Eli would bless Elkanah and his wife, and say, "May Yhwh *repay* [LXX and 4QSam; MT: "grant"] you offspring by this woman in place of the loan [*š'l*] she made to Yhwh. Then they would return home. And [LXX and 4QSam; MT: *kî*] Yhwh visited [*pqd*] Hannah; she conceived and bore three sons and two daughters. Young Samuel meanwhile grew up [*gdl*] in the service of Yhwh. (2:20–21)

Eli seems to think that more children will satisfy Hannah, and maybe keep her away. Whether she welcomes the extra children for whom she has not asked, we cannot determine. The narrator quickly sends her home to her children, but keeps Samuel behind to "grow up" (*gdl*) in the service of Yhwh. The focus of the narrative shifts from Hannah to Samuel, the product of her vow.

Before I return to the regulations over a wife's vow in Num 30, I offer four more observations from Hannah's vow-story. These observations will identify places where this narrative "crosses" the regulations of Num 30.

First, this story presents a woman who is in control of her vow while she is under her husband's (Elkanah's) house. Hannah makes the vow on her own, then fulfills/breaks it despite being rebuked by her (other) "husband" (Eli) (cf. Rakover 1992). The authority of a husband over his wife's vow is not recognized in 1 Sam 1–2. This story presents an alternative to the Num 30 regulations.

Second, the interactions between Hannah and Eli suggest that vows do not always get fulfilled to their minutest details. Hannah compromises her vow in the process of fulfilling it, by loaning the son to Yhwh for only a part of his life, and Eli compromises Hannah's compromise by praying for more children (to distract her from the memory of Samuel). Vows are ways of making compromises, and their fulfillment also involves making compromises, depending on how they compromise the subjects involved. Something is both gained and lost in the process. According to this reading, the possibility (reality?) of compromises unsettles the ideologies behind Num 30.

Third, Hannah's decisive disposition in the story raises the question of subjectivity. In the foregoing reading, Hannah separates herself from her husband's household, by opting to stay behind until Samuel is weaned, and from Yhwh's control, by compromising her vow. But she would not remove herself from both (everyday and ritual) spheres. She returns to Elkanah's house with five more children, and is linked to Yhwh on account of the son she has loaned to his service. She seeks to be apart from Elkanah and Yhwh, and she becomes a_part of both. She complements (or should I say, ambiguates?) her subject position, being on both sides of alternative readings, and she thereby problematizes colonizing readings.

Finally, the tension between the words and deeds of Hannah suggests that this text is ontologically decidable. It has more than one meaning, and it only seems undecidable when one of its meanings does not fit the "larger picture" that critics imagine. Though Hannah performs (*deed*) something different from what she vows (*words*), so that her deeds and words appear to be contradictory, the foregoing reading embraces those differences. I read this text as a complex of twists and turns, promises and compromises.

Changing one's mind and compromising one's vow are crucial elements of vow-events. The tendency to make compromises indicates that words do not have full control over the deeds they trigger. This suggests that texts and subjects may do other than they say; in other words, deeds do not always manifest the words to which they respond.

Hannah's story, vow, and song are ontologically decidable, and decisive. They have already said what they have to say, even to the extent of resisting some of my readings, already, and readers need to cope with the possibility that, as Hannah has done, *texts too may do other than they say.*

5.4 The Wife of Numbers 30

The lure that brought me to the story of Hannah is her vow, which sets the limit in the foregoing reading. I explored the dynamics of Hannah's interactions with her "husbands" (Elkanah, Eli, Yhwh), and there are different ways of applying these dynamics to Num 30.

On the one hand, one may argue, on historical grounds, that Num 30 has nothing to do with 1 Sam 1–2. The two texts come from different contexts, featuring two different genres; they speak past each other (cf. Willis 1997, 59). In that regard, one should not circumread them. On the other hand, drawn by the lure of the vow and the placement of both texts in the same book, another may circumread 1 Sam 1–2 and Num 30. I follow this alternative path for another excuse: I am also interested in the relation between different literary types, between law and narrative. Numbers 30 and the story of Hannah present an opportunity to explore this further, as well as to evaluate Miscall's claim that texts are undecidable. Based on the foregoing readings, the relation between law and narrative may be explained in several ways.

Along the direction I followed in this chapter, the story of Hannah presents a situation in which the regulations over vows that a woman makes while she is in her husband's house (Num 30:11–16) are ineffective. These regulations give the impression that the matter of a wife's vow is simply between the woman and her husband, with Yhwh brought in to release the innocent party. On the other hand, Hannah's story exposes other elements ignored in Num 30.

First, the matter of placement. Strictly speaking, Hannah's vow is not made "in the house of her *'îš*" but somewhere near the doorpost of the temple (1 Sam 1:9),[31] for the purpose of making her an accepted member "in the house of her *'îš*." In this regard, Elkanah does not have full authority over her vow as prescribed in Num 30:11–16. Moreover, he is not always aware of what happens to Hannah, learning of her vow through information she volunteers later (cf. 1 Sam 1:20). The authority of a husband is pacified in this narrative.

Second, the gender code. The story of Hannah's vow overturns the predominant view in Num 30 that a man has authority over his women. Hannah does not allow Eli (who played the role of the husband) to annul her vow, even though he tries on the same day she made it. Hannah's rejection of Eli's rebuke suggests that a woman who makes a vow, in any man's house, is not as naive as the regulations in Num 30 imply. She is decisive, and she resists any man who may try to annul her wishes. Numbers 30 does not take into consideration women like Hannah. Her story exposes both the legislator's simplistic view of "a woman in her man's house," and the imprudence of his regulations. In Hannah's case, she makes the final decision concerning her vow.

Third, the theological question. Hannah involves Yhwh in the event

---

[31] Since the temple was also the house of Eli (cf. 1 Sam 2:22ff.), Eli qualifies as the *'îš* who may annul her vow. In this regard, Hannah is the literal (Miscall) wife of two men.

of the vow, with a share in the problem and its solution. This differs from the mechanical role Yhwh plays in Num 30 of releasing wives from their obligations. Yhwh has an obligation to fulfill: to give Hannah the seeds of men, which releases the closure of her womb. Hannah makes Yhwh work against himself and, according to this reading, she exposes the double effects of his deeds with her song. Hannah makes Yhwh more responsible than Num 30 implies.

And fourth, the limits of the law and the complexity of vow-events. If the foregoing reading incorporating multiple husbands holds, then Num 30 gives Hannah the right both to *fulfill* and *break* her vow. Since Elkanah is not aware of her vow and Yhwh is silent in the process, Hannah must do as she has obliged herself (Num 30:12). On the other hand, she is released from her vow because Eli rebuked her. In light of Num 30, therefore, Hannah is obliged both to fulfill and break her vow. This is just what she did, as proposed above.

Concerning the relationship between law and narrative, this reading explores an instance in which a law *crosses* a narrative. On the one hand, one may argue that the narrative deconstructs the law. On the other hand, reading in the opposite direction, one may argue that the regulations in Num 30:4–9, 11–16 are designed to prevent the kind of situations I read in(to) the story of Hannah. The law aims to put a full stop to that kind of silliness (e.g., Hannah's rejection of Eli's rebuke). After all, it is in the nature of the law to set limits. Both readings are possible, lured by the texts, depending on what direction one takes in exploring the transtextual relation between them.

6

A Woman No Man Unveiled

You shall not ill-treat any widow or orphan. If you do mistreat them, I will heed their outcry as soon as they cry out to Me, and My anger shall blaze forth and I will put you to the sword, and your own wives shall become widows and your children orphans. (Exod 22:21–23 Tanakh)

A widow, or a divorced woman, or one who is degraded by harlotry— such he [a priest] may not marry. Only a virgin of his own kin may he take to wife—that he may not profane his offspring among his kin, for I the LORD have sanctified him. (Lev 21:14–15 Tanakh)

They [priests] shall not marry widows or divorced women; they may marry only virgins of the stock of the House of Israel, or widows who are widows of priests. (Ezek 44:22 Tanakh)

6.0 To Love the Widow and Divorcée More Than the Torah

Without husbands, widows and divorcées are figures of helplessness. They are vulnerable (to others, including other husbands) (cf. Isa 1:23; 10:1–2; Job 24:3; Ps 94:6–7), so God takes them under his care (cf. Deut 10:17–18; 14:28–29; 24:17–22; Hos 14:3; Jer 49:11; Prov 15:25; Mal 3:5). Several biblical critics follow God's lead by demanding responsibility on their behalf (cf. Job 31:16–23). Levinas was devoted to this drive, treating widows, along with orphans, as manifestations of the "face of the other" who always already oblige us:

> One's duty regarding the other who makes appeal to one's responsibility is an investing of one's own freedom. In responsibility, which is, as such, irrecusable and non-transferable, I am instituted as non-interchangeable: I am chosen as unique and incomparable. My freedom and my rights, before manifesting themselves in my opposition to the free-

dom and rights of the other person, will manifest themselves precisely in the form of responsibility, in human fraternity. An inexhaustible responsibility: *for with the other our accounts are never settled.* (1993, 125; my italics)

I add that the accounts of the Hebrew Bible to the widow and divorcée *are not yet settled.* I reiterate Levinas's love for the Torah (1979) with an echo of our *inexhaustible responsibility:* "to love the widow and divorcée more than the Torah."

To love the widow and divorcée requires that I embrace subjects, according to Lev 21:14–15, who may bring profanation and shame. This difficult love is inscribed in the space, the gap, that Lev 21:14–15 demands between priests and widows. At the underside of Lev 21:14–15 is the hint that some priests prefer to marry widows, which the regulation was stipulated to prevent; in other words, this space is sometimes crossed (cf. Ezek 44:22). Leviticus 21:14–15 takes advantage of this opening to set priests apart from nonpriests by associating the widow with impurity in order to assert that priests deserve only (pure) virgins. The spatial demand of Lev 21:14–15 resonates with the delays, the *navels,* that allowed Jephthah's daughter and Hannah to simultaneously fulfill and break their vows (cf. Rakover 1992).

In loving the widow and divorcée one embraces the complexity of Hebrew Bible regulations. In this chapter I imagine that placing responsibility for the widow and divorcée upon Yhwh, who is often, then and now, here and there, silent and absent,[1] gives men space to distance themselves from widows and divorcées. It is an attempt to shift the blame. One arm of the Torah protects the widow, *after* she is abused (Exod 22:21–23), while other sections (Lev 21:14–15; Ezek 44:22) subject her to abuse (see also Menn 1997, 41–48).

I first reiterate a narrative axis I raised in previous chapters, the role of delays in vow-events (§6.1), then turn to the story of Tamar (Gen 38), who is portrayed at once as widow and divorcée (§6.2). By twice becoming a widow, Tamar's story is about broken vows (§6.3), and by coming to face Judah at Enaim, and later challenging his judgment to have her burned, her story is also about the drive to fulfill vows (Judah's pledge). It is a story of sublime (implied) vows and the sublimation of vows. Both these readings result from accounting for the delay that Judah offered (forced upon?) Tamar (§6.4). Materializing (Bal) vows in Tamar's story, therefore, is the upshot of my transtextual obsession with reading for delays.

---

[1] Note in Exod 22:21–23 that widows *have to cry* before Yhwh will listen to them, and that Yhwh's solution is paradoxical, offering to make more widows and orphans.

6.1 Reiterating Delays

Reading for delays is the stuff of islanders, in and beyond Oceania, who are also known for our laid-back personalities. We are carefree not because we do not care, but because we take advantage of delays (to fish and to kick back!). In "coconut time," "time" is not a linear phenomenon that is timed and hurried but a fluctuation of events, good and bad, that is embraced (see also Sugirtharajah 1998, ix–x; Jameson 1998, 51–52).[2] Coconut time is lived time with spatial significance, and we tend not to rush, because laid-back islanders experience time with delays.[3] We are neither surprised nor disappointed when delays occur; most of the time we expect delays. Anticipating delays provides us with opportunities to prepare for the expected arrival or departure, to play, to saunter . . . to be islanders. We embrace delays for the opportunities they provide. In this regard, reading for delays harbors islanders' laid-back ways of life.

I discussed in chapters 4 and 5 the effects of delays in the vows by Jephthah and Hannah. Concerning Jephthah's daughter, I suggested that the two months she requests delays the fulfillment of Jephthah's vow and gives him an opportunity to reassess his vow. The delay is an opportunity, an opening, to break his vow. But Jephthah does not take advantage of this opportunity on behalf of his daughter. Hannah, on the other hand, takes advantage of the delay she demands from Elkanah to both fulfill and break her vow to Yhwh. Both these women show that vows are breakable.

Delays have temporal (two months in Judg 11 and the weaning period in 1 Sam 1) and spatial (to the mountains in Judg 11 and to stay at home in 1 Sam 1) dimensions (compare *différance* in Derrida 1982). For an islander, such delays postpone arrival and embrace (of voyagers to the islands) as well as departure and tears (of wayfarers from the islands). Delays are not realized in temporal terms only, the extra time it takes for travelers to arrive or depart; delays are not abstract moments that are absent. Rather, delays are made present in the faces whose departure/arrival is postponed. Postponement of departure/arrival gives us more/less faces, and spaces, in our island-space. In other words, we also "face" the delays in the space, and faces, that we have.

---

[2] A bunch of ripe coconuts can resist a strong gust because the coconuts hold each other together. But when one coconut is picked, the bunch can easily break up. "Coconut time" has to do with the coconuts' resistance against pressure, delaying their fall, and the instability of the bunch when one coconut falls (instability occurs when the possibility of delay and resistance are removed). Coconut time is about the delay of fulfillment, rather than being late.

[3] This is not to suggest that island cultures are the only ones that embrace delays, or that perceive them in temporal and spatial terms. But our cultures have yet to be presented or embraced in this manner. Of course, this is one islander's attempt to explain (colonize?) our laid-back personality (see also Havea 1995), and I am not the only islander who reads!

Both Jephthah's daughter and Hannah request delays from the men in whose houses they live. Tamar, on the other hand, is offered (forced into?) a delay. After the death of her husbands at the hands of Yhwh (Gen 38:6, 10), Judah sends Tamar to her father's house until Shelah, his third son, is ready for her (Gen 38:11). Judah opts not to observe the levirate rule (cf. Deut 25:5), which requires him to give Tamar to Shelah, but inserts a delay because he is more concerned for his remaining son (Gen 38:11) than for the widow in his house (Gen 38:14).[4] Judah's delay prevents Tamar from continuing as a married woman; in other words, it fixes Tamar as a widow and literally (Miscall), as a woman sent away from "her man's" household, divorces her from the husband she is owed. In the following reading, I explore how Tamar takes advantage of the delay she is provided, re-presenting her as an islander!

Juxtaposing the stories of Jephthah's daughter, Hannah, and Tamar leads me back to the mal(e)practices (Brenner) in/of Num 30. As I indicated in the foregoing chapters, the opportunities that delays provide are recognized, by the denial of delays, in Num 30. Fathers (Num 30:6) and husbands (Num 30:8, 13, 15, 16) must decide on the first day whether to confirm or annul vows made by their women, discouraging them from taking advantage of delays. The period of the delay is limited, but available, and male subjects have more opportunities than their female subjects. But the gift of delays is absent from the regulation concerning the vow of a widow and a divorcée (Num 30:10), robbing them of the opportunity to (kick back, as islanders, and) reconsider their vows. The following reading adds a different twist. Here, I focus on Tamar's courage to take advantage of what the law denies.

6.2 The Complex Tamar

Dominant critics straitjacket Tamar with monotonous characterizations. She is the crafty widow who takes matters into her own hands to produce an heir for her first husband, which makes her "more in the right" than Judah (Gen 38:26). According to this dominant reading, Tamar has always already wanted to bear a child who would restore her into Judah's house (Bellis 1994, 91; Fokkelman 1996, 168; Westermann 1982, 53). As if, like Hannah, Tamar wants her womb opened.

The focus in the opening verses on Judah's household anchors this popular reading. After Judah separates from his brothers, both in space and behavior (cf. Menn 1997, 51–52), he marries a Canaanite wife who soon bears him three children (Gen 38:1–5). Tamar is inserted into this family as a wife for Judah's first son with the expectation, lured by the fertility of Judah's foreign wife, that she will bear children (cf. Gen 38:8b).

---

[4] Judah may be exonerated if, as Soggin argues, the brother of the deceased is not obligated to marry the widow (1993, 285; so Coats 1972, 466; see also Menn 1997, 59).

Her childlessness, like Hannah's, brings suspicion upon her. But when she later produces sons for Judah (Gen 38:24–30), readers admire her for fulfilling her role. She gives Judah two sons, as if to recompense the two sons whom Yhwh killed.

I extend this reading by suggesting that Tamar also wanted sexual intercourse (cf. Ho 1999, 520). Her womb can only be opened if her vagina is also parted, from both sides, and the task of producing children involves both the pleasures of sex and the pains of childbearing.[5] In that regard, Tamar is more in the right than Judah because she is entitled to sex and "the seed of men" from Judah's house, both of which were withheld when she was made a widow and a divorcée.[6]

The following sections address the complexity of Tamar's character, the "Tamar complex," by retelling her interactions with other characters in the story.[7] I seek to free the character of Tamar from monotonous readings (cf. Andrew 1993) with transtextual readings that also inevitably threaten to confine.

6.2.1 *Tamar the Widow*

When Er dies, Tamar is swiftly pushed down the family tree. She is a wife and a widow in the space of two verses, suggesting a conflict of interests between Judah and Yhwh. Judah turns Tamar into a wife for Er and, because Er was "bad" in his eyes, Yhwh makes her a widow (Gen 38:6–7). Judah and Yhwh show no concern for Tamar, who is at the underside of their concerns.

When he instructs his second son Onan to "enter" his dead brother's wife, Judah is concerned that his firstborn be provided with an offspring (Gen 38:8). As a consequence, Tamar's widowhood is terminated. But she is made a widow again two verses later, because Onan does something "bad" in Yhwh's eyes (Gen 38:10). The forces at work in Tamar's life pull in opposite directions. Judah wants to plant the "seeds of men" for Er, while Yhwh drives to clean out "bad" people, and Tamar is caught in the

---

[5] Genesis 38:26b states that Tamar did not bear any more children because Judah ceased to be "intimate with her again" (Tanakh). "This means not only that Judah will never know her again sexually, but, in a more important way, that she is righteous for putting the survival of the family above herself" (Lambe 1998, 108; see also George R. H. Wright 1982, 527). The following reading resists Ulanov's image of a character whose vagina bites and kills (1993, 24–25).

[6] The story is saturated with references to sex and seeds. Onan provides only sex but not his seed, for which Yhwh kills him (Gen 38:9). Judah too was only looking for sex, but was not concerned about planting his seeds (Gen 38:15–16), and he admits that Tamar was more in the right because he did not give her to Shelah, who would have provided both sex and the "seed of men" (Gen 38:26a). Sex and seeds go together, even for those who prefer one and not the other.

[7] This "complex Tamar" is an alternative to Menn's characterization of a "marginal protagonist" who interacts with a (more) complex Judah (1997, 28–41). I read Tamar as equally complex as, if not more complex than, Judah.

middle without a word or a cry. Onan avoids planting his seeds in Tamar, not even for the sake of his brother, and the narrator does not give Tamar (or Er and Onan) access to words. Because of the levirate rule she is at once a wife (to Onan) and a widow (of Er)—she is a wife because she is a widow and a widow because she is a wife; she is both, at once.[8] "She was to remain insecure and unsettled. She is a widow, but also betrothed, and yet unaccepted in the household into which she married" (Morimura 1993, 56). Tossed in between ends, at the meeting point where being a wife and being a widow (con)fuse, Tamar is pushed to the place of delay and of silence.

Yhwh appears unconcerned for this wife-widow, and I cannot determine if she is good or bad in Yhwh's eyes. If what Yhwh does to Er and Onan signifies his gauge, then one may conclude that Tamar is "not bad" in Yhwh's eyes. In Judah's eyes, on the other hand, Tamar is "bad" to his family. Judah blames her for something she does not do—that is, kill his sons—and he unconsciously submits to the consequence of Yhwh's deeds, keeping Tamar as a widow (Gen 38:11). Unaware of Yhwh's role in un-seeding his family, Judah too shows no concern for Tamar. No longer an unmarried virgin and yet to be a child-producing wife (cf. Niditch 1979, 145; Anderson 1993, 35), Tamar is sent to her father's house to be a widow only, also delayed from becoming a wife. The upshot of Judah's command is the disambiguation of Tamar's position (Bird 1989, 122).

The narrative gives the impression that Tamar, at first, accepts her lot as a widow. She dresses as one (cf. Gen 38:14) and keeps a distance from her in-laws. But she is a betrothed widow, destined to remove her widow's garb and to be given to a husband that Judah has lined up for her. So Judah says, but his heart is not where his mouth is.[9] For the time being, so it appears, Tamar silently stays, dwells, as a widow in her father's house (cf. Gen 38:11).

But Tamar is not the only widow in Gen 38. Long after she returns to her father's house, the narrative jumps to Judah and the death of his wife (Gen 38:12). Judah is a widower, but the narrator does not blame Yhwh for the death of Judah's wife. Having been comforted at home, Judah and his friend Hirah set out for Timnah (cf. Noble 2002, 228–29). The purpose of their trip, sheep-shearing, the "disrobing of sheep," sets the tone for my reading of what ensues.

They stop at the entrance to Enaim, where Tamar has taken a place after removing her widow's garb. She has wrapped herself up and put a

---

[8] The narrator continues to refer to Tamar as "his brother's wife" (Gen 38:9) even after she is given to Onan, so she is at once wife and widow (so Carol Smith 1992, 17–18, 25).

[9] What Judah intends to do echoes what Laban did to Judah's father. Judah plans to withhold Shelah from Tamar as Laban withheld Rachel from Jacob (Gen 29:9–30:43).

veil over her head (face?),[10] and she has come because Judah has not kept his words. Shelah has grown up but she has not been given to Judah (Gen 38:13–14). I assume that Tamar comes (alone?)[11] for retribution, but what she plans to do is not revealed (so Bird 1989, 123; in contrast to Schramm 1990, 196; Lockwood 1992, 39). The text lures us to assume that Tamar has come to Enaim in order to seduce Judah (so Black 1991; Andrew 1993, 264; van Wolde 1997, 21), but it is Judah who approaches her; he sees her as a harlot (Gen 38:15–16).[12] One widow (Judah) asks another (Tamar) to let him enter her, to which she replies, "What will you pay for entering me?" In between places, between Judah's home and Timnah, between her "father's house" and Shelah's embrace, between childless widowhood and motherhood, at the entrance to Enaim ("eyes"), at the "opening of the eyes" (cf. Bos 1988, 42; Fokkelman 1996, 179), a place of delays, of recognition (Tamar of Judah) and misrecognition (Judah of Tamar), two widows discuss an "entry" fee. The widow who was sent home holds the key to the opening that the newly widowed wants to enter. Tamar would have probably been satisfied with Shelah, whom Judah already owes her, but he offers her a kid instead, and she demands a pledge (his seal, cord, and staff)[13] until he sends the payment (Gen 38:17–18).[14] After their encounter, Tamar puts on her widow's garb and returns to her father's house (Gen 38:19).

Without her widow's garb Tamar takes a pledge and allows Judah to penetrate her, and Judah shows her that a widow may still have sex. At the opening to Enaim, two widows open their mouths and legs to each other. But they also withhold information from each other. Neither one

---

[10] To put on a veil does not necessarily mean that Tamar covered her face. Genesis 38:14 only states that she "put on a veil," which she "took off from upon her" in Gen 38:19, but Gen 38:15 explains that Judah did not recognize her "for she had covered her face." I am not certain where the veil was placed, but it was certainly not over Judah's eyes. Moreover, what kind of veil did she put on? The veil of a bride, like the one Rebekah wore in Gen 24 (Fewell and Gunn 1993, 88)?

[11] "Anthropology tells us . . . that people in a small tribal Bedouin village [so islanders] almost never act alone. Tribal villagers, especially women, act in groups" (Anderson 1993, 35).

[12] Westenholz suggests that Tamar's veil was not a sign that she was a harlot, because modest women under male control in Near Eastern cultures usually wear veils (1989, 247; so Morimura 1993). Rather, it was her placement on the side of the road/entrance to Enaim, as if she is "a woman available for commerce" (Vawter 1977, 397), that portrays her as a prostitute.

[13] According to *Genesis Rabba* (85:9), the seal signifies kingship, the cord signifies the Sanhedrin, and the staff signifies the king messiah (cf. Menn 1997, 360).

[14] Judah's concurrence is humiliating: "Without even thinking about it, he gives this woman the equivalent of his passport, credit card, and driving license; the reader could hardly think this was the action of prudent or sensible man" (Carol Smith 1992, 19 [drawing on Alter's characterization]). In a sense, Judah handed over his heritage (cf. Lambe 1999, 57).

mentions a predicament from an earlier stage of their lives: the need to provide an offspring for Er. I read their sexual encounter, for both of them, not for the purpose of planting the "seeds of men" but for satisfying a lack in their lives.[15] Assuming that Tamar considers herself barren (in contrast to Carol Smith 1992, 22), since she was entered by two other men but she did not produce a child, I take her justification for the pledge seriously: "You must leave a pledge until you have sent it [payment for sex]" (Gen 38:17). Tamar is not concerned with obtaining something to justify her pregnancy (cf. Menn 1997, 359–60), as she uses the pledge later (Gen 38:25), but making sure to obtain what she is owed (a kid). Tamar demands a pledge because Judah thus far has not kept his commitment (of words) to her (Furman 1985, 111). In other words, she demands a warrant because commitments to widows are often broken. But that does not mean that widows always keep their end of the bargain. It depends on who the widow is! ,

Without her widow's garb Tamar is still a widow, a widow who realizes the fragility of words and who resists people who deceive her. She is not as vulnerable as Judah might have preferred, and not as naïve as dominant readers imagine her.[16] She takes off her widow's garb in order to provide a delay in the path of another widow(er), so she is always already more than a widow.

6.2.2 *Tamar the Divorcée*

Three incidents portray Tamar as one who is literally (Miscall) divorced. The first two incidents involve Yhwh (by his [killing] deeds), and the third involves Judah (by his words and by his deeds).

Yhwh ends Tamar's marriage twice when, according to the narrator, he kills Er and Onan. No justification is given for killing Er, only that he was "bad in the eyes" of Yhwh (Gen 38:7). The narrator does not explain how and why Er was "bad," and I cannot endorse Yhwh's judgment. On account of Er's unexplained death, his removal from Tamar, I delay in retelling Yhwh's deeds.

On the one hand, one may assume that Er must have done something bad to warrant his death. Judging from what his "fathers" did in Gen 37, when they sold their brother and deceived their father, for which Yhwh did not punish them, Er must have done something really bad, worse than marrying a foreign woman, as Judah did. Otherwise, killing

---

[15] The drive to produce an offspring is an M-concern often superimposed over female characters. On the other hand, the sex drive is both M and F.

[16] Menn also views Tamar as a sufficient manipulator: "Twice . . . Tamar actively manipulates the plot, once on a biological level to facilitate conception and again on a social and legal level to save her own life and that of her unborn sons and to establish their paternity. Without the narrative control exerted by this female protagonist in her heroic restoration of a broken lineage, Genesis 38 would lack its fortunate ending" (1997, 29). Tamar is a widow who makes a difference!

him would have been unfair. The text's silence, however, does not allow me to be certain of this reading. Nor does the text reject it. The text simply announces that Yhwh is responsible for ending Er's life and, as a consequence, Tamar's marriage.

On the other hand, seeing that Onan's action (spilling his seed to the ground) was also "bad" in Yhwh's eyes (Gen 38:10) calls into question the unexplained killing of Er. Yhwh's killing of Onan may seem reasonable, but that does not make it right; from Onan's perspective, any children that he had with Tamar would not have counted as his, so he would have been wasting his seed one way or the other. In comparison, how "bad" could Er have been (cf. Steinmetz 1993, 5–6)? In other words, how bad should the "bad in Yhwh's eyes" be to justify taking a life? Although the text does not justify or condemn Yhwh for killing Er, it makes his murder of Onan problematic. Why is it bad in Yhwh's eyes to look out for one's own interests? Whose interests does Yhwh privilege? Whose interests does he ignore in the process?

These questions reveal that Yhwh's deeds have other consequences, in addition to the deaths of two "bad" characters. Yhwh kills Er because of who he is (Gen 38:7) and Onan because of what he does (Gen 38:10), two different reasons that lead to the same effect.[17] I cannot determine if the punishment fits their crime (cf. Soggin 1993, 282–83; Sarna 1989, 267), but the narrator is certain that Yhwh's deeds bring an end to Tamar's marriages.

I cannot rule out the possibility that Judah brought Tamar into his house in the same way that he brought his own wife: she was seen, taken, and entered (Gen 38:2; cf. 2 Sam 11:2–4; Menn 1997, 37). And now Yhwh starts a process that gets her divorced. Tamar's second husband, too, participates in this process. Had Onan given Tamar the "seed of men," and she consequently had borne a male child, she would have found security in her husband's house.

The text lures us to imagine that Yhwh kills Onan because Onan does not want to impregnate Tamar, in other words, not for his actions but because of what he does *not* want to do (cf. Lambe 1998, 113). Killing Onan suggests that Yhwh cares for Er, who will not have an heir because of Onan. Is that also the reason why Yhwh kills Er, because Er could not make a son for himself?[18]

---

[17] Vawter justifies Onan's death: "It was Onan's refusal of the sacred duty of the *go'el*, his selfishness and his lack of love and loyalty to his brother and family that *greatly offended* Yahweh and brought about his speedy demise" (1977, 395; cf. Westermann 1982, 54–55). "Luther suggested an additional reason for Onan's disobedience to his father's command (though the [levirate] command was not merely Judah's but God's). Onan was motivated not only by jealousy of his elder brother, but by a hatred for the commandment itself" (Steinmetz 1993, 8).

[18] In the *Testaments of the Twelve Patriarchs,* Judah's wife, Saba, instructs Er and Onan not to impregnate Tamar and prevents Shelah from marrying her. Tamar

Whatever concern Yhwh may have had with impregnating Tamar is made problematic by his idleness in withholding Shelah. Why doesn't Yhwh sustain lives and enforce marriages (Ulanov 1993, 20–33; cf. Alter 1981, 3–22)? Yhwh's inactivity suggests that he desires the literal (Miscall) divorce of Tamar.

The third incident that portrays Tamar as a divorcée is Judah's statement, aimed to withhold Shelah from Tamar: "'Stay as a widow in your father's house until my son Shelah grows up'—for he thought, 'He too might die like his brothers'" (Gen 38:11, Tanakh). Two forms of speech are in this verse, the spoken word (*said*) and the disguised thought (*saying*), both of which are ideological, again alerting us to differences between what texts *say* and what they *do* (see also Alter 1981, 18). When Judah *said* to Tamar to stay as a widow in her father's house, his words, in effect— that is, in-deed—*divorced* her from Shelah. From a transoceanic perspective, in which boundaries both limit and transcend spatial and temporal limits, Judah's *said* and *saying* do not match up; Judah's words *do* more than they *say* (in addition to what they *said*). Judah himself admits that he intends more than what he *said* when he *thinks* that he does not want Shelah to die like his older brothers. In this reading, Judah helps establish Yhwh's desire to divorce Tamar from her husband.

That a divorce is disguised in Judah's statement is also suggested by the reference to "father's house," as I suggest in the ensuing transtextual reading. I do not seek to determine the function of a parent's house in biblical literature (cf. Bal 1988a), but to explore the effects of juxtaposing three story-moments: Naomi implores Orpah and Ruth to return to their "mother's house" (Ruth 1:8–13), the Levite's concubine returns to her "father's house" (Judg 19:2), and Judah sends Tamar to her "father's house" (Gen 38:11). I read these moments as a pastiche of voices that reverberate and reiterate each other (cf. van Wolde 1997, 1–8),[19] with the assumption that a pastiche can regain its sense of humor in the events of its reception.

Juxtaposing the demands by Naomi and Judah triggers the following reading (see also Büchner 1997). In Ruth 1:8–13, three widows decide what to do. The story focuses on Naomi, the widow who has lost the most

---

falls victim to the deeds of Saba and her sons, instead of Judah, who ends up as a victim of Tamar's seduction (cf. Wassén 1994, 356–59; Menn 1997, 107–8). And in the *Book of Jubilees* (41:27–28), Tamar is still a virgin when she has sexual intercourse with Judah (cf. Wassén 1994, 361). The gender biases of these early interpretations are transparent, with Judah admitting to a sexual liaison with Tamar without acknowledging that he had "wronged" her (cf. Hayes 1995, 67–70; see also §6.4). Both interpretations "sanctify the name" of Judah.

[19] Jameson explains that a "[p]astiche is, like parody, the imitation of a peculiar or unique style, the wearing of a stylistic mask, speech in a dead language: but it is a neutral practice of such mimicry, without parody's ulterior motive, without the satirical impulse, without laughter, without that still latent feeling that there exists something *normal* compared with which what is being imitated is rather comic. Pastiche is blank parody, parody that has lost its sense of humour" (1998, 5).

(a husband and two sons, Ruth 1:5), as she begins to cross between two places, Moab and Judah (Ruth 1:6–7). In between places, Naomi begs her widowed companions to return to their "mother's house." They departed as a trio (Ruth 1:7), with the expected farewells and tears of departure, but Naomi now redirects her daughters-in-law. In between places, the place of delay, Naomi prevents their arrival. She begs her widowed daughters-in-law to return each to her "mother's house," the place to where some men look for wives (cf. Gen 28:2).[20] Naomi gives them a chance to find husbands (Ruth 1:11–13). She turns them from one place of delay to another place of delay, their "mother's house," signifying that Orpah and Ruth are widows who are free to "find security in the house of a husband" (Ruth 1:9).

Naomi admits that she cannot provide husbands for Orpah and Ruth, so she cannot fulfill the levirate responsibilities. In contrast, Judah has a son that he did not want to give Tamar, telling her to "remain a widow" in her "father's house" (Gen 38:11). At the moment of his *saying,* when he returns her to her "father's house," Judah denies Tamar the chance to "find security" in another man. At the moment of speech, Judah divorces Tamar from the husband she is owed.

Juxtaposed with the story of the Levite's concubine (*'išah pîlegeš*) in Judg 19, I imagine another kind of delay in the "father's house" (Judah). The ambiguity of the relation between the Levite and his concubine, whether they were actually married so that their separation could be considered a divorce, is beyond the scope of this reading (cf. Fewell 1992, 75).[21] My interest is with the opportunities that this unnamed woman is allowed and/or denied as the consequence of her decision to return to her "father's house." The violence that takes place at Gibeah after she is retaken from her "father's house"[22] highlights the gift of delay, which she found in her "father's house."

The concubine plays the harlot (*zanah*) against the Levite, maybe in resistance to his control (so Bird 1989; Fewell and Gunn 1993), then she leaves both Ephraim and her "husband's house" to live in her "father's

---

[20] This reading does not deny that some men find wives in their "father's house," as in the case of Isaac's wife (Rebekah), who comes from Abraham's house (Gen 24). Rebekah, however, is also identified with "her mother's house" (24:28), as if to make the "father's house" and the "mother's house" intersect, cross.

[21] The concubine's relation to the Levite is unclear; he is identified as her *'îš,* who got up to woo her back (19:3). By transference, she is his wife.

[22] Müllner finds both the "sexualizing of violence" in the rape of the concubine (a woman and a stranger, a double Other) and the "desexualizing of violence" in the cutting of the (living) concubine into twelve pieces. "Inasmuch as violence is committed against the woman two different times—once by sexualizing her, the other by desexualizing her—the text constitutes a way of dealing with the double threat of her twofold Otherness, namely, the elimination of the Other woman" (1999, 141; cf. Bach 1999, 145).

house" (Judg 19:2; cf. Lev 22:13) in Bethlehem in Judah (cf. Ruth 1:2).[23] Her
departure and arrival, between two personal and tribal places, are fulfilled by her own will and effort. She does not explain why she has
returned to her "father's house," but it is safe to assume that she is seeking security away from her husband. Since she did "play the harlot"
(*zanah*) but did not choose to enter another husband's house, I assume
that she returns to her "father's house" in order that she may *not* be given
to another man, and because she no longer wants to be under the authority of the man she left. Reentering her "father's house," in this reading,
signifies her desire to annul her previous relation, a movement toward a
literal (Miscall) divorce.

For the Levite, on the other hand, she is someone or something that
he can reclaim (see Judg 19:3). After being separated from his concubine
for four months, the Levite seeks to shut the openings that the "father's
house" offers her.[24] At this juncture, the focus of the story shifts to the exchange between the Levite and his father-in-law, neither of whom
consults the concubine/daughter (cf. Gen 34; 2 Sam 13). The father(-in-
law) appears to catch on to the Levite's intentions, and his reaction is to
press him to delay (*hzq*; Judg 19:4) his departure. He succeeds for several
days, but toward the end of the fifth day, the Levite, his concubine, and
his attendant depart.

In her "father's house," two men conduct business as if she is in between being a wife/concubine and being a daughter, so she belongs to
neither man. Insofar as she delays in between two ends in her "father's
house," she is literally divorced. She had returned to her "father's house"
with authority, deciding her own fate, but in the end she is led away.
From her "father's house," the place of the delay of divorce, she is re-
claimed and silenced. The narrative transforms her from a determined
subject into a bargained trophy.

This reading takes the "father's house" as a place to which a divorcée
turns, a place of delay where the subject is not free to be married off to
another person. It is to such a place that Judah sends Tamar. In contrast to
the Levite's concubine, who goes to her father's house on her own will,
Tamar has no control over her situation. She is sent to her "father's house"
as a place for divorcées, but Judah does not intend to "woo and win her
back" for Shelah. Whereas the unnamed concubine is pursued, Tamar is
discarded. I imagine that Tamar feels that she has been divorced and that

---

[23] Placement and names link the stories in this pastiche (cf. Schramm 1990,
191). Naomi and the Levite's concubine are both linked to Bethlehem, which is defined in terms of "Judah."

[24] The concubine gained autonomy during those four months, as indicated by
the reference that "she [by implication, the concubine] admitted him [the Levite]
into her father's house" (Judg 19:3). Compared to Jephthah's daughter, the concubine is not the one who "comes out of the door" but is the one who "opens the
door."

she has come to the entrance to Enaim, also, like the Levite in Judg 19, to claim her husband. It is not until Judah asks to enter her that the story becomes a story about seduction.

In representing Tamar as a divorcée, I also resist the narrator's drive to fix her as a widow only. This alternative view does not lay all of the blame on Yhwh, for killing Er and Onan thus turning Tamar into a widow, but shifts some of the blame to Judah, for divorcing Tamar from Shelah. This transtextual reading finds a patriarchal drive in the narrator's account: the narrative "shifts the blame" to Yhwh as if to free Judah from blame.[25] I resist the narrator's account by laying some of the blame on Judah, but I also participate in the narrator's "blame-shifting" program insofar as I lay some of the blame on Judah; in other words, I shift some of the blame from Yhwh to Judah and so my resistance to the narrator's account is doubly partial. I am partial (biased) out of "love for a widow and divorcée," and I am partial (limited) out of respect for the workings (Miscall) of the text.

This partial reading unveils the complex face of Tamar as a different kind of widow: at once a wife, widow, daughter, and divorcée. At the underside of her complex face are traces of broken vows.

6.3 Restoring Broken Vows

The terms usually uttered in vow-events are absent from Gen 38, but the story lures us to assume that Tamar has experienced the rupture of vows. She has suffered two broken marriages, thanks to Yhwh, and one postponed marriage, thanks to Judah. After weathering those experiences, and at the time when Judah's lot begins to change, Tamar demands a pledge from Judah (Gen 38:17–18) as if to show him that one must keep one's word. I imagine that Tamar's demand also has a chance to break (in a different manner) commitments. I propose that Tamar comes to face Judah at the entrance to Enaim not in order to break a vow,[26] but *to break the breaking of a vow* (cf. Steinmetz 1993, 9).

Silenced thus far, Tamar is characterized as one who does not know the demands and responsibilities of one who has made a vow. But Judah

---

[25] This reading reflects the attempts in *Genesis Rabba* (85:12) and *Targum Neofiti* (of Gen 38:26) to make Yhwh responsible for what happened at Enaim. This was not because of a problem in the biblical account, but "appears to be a response to a problem that pious readers had as they pondered the text" (Menn 1997, 356). This creates a paradox in later interpretive works. On the one hand, the rabbis want to sanctify the divine name (cf. Menn 1997, 214–15). On the other hand, they want to clear Judah of blame. (In the received forms of *Genesis Rabba, Targum Neofiti*, and *Testament of Judah*, the desire to free Judah's name from blame overshadows the concern to sanctify the divine name.)

[26] This is the implication of the dominant reading that Tamar came to seduce Judah, as if she came to violate an agreement between her and Judah to remain sex-free.

insinuates a vow when he sends her back to her father's house; this is an implied vow which he does not plan to fulfill.[27] In that connection, I read Tamar's demand for a pledge as an attempt to break Judah's intention (i.e., commitment) to break his implied vow (cf. Vawter 1977, 397). Just as words may be broken (see chs. 4 and 5), so can words break desires and expose hidden agendas. Words may break and mend, recover and re-cover, heal, revive, and kill, sometimes with the same utterances; and words can also break themselves. Genesis 38 is nourished by the interplay of such words, exposing the complex power of words.[28]

Tamar gets access to words at the entrance to Enaim. Judah ap-proaches her as if she were a harlot, "Here, let me enter you,"[29] and she responds as if she were one, "What will you pay for entering me?" (Gen 38:15–17).[30] In response, Judah delays fulfillment by offering to send a kid later, and before the narrator tells us whether or not Judah intends to send the kid, Tamar demands a pledge to insure that he will oblige. Tamar is not satisfied with words alone, and she drives to assure that deeds will follow. Not only does she demand a pledge but she also determines what the pledge will be: Judah's seal and cord, and the staff that he carries (Gen 38:18).[31] This is a business deal concerning payment and surety for serv-ice requested and rendered, which Judah accepts.

Tamar makes her demand as one who understands the power of words, when used and misused, as if she knows what Job, another victim of an exchange of words, went through. Job is tested because of a wager into which Yhwh lures Ha-Satan, in order to find out if a worshiper

---

[27] The "implied vow" is the "promise, offer" Judah makes to Tamar (she will be given to Shelah). Its conditions fall upon Judah alone, but its fulfillment will in-volve Tamar.

[28] Other critics have explored the power issue in Gen 38: "It is thoroughly ap-propriate to use the word 'power' in connection with the story of Judah and Tamar, since the narrative is profoundly powerful, not least because it is about power and how it is wielded" (Carol Smith 1992, 16). I take a further step, locating the rhetoric of power in the exchange of words.

[29] Whether Judah was "demanding" or "begging," depending on how one reads the na'-particle, cannot be determined from the text. But I imagine that he was more interested in "entering" rather than the face above the "hole he wants to enter" (in contrast to Sarna 1989, 268; see also the distinction between "fuckor" and "fuckee" in Cornell 1991, 119–20).

[30] Judah took Tamar as a harlot (zonah; Gen 38:15), but Hirah asked for a "cult prostitute" (qedešah) when he went to redeem the pledge (Gen 38:21–22). The dif-ferences between these terms have been explored (Astour 1966; Bird 1989; Luther 1991, 89–93; Westenholz 1989), but the text does not acknowledge if Judah too thought of the woman he entered at Enaim as a cult prostitute.

[31] Judah takes his seal, cord, and staff, but does not have a kid. "As he makes his way *up to Timnah* after his *period of mourning*, Judah is, together with *his friend Hirah*, the proverbial out-of-towner, the conventioner, a visiting sheikh with his little entourage, ready for diversion" (Vawter 1977, 397).

would fear Yhwh gratuitously (Gutiérrez 1987). Yhwh initiates the test by bragging about Job, one upright and blameless man who fears God and shuns all evil from himself and his household (Job 1:4–5). Ha-Satan counters that Job fears God because of the rewards and protection that God has provided, without which Job would curse God to his face (Job 1:8–11). Not to be refuted, Yhwh gives Ha-Satan a chance to prove *his* allegation by taking everything that Job owns without laying a hand on him (as if killing his children does not count as "laying a hand on him"). At the end of his first test, Job is shaken but remains undeterred: "He said, 'Naked came I out of my mother's womb, and naked shall I return there; Yhwh has given, and Yhwh has taken away; blessed be the name of Yhwh " (Job 1:21).

The test does not end there. As if to rub it into his face, Yhwh allows Ha-Satan to touch Job's bones and flesh but spares his life (Job 2:1–6). Job's suffering in the second turn of events is gratuitous, and he takes it out on his wife, whose pain is understandable, for she has just lost all of her children:[32] "You talk as any shameless woman might talk! Should we accept only good from God and not accept evil?" (Job 2:10 Tanakh).[33] The narrator quickly suggests that Job "said nothing sinful" in this case, including when Job said that evil also comes from God, implying that Job's responses prove that Yhwh and Ha-Satan are both *partially* (biased and limited) correct.

Job proves Yhwh correct by remaining upright and blameless during the tests (cf. Job 1:22; 2:10). And Job proves Ha-Satan correct when he states that God gave him the things that had been taken away. God did "fence" Job, as Ha-Satan charged. But in claiming that one should expect "evil" from God, Job literally (Miscall) curses God insofar as his "fence" has only been depicted as a buffer of goodness. God fenced Job with good; Job attributes evil to God. And in the dialogue with his friends, afterward, Job again (almost?) curses God (see 6:4, 8–10; 7:11–21; 9:1–24; 10:2–22; 12:9–13:3; 13:21–28; 14:13–22; 16:9–17; 17:6–16; 19:6–20; 23:2–7; 27:7–12; 30:20–31; 31:35–37). Toward the face of God, in the presence of his friends, Job experiences the power of words to challenge and defend perceptions, to destroy and restore life (cf. Job 42:7–10).

Words are not neutral; words are partial. They can influence and change life, they can bring good and evil both (cf. Job 1:10); such is the power of words.

Though Job's suffering is gratuitous, his words are not. Without wealth or children, he turns to what he has remaining, his words. In this

---

[32] The wife's "curse God and die" request (Job 2:9) may be taken as a test to see if Job cared for her children. In that regard, Job passed Yhwh's test but failed his wife's.

[33] Job's wife talks like a "shameless woman" because she fails to see that "good and evil" come from God. As such, a man who does not accept that is a "shameless man" also.

reading, the story of Job is also about the workings of words of power, evident in the dialogue between Job and his friends (Job 3–31), which lures Elihu (Job 32–37) and Yhwh (Job 38–41) into the exchange with their confining words. Like Job's friends, Elihu and Yhwh offer words of power in order to restrain Job's words. They, too, are seized by the illusions of control. Their words too are partial!

To read these verbal battles in order to determine who has the only correct view undermines the dialogical and lively nature of the encounter. I prefer, on the other hand, to read the paradoxical views for the power of words, noting moments when characters insert words of power to end the dialogue, as Yhwh does in Job 42:7–8.[34] This means, of course, reading against the voices of Yhwh, for the sake of Job, and of Judah, for the sake of Tamar.

As in the story of Job, but with fewer words, Tamar alters her situation with words of power. She demands a pledge, and the effect of her demand is soon realized when Judah sends his Adullamite friend with a kid to redeem the pledge from her (Gen 38:20–23). Judging from the narrative, Judah is driven to action not because of what he said but on account of the pledge that Tamar took from him (Gen 38:20). Only when Hirah fails to find Tamar does Judah refer to what he said earlier, the payment (a kid) for entering Tamar: "Let her keep them [the pledge], lest *we* become a laughingstock ["contempt," "shame"]. I did send her this kid, but *you* did not find her" (Gen 38:23). Judah assumes that he will bring contempt upon *them* if it becomes known that he had an affair with a prostitute, more so than in *not* fulfilling his commitment to a woman. It was Hirah's and the woman's fault that she did not get the kid he promised.[35] Judah does not think that a harlot/prostitute/widow/woman would bring any contempt upon him, even if she possesses his personal seal, cord, and staff. He prefers to ignore her, an ignorance that will come back to haunt him.

Three months later Judah erupts to the accusation that his daughter-in-law is pregnant due to harlotry. The accusation lures us to link Judah to Tamar's pregnancy, for he is the only character associated (in his eyes and his actions) with a "harlot" (in Gen 38:15, 24). The deed and conse-

---

[34] Note Alter's advice: "There is no point, to be sure, in pretending that all the contradictions among different sources [read: stories] in the biblical texts can be happily harmonized by the perception of some artful design. . . . Biblical narrative is laconic but by no means in a uniform or mechanical fashion" (1981, 20).

[35] It is not surprising that Hirah did not find Tamar. He was looking for a "sacred prostitute" whom Judah took as a "harlot," but the narrator presents her as a "widow" without her widow's garb. Hirah was looking for only one face of a complex character, so he was doomed to fail (cf. Morimura 1993, 59). On the other hand, taking qdš(h) as "sacred, holy, consecrated one," Hirah "is denying the affair and pretending to take the kid to the קדשה for a sacrifice, as in Hos 4:14" (Westenholz 1989, 248; so Vawter 1977, 398).

quences of harlotry are coupled, pointing at Judah as he passes judgment: "Bring her out and let her be burned" (Gen 38:24).[36] Judah is satisfied with the words of his informers, as if he had not learned anything from the "harlot" at Enaim. Instead of asking for a pledge in support of their claim, Judah passes judgment on Tamar. He wants to do more to Tamar than to the "prostitute" that Hirah could not find (cf. Fokkelman 1996, 171), without realizing that she is the same person: "Whereas he should have acted on her behalf, Judah's actions toward Tamar have been negative and deceptive and finally destructive" (Bos 1988, 47). But Judah's quick judgment to burn Tamar literally brings contempt (cf. Gen 38: 23) into, in other words, "burns," his house.[37] Two moments justify this reading.

First, Judah's selective recognition of the power of words suggests that he is blinded by his desires. He does not hold himself accountable to the standards he expects from Tamar and his informers, as if he is not limited by his words. Had he delivered the kid as promised he would have discovered that Tamar was the woman he had entered. He gives up trying to keep his words with a self-centered excuse that brings contempt upon himself (cf. Menn 1997, 38–41).

The problem with Judah is that he acts as if his words are breakable while the words of others are unbreakable. Judah makes an offer that he does not intend to keep (cf. Gen 38:11) and one that he does not work hard enough to keep (cf. Gen 38:20–23), but he does not question the words of Hirah (cf. Gen 38:22) or the accusation of his informers (cf. Gen 38:24). Like some readers, he embraces the words that he wants to hear but ignores the others.

Second, Judah's misuse of delays for his interests alone also brings contempt upon himself. Judah placed delays upon Tamar earlier, by sending her to her father's house and by keeping her waiting until he had redeemed his pledge, so he knows of the possibilities that delays offer. This time around, he jumps on the opportunity to deny Tamar the gift of delays by passing judgment (Gen 38:24), as if he were trying to cover something up.[38]

Instead of celebrating the news that his daughter-in-law is fertile, so Er may now have descendants, or taking into consideration that harlotry is between two people, Judah commands that Tamar be burned. He does

---

[36] Note that the punishment for playing the harlot, according to Deut 22:21, was stoning. Burning is reserved for cultic offences (cf. Carol Smith 1992, 27).

[37] Had Judah not secured his words to the "prostitute" with a pledge, he could have easily turned Tamar into ashes. If it was up to him, her body and his words would have quickly gone up, consumed, in a flame. Words, however, remain to cry, as Job's did, even from the ashes.

[38] Vawter suggests that "we probably do him [Judah] no injustice if we surmise that he discovered in Tamar's apparent disgrace an easy way out of the continuing embarrassment she caused him by her very existence, and that he pronounced sentence on her the more willingly for this reason" (1977, 399).

not consider the other consequences of his command, such as the denial of descendants for Er, which could end his own lineage, and the loss that it would bring to Tamar's family. Rather, without delay, as if Tamar were still under his authority (cf. Niditch 1979, 147; Maddox 1987), Judah grabs the opportunity to clean up the mess that he could not remedy earlier when he sent her to her father's house.

The unseminated widow/divorcée who was sent to her father's house is led out, having being inseminated, toward a fire built for her dissemination. Instead of the marriage bed of Shelah, Judah commands her toward, and commends her to, a bed of fire. Tamar would have ended up in ashes, in cinders, had she not produced Judah's pledge. She seizes the delay Judah had denied her with fiery words:[39] "I am with child by the man to whom these belong. . . . Examine these: whose seal and cord and staff are these?" (Gen 38:25). She does not deny the charges, but utters a charge of her own.

The delay is an opportunity for Tamar's words of power to stamp contempt upon Judah's face, and to reverse a destructive decision. In this complex story, the same delay effects the restoration of the vow that Judah had made to Tamar earlier. But the implied vow is literally (Miscall) compromised, as if it is substituted,[40] for the narrative does not say if Tamar was given to Shelah.[41] Only that *he* (Judah? Shelah?) was not intimate with her again (Gen 38:26). Still, Tamar takes advantage of the power of words and the opportunity from the delay to restore her place in Judah's house and to bear the fruits of his implied vow. In that regard, I imagine that Tamar would prefer that a commitment/vow, the words, made to a widow and divorcée were fulfilled.

---

[39] The tone of Tamar's charge is stronger in *Targum Neofiti*, in which she could not find Judah's pledge when she "went out [MT: "brought out"] to be burned in the fire." In the Targum, she prays to the "God who answers the distressed" to show her the "witnesses" (cf. Menn 1998, 208). In the Targum, so in *Genesis Rabba* and the *Testament of Judah*, Tamar is determined to face Judah's judgment, trusting that she will not be burned once she finds the pledge (witnesses).

[40] Fokkelman notes that "Genesis 38 is filled to the brim with substitutions. The three objects for identification are substitutes for the kid, which is the substitute for paying, which is the commercial exchange and substitute for the visit to a whore, which is the substitute for intercourse between Shelah and Tamar, which should have been the legal substitute for Onan giving his seed to her, which was the legal substitute for Tamar conceiving from her husband. The searching Hirah replaces Judah, and the twins are also involved in a struggle of substitution (who will be the firstborn?)" (1996, 180).

[41] In the *Book of Jubilees* (41:20), Tamar was not given to Shelah (cf. Hayes 1995, 67–68).

6.4 Uttering Judah's Wrong

Recognizing his seal, cord, and staff, Judah declares that Tamar "is more in the right than I inasmuch as I did not give her to my son Shelah" (Gen 38:26).[42] "Faced with himself [his seal, cord, and staff], he is able to see both himself and Tamar. He sees that what he should have given he did not give and that what he gave set the trap to show his own unrighteousness" (Bos 1988, 47; cf. Bal 1987, 102).

Judah declares that Tamar is more in the right than he, but he does not admit that he was wrong. What he does afterward, ceasing "to know her" further (Gen 38:26b), suggests that Judah may have assumed that he was "not as right as Tamar" in withholding Shelah but that he had been wrong in knowing Tamar.[43] Otherwise, there is no reason for him to stop knowing her.

The narrator too veils how Judah wronged Tamar by turning his attention to the birth of twins (Gen 38:27–30),[44] implying that the concern of the story, and of Tamar, is with bearing sons. But when she names one of the sons Perez,[45] playing on the verb "to breach," the text suggests that Tamar is not at ease with her situation. A breach has taken place, which invites a retelling of the story.[46]

The birth story of Perez and Zerah invokes stories of other brothers like Cain and Abel (Gen 4), Ishmael and Isaac (Gen 16–17, 21), Esau and Jacob (Gen 27:1–28:9), and Joseph and his brothers (Gen 37), sto-

---

[42] Morimura explains that "the feminine form of 'be righteous' (*tsadqah*) is a unique occurrence in the whole Bible, which means that Tamar is the only woman who was declared righteous" (1993, 62; cf. Hayes 1995, 65–67).

[43] The irony is that Judah "did not know" that he was "knowing" Tamar at the entrance to Enaim; he was blinded when the eyes were opened.

[44] In the *Book of Jubilees* and *Testaments of the Twelve Patriarchs*, "Judah's sin is . . . not a sin of deception or ethical unrighteousness towards Tamar, but rather a sin of sexual liaison with his daughter-in-law" (Hayes 1995, 69). Note that in the *Targum Onqelos*, *Targum Pseudo-Jonathan*, and *Targum Neofiti*, Judah's admission that Tamar is "more in the right" is omitted.

[45] I assume that Tamar is the subject who speaks in Gen 38:29a without ruling out the possibility that it could have been the midwife (cf. Furman 1985, 112; Sarna 1989, 270; Menn 1997, 367). The text is also ambiguous concerning who named the child "Perez," for it passively states ". . . and his name was called Perez" (38:29b).

[46] Carmichael, who imagines that Tamar was Canaanite (so Emerton 1975, 1979), because her name is the Canaanite term for "palm tree," argues that this is one of the "breach" stories that gave rise to Deuteronomic laws against the intermixing of different types (e.g., Deut 22:9–11) (Carmichael 1982, 402–3; cf. Bauckham 1995, 314–20). Carmichael's argument derives from his assumption that OT laws, like sayings and proverbs, are "condensed stories." Arbeitman (2000), on the other hand, suggests that Tamar's name derives from the Hittite *dammara-*, which refers to a "cultic functionary" and has become a character's personal name.

ries in which younger brothers are favored (cf. Goldin 1977). In Tamar's story world as well, Judah favors a younger brother over his levirate responsibility to his older sibling (cf. Carol Smith 1992, 16–17). Since Tamar delivers her twins into such a story world, I imagine that there are more to her words—"What a breach you have breached against yourself"—than an explanation for the name of the first son to be cut from her womb. Tamar directs her words to Perez, but Judah too has made a breach against her. I thus direct her response to Judah, who has also made a breach against himself (cf. Fokkelman 1996, 177). The ambiguity over which son was the firstborn justifies this alternative reading.

Although Zerah puts his hand out first, to which the midwife ties a crimson thread to signify that "this came out first" (Gen 38:28), he is not the first to leave his mother's womb. He pulls his hand back in, and out comes his brother. Most readers assume, focusing on the crimson thread, that Zerah should have been the firstborn, so Tamar must be rebuking Perez for infringing on Zerah's position. Perez made a breach by trespassing in the way of "firstborn" Zerah.

But there is more to Zerah than one of his limbs. He is not "born" before Perez comes out, and the midwife's crimson thread may just be an indication of the hand (in contrast to the baby) that comes out first—"this [hand] came out first!" Since Perez is cut from his mother's womb first, he too is a firstborn.[47] Both sons are firstborns in this reading, as twins, and Tamar's remark upon Perez's arrival is evasive. In a story world in which the firstborn does not usually get what he deserves, and insofar as we are not sure of Tamar's emotions at that moment, it is not clear if Tamar was rebuking or praising Perez for what has taken place: "What a breach you have made for yourself!" Three readings are possible. First, Tamar may be expressing excitement for a feisty baby boy who beats his sibling out of the darkness of her womb. She praises him for beating the other child out of her womb. Second, Tamar could be lamenting that Perez had wronged himself by jumping in front of his sibling, who could be a girl. And third, it is possible that the breach to which Tamar is referring is not what Perez did against Zerah but what he has done against her. As her firstborn, Perez breached her womb and private parts from within.[48] These readings witness to the power of words to *do* more than they *say*.

I offer these alternative readings in order to loosen, to release, Tamar's words, and I thus far have submitted to the narrative in directing

---

[47] Genesis 38 is full of this kind of ambiguity. In addition to the confusion over who is born first is the problematic relation of Judah to Tamar's sons, Perez and Zerah. Judah at once is their father and grandfather (so Martin Luther, according to Steinmetz 1993, 9).

[48] Tamar could have been happy that she finally has become a mother and then, seeing that Perez does not have the crimson cord, is not sure if the cord is still inside her or if she has to bear the pain of delivering a second child.

them against Perez. But her words are not against Perez alone.[49] What has a newly born boy done to deserve such powerful words? The power of Tamar's words, her final words in the story, may also be taken as words of power against Judah. This possibility exposes four areas in which Judah made a breach against himself.

First, in withholding Shelah from Tamar he jeopardizes his lineage. Judah refuses sex and the seeds of men from Tamar, which he admits (Gen 38:26), and consequently refuses something from himself. Refusing to give Tamar to Shelah is also a breach against Judah. Figuratively speaking, by announcing that Tamar was more in the right, Judah acknowledges how he almost spilled his seeds to waste. Tamar's words are revealing in their context: "What a breach you [Judah] have made against yourself!"[50]

Second, Judah made a breach against himself by failing to examine the words brought against Tamar as closely as he examines material evidences. It appears that Judah had already decided that Tamar was a "harlot" even before she was charged (cf. Bird 1989, 122–26), and maybe before he "saw her as a harlot" at the opening to Enaim, a misjudgment that invites Nathan's judgment against him: "That man is you!" (2 Sam 12:7; so Rendsburg 1986, 442).[51] Judah too is a harlot driven by desires that blind his judgments. Tamar's rebuke/praise of Perez would, therefore, be appropriate against Judah's behavior.

Third, Judah made a breach against himself by continuing to break his words. He has a history of breaking words and commitments. In the recent turn of events, when he announced that Tamar was more in the right, he broke his earlier words, "Bring her out and let her be burned." Judah literally (Miscall) burns his own words, and he deserves Tamar's fiery words.

Finally, Judah made a breach against himself by announcing that Tamar was more in the right without admitting that he wronged her. This reading uses Tamar's words to force the issue against Judah, and thereby resists drawing the text to closure by embracing Judah's misdeeds against both Tamar and himself. This reading ties a crimson thread to the deeds and words of Judah and exposes the androcentrism of the story, present at several places, as Bos concludes:

---

[49] Tamar's words cannot be directed at the midwife (assuming a female) because the Qal verb and pronominal suffix are in the second-person masculine singular forms.

[50] Fokkelman suggests that the "criminal act of withholding seed is to a certain degree committed by Onan's father as well. The main difference is that Judah thinks he looks much less callous than his second son and is *very skilful in covering his tracks. Fortunately, the only person whom he makes a fool of is himself*" (1996, 177; my italics).

[51] Carol Smith (1992, 24) also situates Gen 38 in the same period as 2 Sam 9–20, and van Dijk-Hemmes reads the story of Tamar in Gen 38 as a midrash on the story of Tamar, daughter of David, in 2 Sam 13. See also the support that Ho gives to Rendsburg's intertextual study.

Where is the androcentrism of this text located? An obvious bias is found
in the lack of open condemnation of Judah, who behaved irresponsibly
and destructively toward Tamar. (1988, 48)

Androcentric bias is also clearly visible in the interpretations of the story
which show difficulty in dealing with a woman as a central character.
(48)

The foregoing readings expose the connectedness of right and
wrong, of good and bad, and the complexity of Tamar's story world.
These readings recognize the power of words to heal and kill, to fix and
break, to create and destroy, to vow and annul, to construct and dismantle, to deconstruct and say otherwise. This is the stuff of transtextuality! I
take the story and words of a widow seriously, and resist the closure desired by the narrator's account. Of course, appealing to Tamar's story, I
produced twin readings by harlotry (cf. Furman 1985, 107–8)![52]

One may apply the words of the astonished midwife [in contrast to the
foregoing reading] to this type of interaction with the biblical text: "What
a breach you have made for yourself!" . . . And this is as it must be, if
scripture is to retain its normative and vital function within living religious communities. (Menn 1997, 367)

At the end of her story, Judah does not right his wrong by giving
Tamar to Shelah. She continues to be a widow and divorcée, at once, leading me back to Num 30:10. I take this shift with what Carol Smith
considers to be "the underlying assumption in the story of Tamar: that the
Law is not absolute" (1992, 26).

6.5 The Widow and Divorcée of Numbers 30

I take advantage of the placement of Gen 38, a story that both belongs and
does not belong within its context (so Bos 1988, 49),[53] to point it toward

---

[52] In that regard, a transtextual reading resonates with Hayes's definition of
midrash as "an approach to text motivated by various needs, which makes possible and encourages the finding of many meanings, even contradictory ones, in
the one text" (1995, 63).

[53] Critics differ on the placement of Gen 38, ranging from reading it as an independent unit (cf. Speiser 1964, 299; von Rad 1972, 351; Brueggemann 1982, 307;
Westermann 1982, 49) to reading it as a crucial component of the Joseph narrative
on literary (cf. Alter 1981, 3–22, esp. 11 [in contrast to Andrew 1993, 266–68]; Ska
1988; Sarna 1989, 263–64; Fokkelman 1996), type-narrative (Noble 2002), thematic
(cf. Goldin 1977; Andrew 1993), and theological (cf. Mathewson 1989) grounds.
Moreover, critics who read Gen 38 as a "historical" account within the nonhistor-
ical Joseph cycle (cf. George R. H. Wright 1982) differ on reading it within its
literary context (cf. Lockwood 1992) and reading it in terms of the assumed context of J (cf. Rendsburg 1986). In the latter case, Gen 38 is a mirror of (Ho 1999), and
a midrash on, David's story (see also Menn 1997, 73–82). It has more to do with
David then Judah (Rendsburg 1986, 441; Ho 1999, 514).

Num 30:10. I insert a delay in order to send the regulations of Num 30 to the house of Tamar.

The foregoing readings suggest that Tamar's behavior affirms that "the vow of a widow and a divorcée, all that she obliges upon herself shall stand upon her" (Num 30:10). Moreover, Tamar acts as if she also wants "the man" to keep his (implied) vow to a widow and divorcée (Num 30:3). On both counts, manifesting the power of words, Tamar's story lures me to five issues to which the legislators in Num 30 were blinded.

First, Tamar's story exposes the complexity of vow-events. Vows and commitments are made within networks of human relations, and of words, so the observance or annulment of one's vow affects the subjects with whom one relates. Moreover, a vow may be made in order to fulfill and/or annul another commitment. Tamar's story exposes the failure of the legislators in Num 30 to take into account the lively contexts of vows, and the complex interrelation of subjects and their interests.

Second, Tamar's story makes the question of agency problematic. Whereas Num 30:10 regulates vows *by* a widow and divorcée, Tamar seeks to assure that the (implied) vow made *to* a widow and divorcée is fulfilled. Numbers 30:10 aims to control the will of a widow and divorcée, but Tamar shows that "concern" for the widow and divorcée must include controlling the subjects who break their commitments to them. As I proposed above, this was one of the reasons why Tamar came to the "entrance to Enaim," to the "opening of eyes." She also came to claim what had been withheld from her. In this transtextual reading, Tamar opens the eyes of Num 30:10 to the fact that vows made to a widow and divorcée are often broken.

Third, Tamar's story exposes androcentric biases in Num 30:10. Whereas Num 30:10 constructs the widow and divorcée as females only, Gen 38 presents the words and deeds of a widower. The complexity of Tamar's character (as wife, widow, daughter, divorcée, prostitute, harlot,

---

Other critics focus on the narrative art of Gen 38 (cf. Luther 1991; Bird 1989, 120). I favor this narrative approach because of the opportunities it provides for readers to make contextual sense out of ancient literature (cf. Maddox 1987; Büchner 1997), a practice that goes back to the rabbinic teachers and Pseudo-Philo (cf. Polanski 1995), to Martin Luther and his medieval predecessors (cf. Steinmetz 1993).

My preference for the narrative does not rule out "historical" findings, such as Emerton's suggestion that the Tamar story originated in Canaanite territories (Shephelah near Adullam) before it was used by J to form a continuous written narrative (1975, 1976; in contrast to Westermann 1982, 50). It is, in this regard, a literary creation, a fiction, rather than a legend (Rendsburg 1986; Ho 1999).

I too presume that Gen 38 is an interested foreign story, providing an opening for my drive in this section to read (re-place) it in relation to Num 30:10. In other words, insofar as I am as neutral as (that is, hardly neutral) the biblical narrator (cf. Furman 1985, 116), I propose to do to Gen 38 what J is said to have done to the Canaanite story of Tamar!

holy person, accused, mother, and accuser) discloses the complexity of the subject "widow and divorcée," which was not considered in Num 30. In that regard, Tamar both upholds and breaks Num 30:10 (cf. Rakover 1992). When she made Judah fulfill his commitments—his implied vow, according to the foregoing reading—she made a widow(er) observe his words; hence, she upholds 30:10. But in extending the regulation in Num 30:10 to a man, she also breaks it.

Fourth, Tamar's story exposes two blind spots in the Num 30:3 regulation: "A man, when he vows a vow to Yhwh or oaths an oath to oblige an obligation upon himself, he must not break his word; according to all that come out of his mouth, he must do." Drawing upon Tamar's interactions with Judah, why should a man (including a widower) keep his vow to Yhwh but not his (implied) vow to a widow and divorcée? And concerning the early deaths of Tamar's husbands, why is Yhwh exempted from laws against breaking vows? Even though it appears that the "widow and divorcée" (Num 30:10) share the same regulation as "the man" (Num 30:3), "the man" is not obligated to fulfill his vows to other human subjects. In that regard, also, Tamar's story discloses the androcentric blindness of Num 30.

Fifth, the story of Tamar goes through the processes of breaking and restoring vows and commitments as if to "open the eyes" of Num 30 to a transtextual demand: *vows must be fulfilled because they are breakable.* In other words, *broken vows are also restorable.* According to this reading, Tamar is "more in the right" for not settling for broken (implied) vows but for grabbing what she is owed.

The story of Tamar (narrative), therefore, both unveils the ignorances in Num 30 (law) and indicates how they are blinding but restorable. I read *a narrative around a law,* and *a law around a narrative,* not unlike a pastiche, transferring the complex character of Tamar upon the widow and divorcée of Num 30. In complicating the face of Tamar I unveil the accounts of the law (Torah) to the "widow and divorcée:" *They are not yet settled!*

Afterword, My Alibi, a Story

The Bible is neither the first nor last word. It is not the first word because its language necessarily borrows from and builds on the language of its time. It is not the last word because [non-]Christians all over the world continue to make the Bible "talk." As a talking book, it depends on the community of faith [and readers] to bring it to life. (Kwok Pui-lan 1995, 43)

[H]istory is not so much a text, as rather a text-to-be-(re-)constructed. Better still, it is an obligation to do so. . . . (Jameson 1988, 107)

The disappearance of truth as presence, the withdrawal of the present origin of presence, is the condition of all (manifestation of) truth. Nontruth is the truth. Nonpresence is presence. Differance, the disappearance of any original presence, is at once *the condition of* impossibility and *the condition of impossibility of truth. At once. 'At once' means that the being-present* (on) *in its truth, in the presence of its identity and in the identity of its presence,* is doubled *as soon as it appears, as soon as it presents itself.* It appears, in its essence, as *the possibility of its own most proper non-truth, of its pseudo-truth reflected in the icon, the phantasm, or the simulacrum. What is is not what it is, identical and identical to itself, unique, unless it* adds to itself *the possibility of being* repeated *as such. And its identity is hollowed out by that addition, withdraws itself in the supplement that presents it.* (Derrida 1981, 168)

[S]tories can be subversive, a means of criticizing dominant patterns of thought and institutions. Indeed, at times, to narrate an implicitly subversive story is the only safe way for social criticism to be spoken and heard. And, of course, such stories have the potential to create new social worlds. (Gunn and Fewell 1993, 1–2)

Leaving the Surfs

In the end, the islander must leave the ocean, the boundary, to dry up and rest while she considers what things to do, and how to do them, the next time she returns. The islander must leave the surfs because she is not a native of the ocean. In that regard, I exit this book by disclosing, releasing, fracturing it in two places.

First, I dipped into the limits of Hebrew Bible law and consequently shifted the limits to different locations. I was not interested in removing the limits, but in exposing their fluidity and place-fullness. I dis-closed the limits as if to re-limit, and to re-move, the Hebrew Bible law. In other words, a transtextual reader dives into, shifts, breaks, and upholds, holds up, limits.

I read Num 30 around and across biblical narratives, and extrabiblical narratives expressed and disguised in representations of Num 30, as if they are a_part of each other. In this regard, I resisted Miscall's sanction against reading the "deep structure" of texts (for he prefers to read their [surface] workings), in order to materialize (Bal) what I imagine to be at the underside of the narratives. On the other hand, I resisted Bal's drive to name (materialize) what resists being named (e.g., naming Jephthah's daughter "Bath") out of respect for the decidability of the text (which depends on its undecidability). These resistances, or *transgressives* (Foucault), reveal how my interests, as in Num 30, determine what to uphold and what to restrain. In other words, my transtextual readings wrapped transoceanic metanarratives around Num 30 as if I, too, drown in the elusions of control.

Second, I disturbed the shifting junctures (limits) of biblical criticism at the points where text meets interpretation, and dis-closed ignorances at several places. And I exit the shifting junctures with a call for responsible reading, paraphrasing Num 30: *if you say it, you must do it; but if you restrain, you annul it . . . and you bear the guilt . . . so you decide!*

The upshot of the transtextual readings that I offer is that texts become soaked, salty, and tanned with each other. In other words, transtextuality, too, is in the business of transformation. In that regard, the call for responsible reading must also include the reminder, to supplement the foregoing readings: *. . . you decide . . . but remember that some words must be kept, upheld, held up . . . and some words belong to other subjects!*

I privileged my understanding of the transoceanic perspectives but I realize, also, that there are transoceanic perspectives beyond my control, and not just because they have not been written. I re-presented "our" transoceanic perspectives in nonnative ways, using foreign concepts to narrate transoceanic readings and consequently to transgress the native faces I set out to introduce. Out of respect to my transoceanic interests, therefore, I rest this project at the place of arrival and departure, oriented toward the limit and in anticipation of further crossings and harvests. In other words, I exit upon another n(arr)ative, a story:

> For many moons before the arrival of pale-face settlers, the voyagers who pierce the sky and club from afar with fire slings, she was a woman in her late years. Old in age but young in spirit, wise in presence but

poor in appearance, she was a midwife by profession and a widow by fate.

She gained wealth when she delivered chiefs, and in the opportunities to hand-over, hand-back, to re-turn, re-lease, lives that came through her hands.

She had hands of deliverance, with which she draws lives out of the darkness. She was in between, setting creatures free from the hold of darkness and setting darkness free from the grab of those creatures. She sets them free. Both of them. Darkness and creatures. She sets them free from each other. Almost.

This midwife's hands were magic hands. Hands that reach out, to penetrate; hands that receive, to give back. She reaches into disturbed wombs to receive noisy creatures. She receives bodies that have been rejected, bodies that struggle to be on the other side. She was not any ordinary woman but the midwife with magic hands, the midwife who is also an ex-wife; a woman of few but mighty words, who did most of her talking with her hands.

She hunches over at the point of transition, the midperson at midpoint, from where she passes on. She sets free. Both of them. Mother and child. She cuts them apart, as they both cry, and she rebinds them. Both of them. Mother and child. She gives them to each other, so that one becomes a_part of the other. She cuts, so that they unite. This delivering woman stands at the point of transition. She is the point of transition. She is transition. She is.

This midwife travels only at night, the space between days. When it was time to leave for the next village, she was endowed with gifts from the families she visited. She was the visitor who was visited, the stranger who was loved, the visitor who was no stranger.

But she did not take anything with her because she traveled at night, and she traveled alone. She left the gifts, so her departure brought riches. She left the gifts; they continue to be gifts. She left the gifts, having been received, and so her departure became her arrival. The gift that is she. She is gift. She was the stranger who was not strange, whose presence was felt when she leaves. And she leaves so that she may arrive. She is arrival.

At one village the chief confronted her, troubled because she refused to take his gifts and concerned because of the dangers of traveling in the dark. He was concerned mostly because she was a woman, old and unattached. The midwife showed respect, "Son, gifts come out of gratitude, not in payment for a task. You gave me wages. I must refuse. But I accept gifts, which can only be given. I travel in the dark, the realm of spirits. In light, one follows a path. But in the dark, one gives a path."

Out of the darkness she arrives. Into the darkness she departs. In between, at the place of deliverance, the place of laboring pangs and freeing cries, she leaves the gift that is, drawn from the darkness of the womb. Whether it is the first or last night of her arrival, her second or last visit to that village, she leaves the gift that is, the gift that gives. She is departure.

So goes her tale. And mine. Of an ordinary woman who also talked with her feet. With hands and feet, she finds her way through the darkness. Not just with words.

So goes the tale, about the dark days of the natives. A tale about a woman whose name shadows this story, a woman whose presence lives in my story, a woman whose gift gives in her story, a woman whose story is at the mercy of my telling, a woman whose life cannot be told in my writing, a woman whose gift I can only accept by giving. So there! Tear! Here! Hear!

Works Cited

Aichele, George, and Gary A. Phillips
1995a   "Introduction: Exegesis, Eisegesis, Intergesis." *Semeia* 69/70: 7–18.
1995b   "Intertextuality and the Bible." *Semeia* 69/70. [The reference is to one issue of the journal, with the given theme. Aichele and Phillips served as editors for this issue.]
Albright, William F.
1925   "The Administrative Divisions of Israel and Judah." *Journal of the Palestine Oriental Society* 5:17–54.
Alexander, Larry, and Emily L. Sherwin
1994   "The Deceptive Nature of Rules." *University of Pennsylvania Law Review* 142:1191–225.
Alter, Robert
1981   *The Art of Biblical Narrative*. New York: Basic Books.
2000   *Canon and Creativity: Modern Writing and the Authority of Scripture*. New Haven and London: Yale University Press.
Amit, Yairah
1994   " 'Am I Not More Devoted to You Than Ten Sons?' (1 Samuel 1.8): Male and Female Interpretations." Pp. 68–76 in *A Feminist Companion to Samuel and Kings*. Edited by Athalya Brenner. FCB 5. Sheffield: Sheffield Academic.
Anderson, Rosemarie
1993   "A Tent Full of Bedouin Women." *Daughters of Sarah* 19 (winter): 34–35.
Andrew, M. E.
1993   "Moving from Death to Life: Verbs of Motion in the Story of Judah and Tamar in Gen 38." *ZAW* 105:262–69.
Arbeitman, Yöel L.
2000   "Tamar's Name or Is It? (Gen 38)." *ZAW* 112:341–55.
Ashley, Timothy R.
1993   *The Book of Numbers*. Grand Rapids: Eerdmans.
Astour, Michael C.
1966   "Tamar the Hierodule: An Essay in the Method of Vestigial Motifs." *JBL* 85:185–96.
Auld, A. Graeme
1984   *Joshua, Judges, and Ruth*. Philadelphia: Westminster.

Bach, Alice
1991   Review of *Murder and Difference: Gender, Genre, and Scholarship on Sis-*
            era's Death and *Death and Dissymmetry: The Politics of Coherence in the*
            Book of Judges, by Mieke Bal. *USQR* 44:333–41.
1999   "Rereading the Body Politic: Women and Violence in Judges 21." Pp.
            143–59 in *Judges: A Feminist Companion to the Bible.* Edited by Athalaya
            Brenner. 2d ser. Sheffield: Sheffield Academic.
Bal, Mieke
1985   *Narratology: Introduction to the Theory of Narrative.* Translated by C. van
            Boheemen. Toronto: University of Toronto Press.
1987   *Lethal Love: Feminist Literary Readings of Biblical Love Stories.* Blooming-
            ton: Indiana University Press.
1988a   *Death and Dissymmetry: The Politics of Coherence in the Book of Judges.*
            Chicago and London: University of Chicago Press.
1988b   *Murder and Difference: Gender, Genre, and Scholarship on Sisera's Death.*
            Bloomington and Indianapolis: Indiana University Press.
1991a   "Murder and Difference: Uncanny Sites in an Uncanny World." *Jour-*
            nal of Literature and Theology 5:11–19.
1991b   *On Story-Telling: Essays in Narratology.* Edited by David Jobling.
            Sonoma, Calif.: Polebridge.
1991c   *Reading "Rembrandt:" Beyond the Word-Image Opposition.* Cambridge:
            Cambridge University Press.
Barnes, Timothy David
1971   *Tertullian: A Historical and Literary Study.* Oxford: Clarendon.
Barré, Michael L.
1992   "Treaties in the ANE." *ABD* 6:653–56.
Bauckham, Richard
1995   "Tamar's Ancestry and Rahab's Marriage: Two Problems in the Mat-
            thean Genealogy." *NovT* 37:313–29.
Bauman, Zygmunt
1995   *Life in Fragments: Essays in Postmodern Morality.* Oxford: Blackwell.
Baur, Chrysostomus
1959   *John Chrysostom and His Time.* Vol. 1: *Antioch.* Translated by M. Con-
            zaga. Westminster, England: Newman.
Beal, Timothy K.
1992   "Ideology and Intertextuality: Surplus of Meaning and Controlling the
            Means of Production." Pp. 27–39 in *Reading between Texts: Intertextual-*
            ity and the Hebrew Bible. Edited by Danna Nolan Fewell. Louisville:
            Westminster John Knox.
1994   "The System and the Speaking Subject in the Hebrew Bible: Reading
            for Divine Abjection." *Biblical Interpretation* 2:171–89.
Begrich, Joachim
1938   *Studien zu Deuterojesaja.* BWANT 4. Stuttgart: W. Kohlhammer.
Bellis, Alice Ogden
1994   *Helpmates, Harlots, and Heroes: Women's Stories in the Hebrew Bible.*
            Louisville: Westminster John Knox.
Berchman, Robert M.
1984   *From Philo to Origen: Middle Platonism in Transition.* Chico, Calif.: Scholars.

Berlinerblau, Jacques
1996   *The Vow and the "Popular Religious Groups" of Ancient Israel: A Philologi-
          cal and Sociological Inquiry.* JSOTS 210. Sheffield: Sheffield Academic.
Berman, Harold J.
1974   *The Interaction of Law and Religion.* Nashville: Abingdon.
Bible and Culture Collective, The
1995   *The Postmodern Bible.* New Haven: Yale University Press.
Bingham, Charles William
1950   Translator's preface to *Commentaries on the Four Last Books of Moses
          Arranged in the Form of a Harmony,* by John Calvin. Vol. 1. Grand Rapids:
          Eerdmans.
Binns, L. Elliot
1927   *The Book of Numbers, with Introduction and Notes.* London: Methuen.
Bird, Phyllis A.
1989   "The Harlot as Heroine: Narrative Art and Social Presupposition in
          Three Old Testament Texts." *Semeia* 46:119–39.
Black, James
1991   "Ruth in the Dark: Folktale, Law, and Creative Ambiguity in the Old
          Testament." *Journal of Literature and Theology* 5:20–36.
Blackman, Philip, trans.
1963   *Tractate Nedarim.* New York: Judaica.
Blaikie, William
1896   *The First Book of Samuel.* New York: A. C. Armstrong.
Bloch-Smith, Elizabeth
1992   *Judahite Burial Practices and Beliefs about the Dead.* JSOTS 123. Sheffield:
          Sheffield Academic.
Bloom, Harold
1990   "The Breaking of Form." Pp. 1–37 in *De-construction and Criticism,* ed-
          ited by Harold Bloom et al. New York: Continuum.
Boecker, Hans Jochen
1980   *Law and the Administration of Justice in the Old Testament and Ancient East.*
          Translated by Jeremy Moiser. Minneapolis: Augsburg.
Boer, Roland
1997   *Novel Histories.* Playing the Text 2. Sheffield: Sheffield Academic.
Boling, Robert G.
1975   *Judges: Introduction, Translation, and Commentary.* AB. Garden City, N.Y.:
          Doubleday.
Bos, Johanna W. H.
1988   "Out of the Shadows: Genesis 38; Judges 4:17–22; Ruth 3." *Semeia*
          42:37–67.
Brenner, Athalya
1993a   "Female Social Behaviour: Two Descriptive Patterns within the 'Birth
          of the Hero' Paradigm." Pp. 204–21 in *The Feminist Companion to Gene-
          sis.* Edited by Athalya Brenner. FCB 2. Sheffield: Sheffield Academic.
1993b   Introduction to *The Feminist Companion to Judges.* Edited by Athalya
          Brenner. FCB 4. Sheffield: Sheffield Academic.
1994   "On Incest." Pp. 113–38 in *The Feminist Companion to Exodus to Deutero-
          nomy.* Edited by Athalya Brenner. FCB 6. Sheffield: Sheffield Academic.

Brett, Mark G.
1991   *Biblical Criticism in Crisis? The Impact of the Canonical Approach on Old Testament Studies.* Cambridge: Cambridge University Press.
Brin, Gershon
1994   *Studies in Biblical Law. From the Hebrew Bible to the Dead Sea Scrolls.* JSOTS 176. Sheffield: Sheffield Academic.
Brown, Cheryl Anne
1992   *No Longer Be Silent: First-Century Jewish Portraits of Biblical Women (Studies in Pseudo-Philo's "Biblical Antiquities" and Josephus's "Jewish Antiquities").* Louisville: Westminster John Knox.
Brueggemann, Walter
1982   *Genesis.* Interpretation. Atlanta: John Knox.
1990   "I Samuel 1: A Sense of a Beginning." *ZAW* 102:33–48.
Büchner, Dirk.
1997   "Patriarchy and Justice for Women in Africa—Ruth, Tamar." *Scriptura* 62:363–71.
Budd, Philip J.
1984   *Numbers.* Word Biblical Commentary. Waco, Tex.: Word Books.
Burden, Terry L.
1994   *The Kerygma of the Wilderness Traditions in the Hebrew Bible.* New York: Peter Lang.
Calmet, Augustin
1730   *Dictionnaire Historique, Critique, Chronologique, Geographique et Litteral de la Bible.* Paris: Emery, Saugrain, P. Martin.
1737   *Histoire de l'Ancien et du Nouveau Testament, et des Juifs, pour Servir d'Introduction à l'Histoire Ècclèsiastique de M. l'Abbè Fleury.* Paris: Chez G. Martin, J.-B. Coignard.
Calvin, John
1950a   "Preface to the Four Last Books of Moses; Arranged by Him in Form of a Harmony, and Illustrated by Commentaries." Pp. xiv–xviii in *Commentaries on the Four Last Books of Moses Arranged in the Form of a Harmony.* Vol. 1. Translated by Charles William Bingham. Grand Rapids: Eerdmans.
1950b   "The Third Commandment." Pp. 408–32 in *Commentaries on the Four Last Books of Moses Arranged in the Form of a Harmony.* Vol. 2. Translated by Charles William Bingham. Grand Rapids: Eerdmans.
Camp, Claudia V.
1985   Review of *The Workings of Old Testament Narrative,* by Peter D. Miscall. *JBL* 104:504–5.
1988   "Wise and Strange: An Interpretation of the Female Imagery in Proverbs in Light of Trickster Mythology." *Semeia* 42:14–36.
1993   "Feminist Theological Hermeneutics: Canon and Christian Identity." Pp. 154–71 in *A Feminist Introduction.* Vol. 1 of *Searching the Scriptures,* edited by Elisabeth Schüssler Fiorenza and Shelly Matthews. New York: Crossroad.
Caputo, John D.
1987   *Radical Hermeneutics: Repetition, Deconstruction, and the Hermeneutic Project.* Bloomington and Indianapolis: Indiana University Press.
1993   *Demythologizing Heidegger.* Bloomington: Indiana University Press.
Caputo, John D., and Michael J. Scanlon
1999   "Apology for the Impossible: Religion and Postmodernism." Pp. 1–19 in

God, the Gift, and Postmodernism, edited by John D. Caputo and Michael J. Scanlon. Bloomington and Indianapolis: Indiana University Press.

Cardozo, Benjamin N.
1921   *The Nature of the Judicial Process.* New Haven: Yale University Press.
1924   *The Growth of the Law.* New Haven: Yale University Press.
1928   *The Paradoxes of Legal Science.* New York: Columbia University Press.

Carmichael, Calum M.
1982   "Forbidden Mixtures." *VT* 32:394–415.
1985   *Law and Narrative in the Bible: The Evidence of the Deuteronomic Laws and the Decalogue.* Ithaca, N.Y.: Cornell University Press.
1992   *The Origins of Biblical Law: The Decalogue and the Book of the Covenant.* Ithaca, N.Y.: Cornell University Press.

Carroll, Robert P.
1998   "Exile! What Exile? Deportation and the Discourses of Diaspora." Pp. 62–79 in *Leading Captivity Captive: "The Exile" as History and Ideology,* edited by Lester L. Grabbe. JSOTS 278. Sheffield: Sheffield Academic.

Cartledge, Tony W.
1989   "Were Nazirite Vows Unconditional?" *CBQ* 51:409–22.
1992   *Vows in the Hebrew Bible and the Ancient Near East.* JSOTS 147. Sheffield: Sheffield Academic.

Cassuto, Umberto
1972   *The Documentary Hypothesis and the Composition of the Pentateuch: Eight Lectures.* Translated by Israel Abrahams. Jerusalem: Magnes.

Childs, Brevard S.
1970   "The Traditio-Historical Study of the Reed Sea Tradition." *VT* 20:406–18.
1979   *Introduction to the Old Testament as Scripture.* Philadelphia: Fortress.

Chrysostomus, Joannes
1857   "Sermones 5 de Anna." PG 54:631–76.

Clark, Michael
1984   "Imagining the Real: Jameson's Use of Lacan." *New Orleans Review* 11 (spring 1984): 67–72.

Clark, W. Malcolm
1974   "Law." Pp. 99–139 in *Old Testament Form Criticism,* edited by John H. Hayes. San Antonio: Trinity University Press.

Clines, David J. A.
1978   *The Theme of the Pentateuch.* JSOTS 10. Sheffield: Sheffield Academic.
1998   "Varieties of Indeterminacy." Pp. 126–37 in *On the Way to the Postmodern: Old Testament Essays, 1967–1998.* Vol. 1. JSOTS 292. Sheffield: Sheffield Academic.

Coats, George W.
1967   "The Traditio-Historical Character of the Reed Sea Motif." *VT* 17:253–65.
1968   *Rebellion in the Wilderness: The Murmuring Motif in the Wilderness Traditions of the Old Testament.* Nashville: Abingdon.
1972   "Widow's Rights: A Crux in the Structure of Gen. 38." *CBQ* 34:461–66.
1979   "The Sea Tradition in the Wilderness Theme: A Review." *JSOT* 12:2–8.

Collins, John J.
1977   *The Apocalyptic Vision of the Book of Daniel.* HSM 16. Chico, Calif.: Scholars.
1992   "Apocalypses and Apocalypticism: Early Jewish Apocalypticism." *ABD* 1:282–88.

Cook, Joan E.
1998   "Hannah's Later Songs: A Study in Comparative Methods of Interpre-
          tation." Pp. 241–61 in *The Function of Scripture in Early Jewish Tradition*,
          edited by Craig E. Evans and James A. Sanders. JSOTS 154. Sheffield:
          Sheffield Academic.
1999   *Hannah's Desire, God's Design: Early Interpretations of the Story of Hannah.*
          JSOTS 282. Sheffield: Sheffield Academic.
Cornell, Drucilla
1991   *Beyond Accommodation: Ethical Feminism, Deconstruction, and the Law.*
          New York: Routledge.
Crenshaw, James L.
1990   "The Human Dilemma and Literature of Dissent." Pp. 235–58 in *Tradi-
          tion and Theology in the Old Testament*, edited by Douglas A. Knight.
          Sheffield: Sheffield Academic.
Croatto, J. Severino
1987   *Biblical Hermeneutics: Toward a Theory of Reading as the Production of
          Meaning.* Translated by Robert R. Barr. Maryknoll, N.Y.: Orbis Books.
Crüsemann, Frank
1996   *The Torah: Theology and Social History of Old Testament Law.* Translated by
          Allan W. Mahnke. Minneapolis: Fortress.
Daube, David
1947   *Studies in Biblical Law.* London: Cambridge University Press.
1981   *Ancient Jewish Law: Three Inaugural Lectures.* Leiden: Brill.
Davies, Eryl W.
1995   *Numbers.* NCBC. Grand Rapids: Eerdmans.
Davies, Graham I.
1979   *The Way of the Wilderness: A Geographical Study of the Wilderness Itiner-
          aries in the Old Testament.* Cambridge: Cambridge University Press.
1983   "The Wilderness Itineraries and the Composition of the Pentateuch."
          VT 33:1–13.
1992   "Wilderness Wanderings." *ABD* 6:912–14.
Davies, Philip R.
1992   *In Search of "Ancient Israel."* JSOTS 148. Sheffield: Sheffield Academic.
1994   "The Society of Biblical Israel." Pp. 22–33 in *Temple Community in the Per-
          sian Period*, edited by Tamara C. Eskenazi and Kent H. Richards. Vol. 2
          of *Second Temple Studies.* JSOTS 175. Sheffield: Sheffield Academic.
1997   "Whose History? Whose Israel? Whose Bible? Biblical Histories, An-
          cient and Modern." Pp. 104–22 in *Can a "History of Israel" Be Written?*
          edited by Lester L. Grabbe. JSOTS 245. Sheffield: Sheffield Academic.
1998   "Exile? What Exile? Whose Exile?" Pp. 128–38 in *Leading Captivity Cap-
          tive: "The Exile" as History and Ideology*, edited by Lester L. Grabbe.
          JSOTS 278. Sheffield: Sheffield Academic.
Dawson, David
1992   *Allegorical Readers and Cultural Revision in Ancient Alexandria.* Berkeley:
          University of California Press.
Day, Peggy L.
1989   "From the Child Is Born the Woman: The Story of Jephthah's Daugh-
          ter." Pp. 58–74 in *Gender and Difference in Ancient Israel*, edited by
          Peggy L. Day. Minneapolis: Fortress.

Derrida, Jacques
1978   *Writing and Difference*. Translated with an introduction by Alan Bass.
         London: Routledge and Kegan Paul.
1981   *Dissemination*. Translated with an introduction by Barbara Johnson.
         London: Athlone.
1982   "Différance." Pp. 1–27 in *Margins of Philosophy*. Translated by Alan Bass.
         Chicago: University of Chicago Press.
1990   "Force of the Law: The 'Mystical Foundation of Authority.'" Translated
         by Mary Quaintance. *Cardozo Law Review* 11:919–1045.
1991   *Cinders*. Edited and translated by Ned Lukacher. Lincoln: University of
         Nebraska Press.
1995   *The Gift of Death*. Translated by David Wills. Chicago and London: Uni-
         versity of Chicago Press.
2002   *Without Alibi*. Edited and translated by Peggy Kamuf. Stanford, Calif.:
         Stanford University Press.
de Tarragon, Jean-Michel
1992   "Ammon." Translated by Gerard J. Norton. *ABD* 1:194–96.
Detweiler, Robert
1991   "Parerga: Homely Details, Secret Intentions, Veiled Threats." *Journal of
         Literature and Theology* 5:1–10.
Dever, William G.
2001   *What Did the Biblical Writers Know, and When Did They Know It? What Ar-
         chaeology Can Tell Us About the Reality of Ancient Israel*. Grand Rapids:
         Eerdmans.
Dodaro, Robert
1999   "Loose Canons: Augustine and Derrida on Their Selves." Pp. 79–111 in
         God, the Gift, and Postmodernism, edited by John D. Caputo and Mich-
         ael J. Scanlon. Bloomington and Indianapolis: Indiana University
         Press.
Doody, Margaret Anne
1994   "Infant Piety and the Infant Samuel." Pp. 103–22, 338, in *Out of the Gar-
         den: Women Writers on the Bible*, edited by Christina Büchmann and
         Celina Spiegel. New York: Fawcett Columbine.
Douglas, Mary
1975   *Implicit Meanings: Essays in Anthropology*. London: Routledge & Kegan
         Paul.
1982   *In the Active Voice*. London: Routledge & Kegan Paul.
1984   *Purity and Danger: An Analysis of the Concepts of Pollution and Taboo*. Lon-
         don: Ark Paperbacks.
1993   *In the Wilderness: The Doctrine of Defilement in the Book of Numbers*.
         JSOTS 158. Sheffield: Sheffield Academic.
Dworkin, Ronald
1996   *Freedom's Law: The Moral Reading of the American Constitution*. Cam-
         bridge: Harvard University Press.
Dyrness, William A.
1994   "Waiting in Hope." *Christian Century* 111, 2 November, 1011.
Eco, Umberto
1983   *Postscript to the Name of the Rose*. Orlando, Fla.: Harcourt, Brace and Jo-
         vanovich.

Eichrodt, Walther
1961   *Theology of the Old Testament.* Translated by J. Baker. Vol. 1. Philadel-
          phia: Westminster.
Ellis, Peter
1968   *The Yahwist: The Bible's First Theologian.* Notre Dame, Ind.: Fides.
Emerton, John A.
1975   "Some Problems in Genesis xxxviii." *VT* 25:338–61.
1976   "An Examination of a Recent Structuralist Interpretation of Genesis
          xxxviii." *VT* 26:79–98.
1979   "Judah and Tamar." *VT* 29:403–15.
Engnell, Ivan
1960   "Methodological Aspects of Old Testament Study." Pp. 13–30 in *Supple-
          ments to Vetus Testamentum, Congress Volume, Oxford 1959,* edited by
          G. W. Anderson et al. Leiden: E. J. Brill.
1969   *A Rigid Scrutiny: Critical Essays of the Old Testament.* Edited and trans-
          lated by John T. Willis and Helmer Ringgren. Nashville: Vanderbilt
          University Press.
Erdmann, David
1877   *Books of Samuel.* Translated by C. H. Troy and John A. Broadus. New
          York: Charles Scribner.
Exum, J. Cheryl
1989   "The Tragic Vision and Biblical Narrative: The Case of Jephthah." Pp.
          59–83 in *Signs and Wonders: Biblical Texts in Literary Focus,* edited by
          J. Cheryl Exum. Semeia Studies. Atlanta: Scholars Press.
1992   *Tragedy and Biblical Narrative: Arrows of the Almighty.* Cambridge: Uni-
          versity Press.
1993   "On Judges 11." Pp. 131–44 in *The Feminist Companion to Judges,* edited
          by Athalya Brenner. FCB 4. Sheffield: Sheffield Academic.
1995   "Feminist Criticism: Whose Interests Are Being Served?" Pp. 65–90 in
          Judges and Method: New Approaches in Biblical Studies, edited by Gale A.
          Yee. Minneapolis: Fortress.
Falk, Marcia
1994   "Reflections on Hannah's Prayer." Pp. 94–102, 337, in *Out of the Garden:
          Women Writers on the Bible,* edited by Christina Büchmann and Celina
          Spiegel. New York: Fawcett Columbine.
Falk, Z.
1964   *Hebrew Law in Biblical Times.* Jerusalem: Wahrmann Books.
Fewell, Danna Nolan
1987   "Feminist Reading of the Hebrew Bible: Affirmation, Resistance and
          Transformation." *JSOT* 39:77–87.
1992   "Judges." Pp. 67–77 in *The Women's Bible Commentary,* edited by
          Carol A. Newsom and Sharon H. Ringe. London: SPCK; Louisville:
          Westminster John Knox.
1995   "Deconstructive Criticism: Achsah and the (E)razed City of Writing."
          Pp. 119–45 in *Judges and Method: New Approaches in Biblical Studies,* ed-
          ited by Gale A. Yee. Minneapolis: Fortress.
———, ed.
1992   *Reading between Texts: Intertextuality and the Hebrew Bible.* LCBI.
          Louisville: Westminster John Knox.

Fewell, Danna Nolan, and David M. Gunn
1990   "Controlling Perspectives: Women, Men, and the Authority of Violence in Judges 4 and 5." *JAAR* 77:389–411.
1993   *Gender, Power, and Promise: The Subject of the Bible's First Story.* Nashville: Abingdon.

Fish, Stanley
1989   *Doing What Comes Naturally: Change, Rhetoric, and the Practice of Theory in Literary and Legal Studies.* Durham, N.C., and London: Duke University Press.

Fishbane, Michael
1985   *Biblical Interpretation in Ancient Israel.* Oxford: Clarendon.
1993a   Introduction to *The Midrashic Imagination: Jewish Exegesis, Thought, and History,* edited by Michael Fishbane. Albany: State University of New York Press.
1993b   "'The Holy One Sits and Roars': Mythopoesis and the Midrashic Imagination." Pp. 60–77 in *The Midrashic Imagination: Jewish Exegesis, Thought, and History,* edited by Michael Fishbane. Albany: State University of New York Press.

Flanagan, James W.
1976   "History, Religion, and Ideology: The Caleb Tradition." *Horizons* 3:175–85.

Fokkelman, Jan P.
1996   "Genesis 37 and 38 at the Interface of Structural Analysis and Hermeneutics." Pp. 152–87 in *Literary Structure and Rhetorical Strategies in the Hebrew Bible.* Assen, the Netherlands: Van Gorcum.

Foucault, Michel
1975   *The Birth of the Clinic.* Translated by A. M. Sheridan Smith. New York: Vintage Books.
1977   "What Is an Author?" Pp. 113–38 in *Language, Counter-Memory, Practice: Selected Essays and Interviews,* edited by Donald F. Bouchard, translated by Donald F. Bouchard and Sherry Simon. Ithaca, N.Y.: Cornell University Press.
1980   *Power/Knowledge: Selected Interviews and Other Writings, 1972–1977.* Edited and translated by Colin Gordon. New York: Pantheon.
1999   *Religion and Culture.* Edited by Jeremy R. Carrette. New York: Routledge.

Fowl, Stephen
1995   "Texts Don't Have Ideologies." *Biblical Interpretation* 3:15–34.

Freedman, H.
1936   *Nedarim.* Translated by H. Freedman. London: Soncino.

Fretheim, Terence E.
1991   *Exodus.* Interpretation. Louisville: John Knox.

Frymer-Kensky, Tikva
1980   "Tit for Tat: The Principle of Equal Retribution in Near Eastern and Biblical Law." *BA* 43:230–34.

Fuchs, Esther
1985   "The Literary Characterization of Mothers and Sexual Politics in the Hebrew Bible." Pp. 116–36 in *Feminist Perspectives on Biblical Scholarship,* edited by Adela Yarbro Collins. Chico, Calif.: Scholars.
1993   "Marginalization, Ambiguity, Silencing: The Story of Jephthah's

Daughter." Pp. 116–30 in *The Feminist Companion to Judges,* edited by Athalya Brenner. FCB 4. Sheffield: Sheffield Academic.

2000   *Sexual Politics in the Biblical Narrative: Reading the Hebrew Bible as a Woman.* JSOTS 310. Sheffield: Sheffield Academic.

Furman, Nelly
1985   "His Story versus Her Story: Male Genealogy and Female Strategy in the Jacob Cycle." Pp. 107–16 in *Feminist Perspectives on Biblical Scholarship,* edited by Adela Yabro Collins. Chico, Calif.: Scholars.

Gammie, John G.
1970   "Theology of Retribution in the Book of Deuteronomy." *CBQ* 32:1–12.

Geertz, Clifford
1973   *The Interpretation of Cultures.* New York: Basic Books.

Gerstenberger, Erhard
1965   "Covenant and Commandment." *JBL* 84:38–51.

Goldin, Judah
1977   "The Youngest Son or Where Does Genesis 38 Belong." *JBL* 96:27–44.

Good, Edwin M.
1988   "Deception and Women: A Response." *Semeia* 42:116–32.

Goodenough, Erwin R.
1935   *By Light, Light: The Mystic Gospel of Hellenistic Judaism.* New Haven, Conn.: Amsterdam.
1962   *An Introduction to Philo Judaeus.* 2d ed. Oxford: Basil Blackwell.

Goodman, L. E.
1986   "The Biblical Laws of Diet and Sex." Pp. 17–57 in *Jewish Law Association Studies II: The Jerusalem Conference,* edited by Bernard S. Jackson. Atlanta: Scholars.

Gottwald, Norman K.
1979   *The Tribes of Yahweh: A Sociology of the Religion of Liberated Israel, 1250– 1050 B.C.E.* London: SCM.
1985   *The Hebrew Bible: A Socio-literary Introduction.* Philadelphia: Fortress.

Gray, George B.
1903   *A Critical and Exegetical Commentary on Numbers.* ICC. New York: Charles Scribner's Sons.

Gray, John
1986   *Joshua, Judges, Ruth.* NCBC. Grand Rapids: Eerdmans.

Greengus, Samuel
1992   "Law: Biblical and ANE Law." *ABD* 4:242–52.

Gregory I
1989   *Commentaire sur le Premier Livre des Rois.* Translated by Adalbert de Vogüé. SC 351. Paris: Cerf.
1993   *Commentaire sur le Premier Livre des Rois.* Translated by Christophe Vuillaume. SC 391. Paris: Cerf.

Greimas, A. J.
1983   *Structural Semantics: An Attempt at a Method.* Lincoln: University of Nebraska Press.

Gruenwald, Ithamar
1993   "Midrash and the 'Midrashic Condition': Preliminary Considerations." Pp. 6–22 in *The Midrashic Imagination: Jewish Exegesis, Thought, and History,* edited by Michael Fishbane. Albany: State University of New York Press.

Gunn, David M.
1980   *The Fate of King Saul: An Interpretation of a Biblical Story.* JSOTS 14.
            Sheffield: JSOT.
1984   Review of *The Art of Biblical Narrative,* by Robert Alter. *JSOT* 29:109–16.
1987   "Joshua and Judges." Pp. 102–21 in *The Literary Guide to the Bible,* edited
            by Robert Alter and Frank Kermode. Cambridge: Harvard University
            Press.
1989   "In Security: The David of Biblical Narrative." Pp. 133–51 in *Signs and
            Wonders: Biblical Texts in Literary Focus,* edited by J. Cheryl Exum. Se-
            meia Studies. Atlanta: Scholars Press.
Gunn, David M., and Danna Nolan Fewell
1993   *Narrative in the Hebrew Bible.* OBS. Oxford: Oxford University Press.
Gutiérrez, Gustavo
1983   *The Power of the Poor in History.* Translated by Robert R. Barr. Maryknoll,
            N.Y.: Orbis Books.
1987   *On Job: God-Talk and the Suffering of the Innocent.* Translated by Matthew
            J. O'Connell. Maryknoll, N.Y.: Orbis Books.
Hamlin, E. John
1990   *At Risk in the Promised Land: A Commentary on the Book of Judges.* ITC.
            Grand Rapids: Eerdmans.
Hanson, A. T.
1989   "Origen's Treatment of the Sacrifice of Jephthah's Daughter." *Studia pa-
            tristica* 21:298–300.
Hanson, Paul
1987   *Old Testament Apocalyptic.* Interpreting Biblical Texts. Nashville: Abingdon.
Harrelson, Walter
1990   "Life, Faith, and the Emergence of Tradition." Pp. 11–30 in *Tradition and
            Theology in the Old Testament,* edited by Douglas A. Knight. Sheffield:
            Sheffield Academic.
Harris, J. Gordon
1987   *Biblical Perspectives on Aging: God and the Elderly.* OBT. Philadelphia:
            Fortress.
Harris, Scott L.
1992   "Hannah's Vow to Yahweh in I Samuel 1: An Issue of Faithfulness."
            Lutheran Forum 26:28–33.
Harrison, R. K.
1990   *Numbers.* Wycliffe Exegetical Commentary. Chicago: Moody.
Hart, Kevin
1989   *The Trespass of the Sign: Deconstruction, Theology, and Philosophy.* Cam-
            bridge: Cambridge University Press.
Havea, Jione
1995   "The Future Stands between Here and There: Towards an Island(ic)
            Hermeneutic." *The Pacific Journal of Theology,* ser. 2, no. 13: 61–68.
1998   *"Tau lave!* [Let's Talk]." *The Pacific Journal of Theology,* ser. 2, no. 20:
            63–73.
2000   "Keep Your Vow: A Transtextual Reading of Numbers 30." Ph.D. diss.,
            Southern Methodist University.
Hayes, C. E.
1995   "The Midrashic Career of the Confession of Judah (Genesis xxxviii
            26)." *VT* 45:62–81.

Heard, R. Christopher
2001   *Dynamics of Diselection: Ambiguity in Genesis 12–36 and Ethnic Boundaries in Post-exilic Judah.* Semeia Studies 39. Atlanta: Society of Biblical Literature.
Herberg, Will
1964   "Five Meanings of the Word 'Historical.'" *The Christian Scholar* 47:327–30.
Heym, Stefan
1973   *The King David Report.* New York: G. P. Putnam.
Ho, Graig Y. S.
1999   "The Stories of the Family Troubles of Judah and David: A Study of Their Literary Links." *VT* 49:514–31.
Houston, Walter
1993   *Purity and Monotheism: Clean and Unclean Animals in Biblical Law.* JSOTS 140. Sheffield: Sheffield Academic.
Hyatt, J. Philip
1971   *Exodus.* Grand Rapids: Eerdmans.
Idel, Moshe
1993   "Midrashic versus Other Forms of Jewish Hermeneutics: Some Comparative Reflections." Pp. 45–58 in *The Midrashic Imagination: Jewish Exegesis, Thought, and History,* edited by Michael Fishbane. Albany: State University of New York Press.
Ingalis, Alan Dean
1991   "The Literary Unity of the Book of Numbers." Th.D. diss., Dallas Theological Seminary.
Irigaray, Luce
1980   "When Our Lips Speak Together." Translated by Carolyn Burke. *Signs: Journal of Women in Culture and Society* 6:69–79.
Iser, Wolfgang
1974   *The Implied Reader: Patterns of Communication in Prose Fiction from Bunyan to Beckett.* Baltimore and London: Johns Hopkins University Press.
1978   *The Act of Reading: A Theory of Aesthetic Response.* Baltimore and London: Johns Hopkins University Press.
Jackson, Bernard S.
1973   "Reflections on Biblical Criminal Law." *Journal of Jewish Studies* 24:8–38.
1987   "Some Semiotic Questions for Biblical Law." Pp. 1–25 in *Jewish Law Association Studies III: The Oxford Conference Volume,* edited by A. M. Fuss. Atlanta: Scholars.
Jameson, Fredric
1981   *The Political Unconscious: Narrative as a Socially Symbolic Act.* Ithaca, N.Y.: Cornell University Press.
1988   *The Ideologies of Theory: Essays, 1971–1986.* Vol. 1: *Situations of Theory.* London: Routledge.
1998   *The Cultural Turn: Selected Writings on the Postmodern, 1983–1998.* London and New York: Verso.
Jastram, Nathan Ray
1990   "The Book of Numbers from Qumran, Cave IV (4QNum[b])." Ph.D. diss., Harvard University.
1994   "4QNum[b]." Pp. 248–51 in *Qumran Cave 4, VII,* edited by Eugene Ulrich et al. Discoveries in the Judaean Desert 12. Oxford: Clarendon.

Jobling, David
1980   "'The Jordan a Boundary': A Reading of Numbers 32 and Joshua 22."
          Pp. 183–207 in *Society of Biblical Literature 1980 Seminar Papers*, edited by
          Paul J. Achtemeier. Chico, Calif.: Scholars.
1986   *The Sense of Biblical Narrative: Structural Analyses in the Hebrew Bible II.*
          JSOTS 39. Sheffield: JSOT.
1991a   "Feminism and 'Mode of Production in Ancient Israel: Search for a
          Method." Pp. 239–51 in *The Bible and the Politics of Exegesis: Essays in
          Honor of Norman K. Gottwald on His Sixty-fifth Birthday*, edited by David
          Jobling, Peggy L. Day, and Gerald T. Sheppard. Cleveland: Pilgrim.
1991b   "Mieke Bal on Biblical Narrative." *Religious Studies Review* 17:1–10.
1994   "Hannah's Desire." *The Canadian Society of Biblical Studies Bulletin*
          53:19–32.
1998   *1 Samuel.* Berit Olam: Studies in Hebrew Narrative and Poetry. Col-
          legeville, Minn.: Liturgical Press.
Josephus, Flavius
1998   *Jewish Antiquities.* Translated by Henry St. John Thackeray. Cambridge:
          Harvard University Press.
Kaiser, Otto
1977   *Introduction to the Old Testament.* Minneapolis: Augsburg.
Kaufmann, Yehezkel
1966   *The Religion of Israel.* Translated by Moshe Greenberg. Abridged ed.
          Chicago: University of Chicago Press.
Keefe, Alice A.
1995   "The Female Body, the Body Politic, and the Land: A Sociopolitical
          Reading of Hosea 1–2." Pp. 70–100 in *A Feminist Companion to The Lat-
          ter Prophets*, edited by Athalya Brenner. FCB 8. Sheffield: Sheffield Aca-
          demic.
King, Richard
1999   *Orientalism and Religion: Postcolonial Theory, India, and "the Mystic East."*
          London and New York: Routledge.
Kirkpatrick, Alexander Francis
1886   *The First Book of Samuel: With Map, Notes, and Introduction.* Cambridge:
          Cambridge University Press.
Klein, Lillian R.
1994   "Hannah: Marginalized Victim and Social Redeemer." Pp. 77–92 in *A
          Feminist Companion to Samuel and Kings*, edited by Athalya Brenner.
          FCB 5. Sheffield: Sheffield Academic.
Knierim, Rolf P.
1989   "The Problem of Ancient Israel's Prescriptive Legal Traditions." *Semeia*
          45:7–25.
Knight, Douglas A.
1990   "Tradition and Theology." Pp. 1–8 in *Tradition and Theology in the Old
          Testament*, edited by Douglas A. Knight. Sheffield: Sheffield Academic.
Kottsieper, Ingo
1973   "שבע." *ThWAT* 7: 974–1000.
Kramer, Phyllis Silverman
1999   "Jephthah's Daughter: A Thematic Approach to the Narrative as Seen
          in Selected Rabbinic Exegesis and in Artwork." Pp. 67–92 in *Judges: A*

Feminist Companion to the Bible, edited by Athalaya Brenner. 2d ser.
Sheffield: Sheffield Academic.

Kristeva, Julia
1991   _Strangers to Ourselves._ Translated by Leon S. Roudiez. New York: Columbia University Press.

Kutz, Christopher L.
1994   "Just Disagreement: Indeterminacy and Rationality in the Rule of Law." _Yale Law Journal_ 103:997–1030.

Kwok Pui-lan
1995   _Discovering the Bible in the Non-biblical World._ Maryknoll, N.Y.: Orbis Books.

Lacan, Jacques
1977   _Écrits: A Selection._ Translated by Alan Sheridan. New York: W. W. Norton.

LaCocque, André
1998   "Thou Shall Not Kill." Pp. 71–109 in _Thinking Biblically: Exegetical and Hermeneutical Studies,_ edited by André LaCocque and Paul Ricoeur, translated by David Pellauer. Chicago and London: University of Chicago Press.

Lambe, Anthony J.
1998   "Genesis 38: Structure and Literary Design." Pp. 102–20 in _The World of Genesis: Persons, Places, Perspectives,_ edited by Philip R. Davies and David J. A. Clines. JSOTS 257. Sheffield: Sheffield Academic.
1999   "Judah's Development: The Pattern of Departure-Transition-Return." _JSOT_ 83:53–68.

Lamberton, Robert
1986   _Homer, the Theologian: Neoplatonist Allegorical Reading and the Growth of the Epic Tradition._ Berkeley: University of California Press.

Landers, Solomon
1991   "Did Jephthah Kill His Daughter?" _Bible Review_ 7, no. 4: 28–31, 42.

Lasine, Stuart
1986   "Indeterminacy and the Bible: A Review of Literary and Anthropological Theories and Their Application to Biblical Texts." _Hebrew Studies_ 27:48–80.

Lee, Jung Young
1995   _Marginality: The Key to Multicultural Theology._ Minneapolis: Fortress.

Lemche, Niels Peter
1998   _The Israelites in History and Tradition._ Louisville: Westminster John Knox.

Levenson, Jon D.
1988   _Creation and the Persistence of Evil: The Jewish Drama of Divine Omnipotence._ San Francisco: Harper and Row.

Levinas, Emmanuel
1979   "To Love the Torah More Than God." Translated by Helen A. Stephenson and Richard I. Sugarman. _Judaism_ 28:216–20.
1981   _Otherwise Than Being or Beyond Essence._ Translated by Alphonso Lingis. The Hague: Nijhoff.
1985   _Ethics and Infinity._ Translated by Richard Cohen. Pittsburgh: Duquesne University Press.
1987   _Time and the Other._ Translated by Richard A. Cohen. Pittsburgh: Duquesne University Press.

1993   *Outside the Subject.* Translated by Michael B. Smith. Stanford, Calif.:
            Stanford University Press.

Levine, Baruch A.

1993   *Numbers 1–20: A New Translation with Introduction and Commentary.* AB.
            New York: Doubleday.

2000   *Numbers 21–36: A New Translation with Introduction and Commentary.* AB.
            New York: Doubleday.

Levinson, Bernard M.

1997   *Deuteronomy and the Hermeneutics of Legal Innovation.* New York and
            Oxford: Oxford University Press.

Lewis, Theodore J.

1985   "The Songs of Hannah and Deborah: *HDL*-II ('Growing Plump')." *JBL*
            104: 105–14.

Linton, Gregory

1991   "Reading the Apocalypse as an Apocalypse." Pp. 161–86 in *Society of
            Biblical Literature 1991 Seminar Papers,* edited by Eugene H. Lovering, Jr.
            Atlanta: Scholars.

Lockwood, Peter F.

1992   "Tamar's Place in the Joseph Cycle." *Lutheran Theological Journal* 26:35–43.

Long, Burke O.

1984   Review of *The Workings of Old Testament Narrative,* by Peter D. Miscall.
            CBQ 46:767–69.

1997   *Planting and Reaping Albright: Politics, Ideology, and Interpreting the Bible.*
            University Park: Pennsylvania State University Press.

Luther, Bernhard

1991   "The Novella of Judah and Tamar and Other Israelite Novellas." Pp.
            89–118 in *Narrative and Novella in Samuel: Studies by Hugo Gressmann
            and Other Scholars, 1906–1922,* edited by David M. Gunn. JSOTS 116.
            Historic Texts and Interpreters in Biblical Scholarship 9. Sheffield: Al-
            mond.

Lyotard, Jean-François

1984   "The Unconscious, History, and Phrases: Notes on *The Political Uncon-
            scious.*" Translated by Michael Clark. *New Orleans Review* 11 (spring):
            73–79.

Maddox, Randy L.

1987   "Damned if You Do and Damned if You Don't: Tamar—A Feminist
            Foremother. Genesis 38:6–26." *Daughters of Sarah* 13 (August): 14–17.

Magnetti, Donald L., S.J.

1969   "The Oath in the Old Testament in the Light of Related Terms and in
            the Legal and Covenantal Context of the Ancient Near East." Ph.D.
            diss., John Hopkins University.

Markus, Robert A.

1995   "The Jew as a Hermeneutic Device: The Inner Life of a Gregorian Topos."
            Pp. 1–15 in *Gregory the Great: A Symposium,* edited by John C. Cavadini.
            Notre Dame, Ind., and London: University of Notre Dame Press.

Mathew, Aley

1984   "Administration of Law and the Oppressed, Particularly Women." *Re-
            ligion and Society* 31:48–52.

Mathewson, Steven D.

1989   "An Exegetical Study of Genesis 38." *Bibliotheca Sacra* 146:373–92.

Matthewson, Daniel B.
2002   "A Critical Binarism: Source Criticism and Deconstructive Criticism."
        JSOT 98:3–28.
Mattingly, Gerald L.
1992   "Chemosh." *ABD* 1:895–97.
Mayes, A. D. H.
1974   *Israel in the Period of the Judges.* Naperville, Ill.: Alec R. Allenson.
McCarthy, Dennis J., S.J.
1963   *Treaty and Covenant: A Study in the Ancient Oriental Documents and in the
        Old Testament.* Analecta biblica 21. Rome: Pontifican Biblical Institute.
1972   *Old Testament Covenant: A Survey of Current Opinions.* Richmond: John
        Knox.
McCurley, Foster R.
1979   *Genesis, Exodus, Leviticus, Numbers.* Proclamation. Philadelphia: Fortress.
McEvenue, Sean E.
1971   *The Narrative Style of the Priestly Writer.* Rome: Biblical Institute Press.
McKenzie, Steven L.
1984   *The Chronicler's Use of the Deuteronomistic History.* HSM 33. Atlanta:
        Scholars.
McKnight, Edgar V.
1988   *Postmodern Use of the Bible: The Emergence of Reader-Oriented Criticism.*
        Nashville: Abingdon.
Mendenhall, George E.
1954   "Ancient Oriental and Biblical Law." *BA* 17:26–46.
1955   *Law and Covenant in Israel and the Ancient Near East.* Pittsburgh: Biblical
        Colloquium.
1958   "The Census Lists of Numbers 1 and 26." *JBL* 77:52–66.
1962   "The Hebrew Conquest of Palestine." *BA* 25, no. 3: 66–87.
1992   "Amorites." *ABD* 1:199–202.
Mendenhall, George E., and Gary A. Herion
1992   "Covenant." *ABD* 1:1179–1202.
Menn, Esther M.
1997   *Judah and Tamar (Genesis 38) in Ancient Jewish Exegesis: Studies in Liter-
        ary Form and Hermeneutics.* Leiden: Brill.
1998   "Sanctification of the (Divine) Name: *Targum Neofiti*'s 'Translation' of
        Genesis 38.25–26." Pp. 206–40 in *The Function of Scripture in Early Jew-
        ish and Christian Tradition,* edited by Craig A. Evans and James A.
        Sanders. JSNTS 154. Sheffield: Sheffield Academic.
Meyer, Linda Ross
1996   "When Reasonable Minds Differ." *New York University Law Review*
        71:1467–528.
Meyers, Carol
1988   *Discovering Eve: Ancient Israelite Women in Context.* New York and Ox-
        ford: Oxford University Press.
1994   "Hannah and Her Sacrifice: Reclaiming Female Agency." Pp. 93–104 in
        A Feminist Companion to Samuel and Kings, edited by Athalya Brenner.
        FCB 5. Sheffield: Sheffield Academic.
Milgrom, Jacob
1990   *Numbers.* JPS Torah Commentary. Philadelphia and New York: Jewish
        Publication Society.

Miller, J. I.
1967   "Use and Abuse of the Bible." *The Morningside Review* 6:72–75.
Miscall, Peter D.
1972   "The Concept of the Poor in the Old Testament." Ph.D. diss., Harvard University.
1978   "The Jacob and Joseph Stories as Analogies." *JSOT* 6:28–40.
1979   "Literary Unity in the Old Testament Narrative." *Semeia* 15:27–44.
1983   *The Workings of Old Testament Narrative.* Chico, Calif.: Scholars.
1986   *1 Samuel: A Literary Reading.* Indiana Studies in Biblical Literature. Bloomington: Indiana University Press.
1992   "Biblical Narrative and Categories of the Fantastic." *Semeia* 60:39–51.
1998   "Introduction to Narrative Literature." Pp. 539–52 in *The New Interpreter's Bible,* edited by Leander E. Keck et al. Vol. 2. Nashville: Abingdon.
1999   *Isaiah 34–35: A Nightmare/A Dream.* JSOTS 281. Sheffield: Sheffield Academic.
Moore, George Foot
1901   *A Critical and Exegetical Commentary on Judges.* ICC. New York: Charles Scribner.
Moore, Stephen D.
1994   *Poststructuralism and the New Testament: Derrida and Foucault at the Foot of the Cross.* Minneapolis: Fortress.
Morden, John W.
1984   "An Essay on the Connections between Law and Religion." *The Journal of Law and Religion* 2:7–39.
Morimura, Nobuko
1993   "The Story of Tamar: A Feminist Interpretation of Genesis 38." *Japan Christian Review* 59:55–67.
Mowinckel, Sigmund
1964   *Tetrateuch-Pentateuch-Hexateuch: Die Berichte über die Landnahme in den drei altisraelitischen Geschichtswerken.* BZAW 90. Berlin: Walter de Gruyter.
Mudge, Lewis S.
1980   "Paul Ricoeur on Biblical Interpretation." Pp. 1–40 in *Essays on Biblical Interpretation,* by Paul Ricoeur. Philadelphia: Fortress.
Müllner, Ilse
1999   "Lethal Differences: Sexual Violence as Violence against Others in Judges 19." Pp. 126–42 in *Judges: A Feminist Companion to the Bible,* edited by Athalya Brenner. 2d ser. Sheffield: Sheffield Academic.
Muraoka, T.
1996   "1 Sam 1, 15 Again." *Biblica* 77:98–99.
Nahkola, Aulikki
2001   *Double Narratives in the Old Testament: The Foundations of Method in Biblical Criticism.* BZAW 290. Berlin and New York: Walter de Gruyter.
Neusner, Jacob
1973   *The Idea of Purity in Ancient Judaism.* The Haskell Lectures, 1972–1973. With a critique and a commentary by Mary Douglas. Studies in Judaism and Late Antiquity: From the First to the Seventh Century 1. Leiden: E. J. Brill.
1991   *The Talmud: A Close Encounter.* Minneapolis: Fortress.
1992   *The Mishnah: Introduction and Reader.* Philadelphia: Trinity Press International.

1995a   *The Talmud of Babylonia: A Complete Outline.* Pt. 2, *The Division of Women.*
           Vol. B, *From Tractate Nedarim through Tractate Qiddushin.* Atlanta: Schol-
           ars.
1995b   *The Talmud of Babylonia: An Academic Commentary, XV Bavli Tractate
           Nedarim.* Atlanta: Scholars.
1996   *The Two Talmuds Compared.* Pt. 2, *The Division of Women in the Talmud of
           the Land of Israel and the Talmud of Babylonia.* Vol. B, *Tractates Nedarim,
           Nazir and Sotah.* Atlanta: Scholars.
1998   *How the Rabbis Liberated Women.* Atlanta: Scholars.
Niditch, Susan
1979   "The Wronged Woman Righted: An Analysis of Genesis 38." *HTR*
           72:143–49.
1987   *Underdogs and Tricksters: A Prelude to Biblical Folklore.* New Voices in Bib-
           lical Studies. New York and San Francisco: Harper and Row.
Noble, Paul R.
2002   "Esau, Tamar, and Joseph: Criteria for Identifying Inner-Biblical Allu-
           sions." *VT* 52:219–52.
Noth, Martin
1960   *The History of Israel.* 2d ed. London: Adam & Charles Black.
1962   *Exodus: A Commentary.* Translated by J. S. Bowden. OTL. Philadelphia:
           Westminster.
1968   *Numbers: A Commentary.* OTL. Philadelphia: Westminster.
1981a   *The Deuteronomistic History.* JSOTS 15. Sheffield: JSOT.
1981b   *A History of Pentateuchal Traditions.* Translated by Bernhard W. Ander-
           son. Chico, Calif.: Scholars.
Olson, Dennis T.
1985   *The Death of the Old and the Birth of the New: The Framework of the Book of
           Numbers and the Pentateuch.* Chico, Calif.: Scholars.
1994   *Deuteronomy and the Death of Moses: A Theological Reading.* OBT. Min-
           neapolis: Fortress.
1996   *Numbers.* Interpretation. Louisville: John Knox.
Ostriker, Alicia Suskin
1993   *Feminist Revision and the Bible.* Oxford: Basil Blackwell.
1997   "A Triple Hermeneutic: Scripture and Revisionist Women's Poetry." Pp.
           164–89 in *A Feminist Companion to Reading the Bible: Approaches, Methods,
           and Strategies,* edited by Athalya Brenner and Carole Fontaine.
           Sheffield: Sheffield Academic.
Ozick, Cynthia
1994   "Hannah and Elkanah: Torah as the Matrix of Feminism." Pp. 88–93 in
           Out of the Garden: Women Writers on the Bible, edited by Christina Büch-
           mann and Celina Spiegel. New York: Fawcett Columbine.
Pardes, Ilana
1992   *Countertraditions in the Bible: A Feminist Approach.* Cambridge: Harvard
           University Press.
Patrick, Dale
1985   *Old Testament Law.* Atlanta: John Knox.
———, ed.
1989   "Thinking Biblical Law." *Semeia* 45. [The reference is to one issue of the
           journal, with the given theme.]

Patrick, Simon

1702   *A Commentary upon the Books of Joshua, Judges, and Ruth.* London: Ri
        Chiswell.

1703   *A Commentary upon the Two Books of Samuel.* London: Ri Chiswell.

Penchansky, David

1990   *The Betrayal of God: Ideological Conflict in Job.* LCBI. Louisville: Westmin-
        ster John Knox.

1992   "Up for Grabs: A Tentative Proposal for Doing Ideological Criticism."
        Semeia 59:35–41.

Peters, F. E.

1970   *The Harvest of Hellenism: A History of the Near East from Alexander the
        Great to the Triumph of Christianity.* New York: Simon and Schuster.

Phillips, Gary A., and Danna Nolan Fewell

1997   "Ethics, Bible, Reading as If." *Semeia* 77:1–21.

Pixley, George V., and Clodovis Boff

1989   *The Bible, the Church, and the Poor.* Translated by Paul Burns. Maryknoll,
        N.Y.: Orbis Books.

Plaut, W. Gunther

1981   *The Torah: A Modern Commentary.* New York: Union of American He-
        brew Congregations.

Polanski, Donald C.

1995   "On Taming Tamar: Amram's Rhetoric and Women's Roles in Pseudo-
        Philo's *Liber Antiquitatum Biblicarum 9.*" *Journal for the Study of the
        Pseudepigrapha* 13:79–99.

Polzin, Robert

1980   *Moses and the Deuteronomist: A Literary Study of the Deuteronomistic His-
        tory.* Pt. 1, *Deuteronomy, Joshua, Judges.* Bloomington and Indianapolis:
        Indiana University Press.

Pomeroy, Sarah B.

1975   *Goddesses, Whores, Wives and Slaves: Women in Classical Antiquity.* New
        York: Schocken.

Power, William J. A.

1961   "A Study of Irony in the Book of Job." Ph.D. diss., University of Toronto.

1992   *Once upon a Time: A Humorous Re-telling of the Genesis Stories.* Nashville:
        Abingdon.

Pressler, Carolyn

1993   *The View of Women Found in the Deuteronomic Family Laws.* Berlin and
        New York: Walter de Gruyter.

Pseudo-Philo

1917   *Biblical Antiquities.* Edited and translated by Montaque Rhodes James.
        London: SPCK.

Qimron, Elisha

1996   *The Temple Scroll: A Critical Edition with Extensive Reconstructions, Judean
        Desert Studies.* Jerusalem: Israel Exploration Society.

Rahlfs, Alfred, ed.

1935   *Septuaginta id est Vetus Testamentum Graece Iuxta LXX Interpretes.*
        Stuttgart: Privilegierte Württembergische Bibelanstalt.

Rakover, Nahum

1992   "Violation of the Law in Order to Preserve It: *Gedolah Averah Lishman.*"

Pp. 107–23 in *Jewish Law Association Studies VI: The Jerusalem 1990 Conference Volume*, edited by Bernard S. Jackson and S. M. Passamaneck. Atlanta: Scholars.

Rendsburg, Gary A.
1986   "David and His Circle in Genesis xxxviii." *VT* 36:438–46.
Ricoeur, Paul
1967   *The Symbolism of Evil*. Translated by Emerson Buchanan. Boston: Beacon.
1978   "Existence and Hermeneutics." Pp. 97–108 in *The Philosophy of Paul Ricoeur: Anthology of His Work*, edited by Charles E. Reagan and David Stewart. Boston: Beacon.
1980   *Essays on Biblical Interpretation*. Edited by Lewis S. Mudge. Philadelphia: Fortress.
1984   "Dialogues with Paul Ricoeur." Pp. 15–46 in *Dialogues with Contemporary Continental Thinkers: The Phenomenological Heritage*, edited by Richard Kearney. Manchester, England: Manchester University Press.
1998   "From Interpretation to Translation." Pp. 331–61 in *Thinking Biblically: Exegetical and Hermeneutical Studies*, edited by André LaCocque and Paul Ricoeur, translated by David Pellauer. Chicago and London: University of Chicago Press.
Rieger, Joerg M.
1994   "Approaches to the Real: Liberation Theology and Spirituality in Latin America and North America (A Comparison of the Works of Gustavo Gutiérrez and Frederick Herzog)." Ph.D. diss., Duke University.
1998a   "Developing a Common Interest Theology from the Underside." Pp. 124–42 in *Liberating the Future: God, Mammon, and Theology*, edited by Joerg M. Rieger. Minneapolis: Fortress.
1998b   *Remember the Poor: The Challenge to Theology in the Twenty-first Century*. Harrisburg, Pa.: Trinity Press International.
Ringgren, Helmer
1990   "The Impact of the Ancient Near East on Israelite Tradition." Pp. 31–46 in *Tradition and Theology in the Old Testament*, edited by Douglas A. Knight. Sheffield: Sheffield Academic.
Robbins, Vernon K.
1994   "The Ritual of Reading and the Reading of Texts as a Ritual: Observations on Mieke Bal's *Death and Dissymmetry*." Pp. 385–401 in *In Good Company: Essays in Honor of Robert Detweiler*, edited by David Jasper and Mark Ledbetter. Atlanta: Scholars.
Rofé, Alexander
1986   "Methodological Aspects of the Study of Biblical Law." Pp. 1–16 in *Jewish Law Association Studies II: The Jerusalem Conference Volume*, edited by Bernard S. Jackson. Atlanta: Scholars.
Rogers, Richard
1615   *A commentary upon the whole booke of Judges preached first and delivered in sundrie lectures*. London: Felixkyngston for Thomas Man.
Rosenzweig, Franz
1935   *Briefe und Tagenbücher*. Edited by Edith Rosenzweig and Ernst Simon. Berlin: Schocken.

Rost, Leohard
1982   *The Succession to the Throne of David.* Translated by Michael D. Rutter
          and David M. Gunn, with an introduction by Edward Ball. Historic
          Texts and Interpreters in Biblical Scholarship 1. Sheffield: Almond.
Ruether, Rosemary Radford
1982   "Woman as Oppressed, Woman as Liberated in Scriptures." Pp.181–86
          in *Spinning a Sacred Yarn: Women Speak from the Pulpit.* New York: Pil-
          grim.
Sakenfeld, Katharine Doob
1988   "Zelophehad's Daughters." *Perspectives in Religious Studies* 15, no. 4:
          37–47.
1995   *Journeying with God: A Commentary on the Book of Numbers.* International
          Theological Commentary. Grand Rapids: Eerdmans.
Salmond, Charles A.
1904   *Eli, Samuel, and Saul: A Transition Chapter in Israelitish History.* Edin-
          burgh: T. & T. Clark.
Sandmel, Samuel
1956   *Philo's Place in Judaism: A Study of Conceptions of Abraham in Jewish Liter-
          ature.* Cincinnati: Hebrew Union College.
1979   *Philo of Alexandria. An Introduction.* New York: Oxford University Press.
Sandy, D. Brent, and Ronald L. Giese, Jr.
1995   *Cracking Old Testament Codes.* Nashville: Broadman & Holman.
Sarna, Nahum M.
1988   "Israel in Egypt: The Egyptian Sojourn and the Exodus." Pp. 31–52 in
          *Ancient Israel: A Short History from Abraham to the Roman Destruction of
          the Temple,* edited by Hershel Shanks. Washington, D.C.: Biblical Ar-
          chaeology Society.
1989   *Genesis: The Traditional Hebrew Text with the New JPS Translation Com-
          mentary.* Philadelphia: Jewish Publication Society.
Scarry, Elaine
1994   *Resisting Representation.* New York and Oxford: Oxford University
          Press.
Scheppele, Kim Lane
1994   "Legal Theory and Social Theory." *Annual Review of Sociology* 20:383–
          407.
Schramm, Gene M.
1990   "Ruth, Tamar, and Levirate Marriage." Pp. 191–200 in *Studies in Near
          Eastern Culture and History: In Memory of Ernest T. Abdel-Massih,* edited
          by James A. Bellamy. Ann Arbor: University of Michigan Press.
Seely, Jo Ann H.
1992   "Succoth (Place)." *ABD* 6:217–18.
Shanks, Hershel
1988   Introduction to *Ancient Israel: A Short History from Abraham to the Roman
          Destruction of the Temple.* Washington, D.C.: Biblical Archaeology Soci-
          ety.
———, ed.
1997   "Face to Face: Biblical Minimalists Meet Their Challengers." *BAR* 23,
          no. 4: 26–29, 32–38, 40–42, 66.

Sheridan, Alan
1977   "Translator's Note." Pp. vii–xii in *Écrits: A Selection,* by Jacques Lacan.
            New York: W. W. Norton.
Sibley, Mulford Q.
1984   "Religion and Law: Some Thoughts on Their Intersections." *The Jour-
            nal of Law and Religion* 2:41–67.
Sider, Robert Dick
1971   *Ancient Rhetoric and the Art of Tertullian.* London: Oxford University Press.
Silber, David
1988   "Kingship, Samuel, and the Story of Hanna." *Tradition* 23 , no. 2: 64–75.
Ska, Jean Louis
1988   "L'Ironie de Tamar (Gen 38)." *ZAW* 100:261–63.
Slater, Susan
1999   "Imagining Arrival: Rhetoric, Reader, and Word of God in Deutero-
            nomy 1–3." Pp. 107–22 in *The Labour of Reading: Desire, Alienation, and
            Biblical Interpretation.* Edited by Fiona C. Black, Roland Boer, and Erin
            Runions. Semeia Studies 36. Atlanta: Society of Biblical Literature.
Slotki, Judah J.
1959   "Judges: Introduction and Commentary." Pp. 152–318 in *Joshua and
            Judges,* edited by A. Cohen. London: Soncino.
Smith, Carol
1992   "The Story of Tamar: A Power-Filled Challenge to the Structures of
            Power." Pp. 16–28 in *Women in the Biblical Tradition,* edited by George J.
            Brooke. Lewiston, N.Y.: Mellen.
Smith, Henry Preserved
1899   *A Critical and Exegetical Commentary on the Books of Samuel.* ICC. New
            York: C. Scribner.
Snaith, Norman H.
1966   "The Daughters of Zelophehad." *VT* 16:124–27.
1967   *Leviticus and Numbers.* The Century Bible. London: Nelson.
Soggin, J. Alberto
1981   *Judges: A Commentary.* OTL. Philadelphia: Westminster.
1993   "Judah and Tamar (Genesis 38)." Pp. 281–87 in *Of Prophets' Visions and
            the Wisdom of Sages: Essays in Honour of R. Norman Whybray on His Sev-
            entieth Birthday,* edited by Heather A. McKay and David J. A. Clines.
            JSOTS 162. Sheffield: JSOT.
Sowers, Sidney G.
1965   *The Hermeneutics of Philo and Hebrews: A Comparison of the Interpretation
            of the Old Testament in Philo Judaeus and the Epistle to the Hebrews.* Rich-
            mond: John Knox.
Speiser, E. A.
1964   *Genesis: Introduction, Translation, and Notes.* AB. Garden City, N.Y.: Dou-
            bleday.
Sperber, Alexander, ed.
1959   *The Bible in Aramaic Based on Old Manuscripts and Printed Texts.* Vol. 1:
            The Pentateuch according to Targum Onkelos. Leiden: E. J. Brill.
Spivak, Gayatri C.
1980   "Revolutions That as Yet Have No Model: Derrida's *Limited Inc.*" *Dia-
            critics* 10, no. 4: 29–49.

Sprinkle, Joe M.
1990   "A Literary Approach to Biblical Law: Exodus 20:22–23:19." Ph.D. diss.,
          Jewish Institute of Religion, Cincinnati.
Stahl, Nanette
1995   *Law and Liminality in the Bible.* JSOTS 202. Sheffield: Sheffield Academic.
Steinmetz, David C.
1993   "Luther and Tamar." *Lutheran Theological Seminary Bulletin* 73:3–15.
Steinsaltz, Adin
1989   *The Talmud: The Steinsaltz Edition.* Reference Guide. New York: Ran-
          dom House.
Stern, David
1993   "The Rabbinic Parable and the Narrative of Interpretation." Pp. 78–95
          in *The Midrashic Imagination: Jewish Exegesis, Thought, and History,* ed-
          ited by Michael Fishbane. Albany: State University of New York
          Press.
Sternberg, Meir
1985   *The Poetics of Biblical Narrative: Ideological Literature and the Drama of
          Reading.* Bloomington: Indiana University Press.
Sterring, Ankie
1994   "The Will of the Daughters." Pp. 11–99 in *A Feminist Companion to Exo-
          dus to Deuteronomy,* edited by Athalya Brenner. FCB 6. Sheffield:
          Sheffield Academic.
Sturdy, John
1976   *Numbers.* Cambridge Bible Commentary. New York: Cambridge Uni-
          versity Press.
Sugirtharajah, Rasiah S.
1998   *Asian Biblical Hermeneutics and Postcolonialism: Contesting the Interpreta-
          tions.* Maryknoll, N.Y.: Orbis Books.
Tertullian
1972   *Adversus Marcionem.* Edited and translated by Ernest Evans. Bks. 1–5.
          Oxford: Clarendon.
Tracy, David
1999   "Fragments: The Spiritual Situation of Our Times." Pp. 170–74 in *God,
          the Gift, and Postmodernism,* edited by John D. Caputo and Michael J.
          Scanlon. Bloomington and Indianapolis: Indiana University Press.
Trible, Phyllis
1978   "Love's Lyrics Redeemed." Pp. 144–65 in *God and the Rhetoric of Sexual-
          ity.* OBT. Philadelphia: Fortress.
1984   *Texts of Terror: Literary-Feminist Readings of Biblical Narratives.* OBT.
          Philadelphia: Fortress.
Ulanov, Ann Belford
1993   *The Female Ancestors of Christ.* Boston and London: Shambhala.
Valler, Shulamit
1999   "The Story of Jephthah's Daughter in the Midrash." Pp. 48–66 in
          Judges: A Feminist Companion to the Bible, edited by Athalaya Brenner. 2d
          ser. Sheffield: Sheffield Academic.
van der Ploeg, J.
1950–51   "Studies in Hebrew Law." 5 parts. *CBQ* 12 (1950): 248–59, 416–27; 13
          (1951): 28–43, 164–71, 296–307.

van der Toorn, Karel
1996   *Family Religion in Babylonia, Syria, and Israel: Continuity and Change in the Forms of Religious Life.* Leiden: E. J. Brill.
van Dijk-Hemmes, Fokkelien
1989   "Tamar and the Limits of Patriarchy: Between Rape and Seduction (2 Samuel 13 and Genesis 38)." Pp. 135–56 in *Anti-Covenant: Counter-Reading Women's Lives in the Hebrew Bible,* edited by Mieke Bal. JSOTS 81, Bible and Literature Series 22. Sheffield: Almond.
van Gennep, Arnold
1960   *The Rites of Passage.* Chicago: University of Chicago Press.
van Ommeslaeghe, F., S.J.
1987   "Chrysostom." Pp. 466–67 in vol. 3 of *The Encyclopedia of Religion,* edited by Mircea Eliade et al. New York: Macmillan.
van Seters, John
1975   *Abraham in History and Tradition.* New Haven: Yale University Press.
1977   "The Yahwist as Theologian? A Response." *JSOT* 3:15–20.
1992   *Prologue to History: The Yahwist as Historian in Genesis.* Louisville: Westminster John Knox.
van Wolde, Ellen
1997   "Texts in Dialogue with Texts: Intertextuality in the Ruth and Tamar Narratives." *Biblical Interpretation* 5:1–28.
Vawter, Bruce
1977   *On Genesis: A New Reading.* Garden City, N.Y.: Doubleday.
von Rad, Gerhard
1958   *Der heilige krieg im alten Israel.* 3d ed. Göttingen: Vandenhoeck & Ruprecht.
1962   *Old Testament Theology.* Vol. 1: *The Theology of Israel's Historical Traditions.* Translated by D. M. G. Stalker. New York: Harper and Row.
1966   *The Problem of the Hexateuch and Other Essays.* Translated by E. W. Trueman Dicken. London: SCM.
1972   *Genesis: A Commentary.* OTL. Translated by J. H. Marks. Rev. ed. Philadelphia: Westminster.
Waldron, Jeremy
1994   "Vagueness in Law and Language: Some Philosophical Issues." *California Law Review* 82:509–40.
Walters, Stanley D.
1988   "Hannah and Anna: The Greek and Hebrew Texts of 1 Samuel 1." *JBL* 107:385–412.
1994   "The Voice of God's People in Exile." *Ex auditu* 10:73–86.
Wassén, Cecilia
1994   "The Story of Judah and Tamar in the Eyes of the Earliest Interpreters." *Literature & Theology* 8:354–66.
Weems, Renita J.
1995   *Battered Love: Marriage, Sex, and Violence in the Hebrew Bible.* OBT. Minneapolis: Fortress.
Wegner, Judith Pomeroy
1988   *Chattel or Person? The Status of Women in the Mishnah.* New York and Oxford: Oxford University Press.
1990   "Public Man, Private Woman: The Sexuality Factor and the Personal

Status of Women in Mishnaic Law." Pp. 22–54 in *Jewish Law Association Studies IV: The Boston Conference Volume*, edited by Bernard S. Jackson. Atlanta: Scholars.

Weinfeld, Moshe
1967   "Deuteronomy: The Present State of Inquiry." *JBL* 86:249–62.
1991   *Deuteronomy 1–11: A New Translation with Introduction and Commentary.* AB. New York: Doubleday.

Weingreen, J.
1966   "The Case of the Daughters of Zelophchad." *VT* 16:518–22.

Wellhausen, Julius
1957   *Prolegomena to the History of Ancient Israel.* Translated by J. S. Black and A. Menzies. New York: Meridian Library.

Wendel, A.
1931   *Das israelitisch-jüdische Gelübde.* Berlin: Philo Verlag GMBH.

Wenham, Gordon J.
1981   *Numbers: An Introduction.* Leicester, England: Inter-Varsity.

West, Gerald O.
1990   "Reading 'the Text' and Reading 'behind the Text': The 'Cain and Abel' Story in a Context of Liberation." Pp. 299–320 in *The Bible in Three Dimensions: Essays in Celebration of Forty Years of Biblical Studies in the University of Sheffield*, edited by David J. A. Clines, Stephen E. Fowl, and Stanley E. Porter. JSOTS 87. Sheffield: Sheffield Academic.
1995   *Biblical Hermeneutics of Liberation: Modes of Reading the Bible in the South African Context.* 2d rev. ed. Pietermaritzburg, South Africa: Cluster Publications.
1999   *The Academy of the Poor: Towards a Dialogical Reading of the Bible.* Interventions 2. Sheffield: Sheffield Academic.

Westbrook, Raymond
1985   "Biblical and Cuneiform Law Codes." *Revue biblique* 92:247–64.

Westenholz, Joan Goodnick
1989   "Tamar, *Qedesa, Qadistu,* and Sacred Prostitution in Mesopotamia." *HTR* 82:245–65.

Westermann, Claus
1982   *Genesis 37–50: A Commentary.* Translated by John J. Scullion, S.J. Minneapolis: Augsburg.
1995   *Genesis 12–36: A Continental Commentary.* Translated by John J. Scullion, S.J. Minneapolis: Fortress.

Whybray, R. N.
1987   *The Making of the Pentateuch: A Methodological Study.* JSOTS 53. Sheffield: Sheffield Academic.

Wiesel, Elie
1979   *A Jew Today.* Translated by Marion Wiesel. New York: Vantage.
1990   *Evil and Exile.* With Philippe-Michaël de Saint-Cheron. Translated by Jon Rothschild. Notre Dame, Ind., and London: University of Notre Dame Press.

Willis, John T.
1972   "Cultic Elements in the Story of Samuel's Birth and Dedication." *Studia Theologica* 26:33–61.

Willis, Timothy M.
1997   "The Nature of Jephthah's Authority." *CBQ* 59:33–44.
Wink, Walter
1973   *The Bible in Human Transformation: Toward a New Paradigm for Biblical Study*. Philadelphia: Fortress.
Winston, David
1991   "Aspects of Philo's Linguistic Theory." *The Studia Philonica Annual* 3:109–25.
Wright, C. J. H.
1992   "Family." *ABD* 2:761–69.
Wright, George R. H.
1982   "The Positioning of Genesis 38." *ZAW* 94:523–29.
Yadin, Yigael
1983   *The Temple Scroll*. Vol. 2: *Text and Commentary*. Jerusalem: Israel Exploration Society.
Zimmerli, Walther
1965   *The Law and the Prophets: A Study of the Meaning of the Old Testament*. Translated by R. E. Clements. New York: Harper and Row.
1978   *Old Testament Theology in Outline*. Translated by David E. Green. Atlanta: John Knox.
Žižek, Slavoj
1989   *The Sublime Object of Ideology*. London and New York: Verso.
1992   *Looking Awry: An Introduction to Jacques Lacan through Popular Culture*. Cambridge, Mass.: MIT Press.
1996   *The Indivisible Remainder: An Essay on Schelling and Related Matters*. London and New York: Verso.

Index of Biblical References

Index of Authors

Index of Biblical Characters